ELIZABETHAN AND JACOBEAN
PLAYWRIGHTS

ELIZABETHAN AND JACOBEAN PLAYWRIGHTS

HENRY W. WELLS

COLUMBIA UNIVERSITY

IN LITTERIS LIBERTAS

1754·1893

NEW YORK

COLUMBIA UNIVERSITY PRESS

1939

TO

WILLIAM WITHERLE LAWRENCE

PREFACE

THIS book has been called *Elizabethan and Jacobean Playwrights* out of deference to literary tradition. In the Introduction to his recent book, *Cavalier Drama*, Professor Alfred Harbage offers an apology for the adjective used in his title. Truly, any author of a work dealing with English drama between 1576 and 1642 is hard pressed to find a title that is entirely satisfactory. Books about "Elizabethan" and "Shakespearean" drama almost always discuss plays written before or after the reign of Gloriana and the days of the chief dramatist in her realm. Discussion of "Jacobean" drama never stops at 1625, the year that James I died. The term "Cavalier" in relation to plays has only limited currency, and there is no general agreement as to its precise application. No single term adequately describes the era of dramatic history that began with the opening of the Theatre, the Rose, the Swan, and the Globe and ran continuously till the closing of all the theatres by the Puritans. The terms that have the widest usage and that indicate most unmistakably the inclusive scope of the present book are "Elizabethan and Jacobean," and they have been adopted, even though the chapters deal with a few playwrights—as Ford and Shirley—who flourished in the time of Charles I and fail to consider in detail those of the first fifteen or twenty years of Elizabeth's reign.

In the course of the book the words "Cavalier drama" are nevertheless often used because of their aptness, but they are used in a less limited sense than that defined by Professor Harbage. In his book the words signify the work of playwrights directly or indirectly associated with the

Court from 1625 to 1660. My own use of the term is more broadly critical. About 1611, or the time of Shakespeare's retirement from active play-writing, a new spirit appears in the English drama. Plays begin to be less national and are addressed more narrowly to an aristocratic audience. They grow more sentimental and genteel, less realistic and poetic. The school of Beaumont and Fletcher succeeds to the tradition of Marlowe and Shakespeare. This change obviously begins in the midst of the reign of James I. But it has seemed convenient at times to refer to the earlier tradition as "Elizabethan" and to the later as "Cavalier." The words have, I think, appropriate connotations. For literary and dramatic students "Elizabethan" still means "Shakespearean," and it is equally true that the Cavalier faction in English life was the chief one to direct and to enjoy the plays of the Fletcherian movement.

The book as a whole analyzes major tendencies in the drama from 1576 to 1642 The earlier chapters deal with the graver, the later with the lighter, plays. In each successive chapter I have sought to find a dominating quality in a new group of plays and to discuss these plays both collectively for this common quality and individually for their special characteristics. Neither my space nor my desire has led me to mention all the five hundred extant plays of the period. Instead I have emphasized the better plays and attempted to give some explanation for my choice. The Introduction and the final chapter deal with larger issues transcending the qualities of any single dramatic group.

The book is addressed to anyone who shares my desire to achieve a more rounded understanding of the most abundant period in the history of the theatre. As I have written, I have tried to bear in mind the needs of the general reader and the graduate and undergraduate student as

well as those of the teacher and specialist in the field. My
treatment has been critical, not chronological. While it
represents no new research, it does, I trust, approach a
large number of major and minor matters in ways that
are either wholly new or at least novel in emphasis. And
while I cannot pretend to give a radically new interpretation of the entire movement, I have attempted to present
a fresh picture. I have followed no single course, as a
study of the philosophical, historical, political, theatrical,
linguistic, or aesthetic aspects, but have chosen to discuss
whatever seems uppermost in importance. Although we
have had many studies of individual playwrights and of
a few obvious types of plays, no previous study resembles
the general analysis given here.

In this approach, then, the book is not traditional. But
even a modest understanding of any literary period necessarily involves a classification that goes beyond a mere
author-by-author analysis and marks out the similarities
in the work of different authors as well as the dissimilari-
ties in the work of one author. Such an analysis of content
is imperative where the works considered are the output
of two-thirds of a century of constant activity by very prolific writers, many of whom—Shakespeare preëminently
—satisfied shifting taste or their own creative need for
experiment by producing plays of widely differing technical form and human significance. And there seems a special virtue in "breaking down" the dramatic output of this
entire period so that the continuity of its activity and its
community of interests may be emphasized and at the same
time perspective on individual authors maintained. Important as it certainly is to follow Shakespeare's growth
from play to play, only a two-dimensional picture of an
isolated genius results when, as is the custom, Shakespeare's plays are considered almost wholly in relation to

one another and to the poet's personal history. Familiar as we are with the products of Shakespeare's genius, they glow with no less enchantment if we look on them very much as the theatregoers of his day did and as we view plays and all other works of art today—in an organic association with the works of other men, in a relationship determined by the factors of time and similarity of effect.

Many friends who have aided me in my work I remember with gratefulness, even though I omit to mention their names. Both they and I know how heavily I have leaned upon them. I cannot, however, omit to acknowledge in particular the valuable help given me by Professor Oscar J. Campbell.

HENRY W. WELLS

Columbia University
January 18, 1939

CONTENTS

ELIZABETHAN AND JACOBEAN PLAYWRIGHTS

CHAPTER ONE

INTRODUCTION

A THEATRICAL MOVEMENT commonly regarded as the most brilliant in over two thousand years of Europe's history arose in London during the lifetime of Shakespeare. This book aims to give an account of that peculiarly vital dramatic literature from its earliest years to its latest, from its gravest tragedy to its gayest farce. Its purpose is to examine carefully and to reëstimate the plays, to avoid time-worn and specious simplifications, and to bring some new order into the field. A critical and judicial approach is preferred to a chronological or biographical one. In viewing a brief movement remarkable for collaboration and coöperation among playwrights of whose intimate lives little is known, this analytical and impersonal method especially recommends itself. The development of style and ideas becomes more important than literary or personal biography. Proprietary rights mean but little more in Elizabethan drama than commonly in medieval art and literature. In the conclusion we shall examine the relation of the Elizabethan drama to the notably dissimilar Cavalier drama and Shakespeare's relation to both schools. His chief allegiance will be shown to be to the earlier.

The entire movement rose and fell with remarkable rapidity. No plays closely resembling those of the great Elizabethans appeared before the last quarter of the sixteenth century, before the tragedies of Kyd and Marlowe and the comedies of Lyly and Greene. The public theatres began to be erected in 1576; the first powerful plays appeared about 1587. The movement reached maturity a little after the death of Elizabeth in 1603, or in the first

decade of the seventeenth century, which witnessed masterpieces by Shakespeare, Jonson, Beaumont and Fletcher,
and their associates. Its peak was clearly passed when
Shakespeare and Beaumont died in 1616 and Jonson gave
evidence that his genius was fully spent. Talented playwrights and inspired actors enabled the playhouses to exist
on their powerful momentum for nearly a quarter of a
century more but with constantly diminishing glory.
Fletcher died in 1625, Middleton two years after. When
in 1642 Puritan propaganda closed the public theatres,
almost all the eminent playwrights were dead and the
few who survived had long finished their important work.
Eighteen years thereafter the restoration of the Stuarts
to the throne gave new life to the English stage, with new
men, new manners, and new dramatic forms. It is true that
the Restoration stage evolved from the Cavalier stage as
the latter was ornamented by Massinger, Shirley, and
Davenant; but it remains none the less clear that the break
of nearly two decades is highly important in theatrical
history. A continuity runs through the drama of three
reigns, those of Elizabeth, James I, and Charles I, like the
work of one mind in youth, maturity, and decline. Literally speaking, one generation witnessed the entire development. Ben Jonson probably saw every playwright from
Marlowe to Shirley. Marlowe died prematurely in 1593,
and Shirley began play-writing about thirty years later.
These are terminal figures. Most of the dramatists enjoyed personal acquaintance with the great majority of
their fellow craftsmen. Their relations on the whole seem
to have been remarkably cordial and about half their plays
were written in collaboration, so that the drama of the
period may be described as the product of a circle of
friends; romantic fancy has painted them grouped about
a table in the Mermaid Tavern. What can have caused the

emergence of such a group of men and what fate denied them the power to produce further generations for the theatre?

The English theatre from 1576, when the first popular playhouse was built in London, till about 1611, when Shakespeare retired, represents one of the last artistic movements addressing all classes of society. The medieval theatre had also been communal, its piety and ribaldry enjoyed alike by king and countryman. Richard II witnessed at York in the great mystery cycle of that city the homely pageants representing the Christian story. Circumstances favored the rebirth of a really national theatre in Shakespeare's England, whereas no such theatre was destined to arise on the Continent.

The great cycles of the mystery plays performed in all the larger towns of Europe and England from the fourteenth century to the sixteenth show as warm and popular a love for theatrical entertainment as history anywhere records. It is a drama of, for, and by the people. Notably enough this most catholic form of drama flourished nowhere more lustily than in England. A court theatre is seldom so vital as a popular one. When the princes and nobles of the Renaissance took theatrical entertainment under their patronage in their own houses, they cut off much of the vitality of the older tradition and suffered a repression in their own. The farces and moral interludes played abroad or in England before Cardinal Morton at the close of the fifteenth century and before Henry VIII at the beginning of the sixteenth surpassed the earlier popular drama in wit but not in power or inspiration. The old communal soil was ready in England for one more new crop.

The Renaissance or, more specifically, the sixteenth-century drama in Europe all too frequently evolved into a somewhat bookish following of the none too inspired Seneca or a fairly close imitation of Plautus and Terence, of which the tragedies of Garnier in French and the comedies of Ariosto in Italian were the most influential in England. As a power behind such plays lay the Renaissance mind increasingly weaning itself from religious preoccupations and seeking fresh personal expression. The new drama became noble and intellectual. But the serious plays commonly remained, after the Senecan models, more declamatory than dramatic or even poetic, and the comedies relatively stereotyped and traditional. Very gradually gaining in richness and power, the drama of the Continent ultimately reached its climax during the mid-seventeenth century in the tragedies of Corneille and the comedies of Molière. Had no peculiar factors been at work in England, there is small reason to suppose that any other than the more conservative phases of Restoration drama would ultimately have appeared. Quite without the aid of an Elizabethan tradition English wit and intelligence might have created a Congreve and sheer imitativeness have produced the neoclassical tragedies of James Thomson and William Mason. But happily England had a theatrical inspiration of her own.

A theatrical movement is to be explained as much by the audience as by the actors and playwrights. The English Court under Elizabeth enjoyed, but did not direct, the British theatre. So long as theatrical entertainment remained in the hands of the Crown or of the great nobles and ecclesiastics, it made no progress beyond that attained under similar circumstances abroad. Moral shows were produced in the household of Cardinal Morton, farces in the even wittier household of Sir Thomas More, while the Inns of Court and the Court itself harbored many typical entertainments grave and gay. Play-writing became one of the acknowledged avocations of gentility, befitting a great lady or a privy councilor. Tragedies were commonly on the Senecan model, as *Gorboduc,* by Thomas Norton and Thomas Sackville, who afterwards became Lord Buckhurst. Comedies ranged from medieval farce to Terencian satire. All these types of plays were also produced in the schools and colleges, where the works of Seneca and Terence were acted and original plays based upon them were given not only in English but in Latin. Medieval mystery and morality plays were still being acted during the first half of Elizabeth's reign. Then, in 1576, the first popular theatre was built in London, and a new epoch in drama suddenly arose. The new plays were, of course, at first based upon the old, but rapidly developed along novel lines.

The more self-contained spirit of the Continent was owing in great part to the logical and consistent course of Renaissance thought among the continental scholars and aristocracy. There is little evidence that they were interested in the fantastic doings of the London stage. In England the public and the playwrights were for the most part either innocent of the rigid critical theories abroad or, like Ben Jonson, superior to them. The playwrights used a freedom enjoyed by the authors of the plays on the saints' legends during the Middle Ages but with a subject matter almost wholly secular. Their plays were highly eclectic, half medieval and half modern. The popular English theatre called for much more action and for less moralizing and declamation than the aristocratic continental theatre. Moreover, even the new aristocracy in England proved in most respects far more liberal and experimental than the leaders abroad. The coming of the Tudors and the policy of Henry VIII created a group of new families enriched by the spoils of war and the desecration of the monasteries.

The *nouveaux riches* of the Western World, they were the less staid and reactionary in upholding tradition of any sort. Both classical Renaissance and Protestant Reformation burst upon them suddenly and disturbingly, less as an evolution than as a revolution. Such men, already keenly sensitized by changes in thought and life, proved ready for any new adventure, whether at Darien with Drake or at the Globe with Shakespeare. Under Elizabeth Protestantism had been successfully established as the religion of state, with a measure of toleration which even invited skepticism. Doubtful as to matters of religion and still religious, although generally persuaded that faith was in any case not the greatest thing in life, the average Elizabethan was ideally poised for new emotional and aesthetic experiences. Old standards in society, belief, education, and conduct were breaking down. Europe itself appeared to the true-born Englishman of the day as a vast, newly opened treasure house of the most varied riches from which he might pick his fill with lavish hand. Whatever might be the ambiguous position of the Anglican Church, the country was still more Catholic in spirit than puritanical in the sense that it was pleasure-loving and aesthetic as England has never been since. Trade had won new freedom and horizons for the enterprising Londoner, but had not as yet frozen into dull commercialism. It was still a merry England, more a land of artists than of shopkeepers. Indeed the very people who kept the shops flocked to the theatres. London was wealthy but hardly sober. While its empire was still a dream it could afford to make its dreams imperial. No deadening weight of hollow and unreal dignity crushed the spirit of those who listened for the first time to plays by the Swan of Avon.

Elizabethan inventiveness is brilliantly reflected in the dynamic language of the dramatists. Blank verse, in which the plays are largely written, was a new medium for English poetry. The poetical language itself, though certainly based upon medieval poetry, was a notable departure from anything which had gone before. The towering images and metaphors of Marlowe and Shakespeare, even the pleasant wit of Lyly and Greene, were new things. So in their turn were the epic style of Chapman, the torrential manner of Jonson, the biting words of Webster, the liquid language of Fletcher, and even the eloquence of Massinger and the lucidity of Shirley. The English language was undergoing a rich series of transformations difficult to parallel in any contemporary tongue. Above all others the dramatists took full advantage of this golden hour for English speech. Shakespeare's language is far more poetical than that of either Chaucer or Congreve, for it is neither immature nor oversophisticated. So inspiring was the instrument of English speech which destiny placed in the playwrights' hands.

The stage is an ideal medium for storytelling. Chaucer had lived in a fine age of storytelling too, but at a time when few tales besides those of the Bible found theatrical expression. Public assembly for other purposes than those of Church or State would doubtless have seemed dangerous and irreligious to the fourteenth century. But London must have been even gayer in Shakespeare's time than in Chaucer's. It passionately loved stories, classical, Italian, and modern, and took a more mature attitude toward storytelling than the English of the fourteenth century. The human spirit and the narrative art reserved in Chaucer for the written page were suddenly released by Shakespeare and his companions for the stage. Our own age attempts to use more complex matter for theatrical purposes with much less confidence of success.

The bold experimentation of the Elizabethan theatre

cannot be overemphasized. So long as it kept its freshness
and explorative spirit, it was masterly. While it combined
on an almost equal footing the medieval and the modern,
it remained emancipated and alive. But when Jonson produced a school of realists, when Fletcher succeeded to the
laurels of Shakespeare and was followed in turn by Massinger and by Shirley, the period of experimentation had
passed and that of decadence and imitativeness arrived. It
was not the Puritans who killed the Elizabethan stage, but
the want of that free, invigorating, and windswept air that
the great dramatists breathed as the birthright of their age.
Changing times allayed the winds, weighed the atmosphere
with heaviness, and induced the playwrights to copy their
predecessors, who had themselves been copyists only in
minor matters. The theatre ceased to be national and became aristocratic. Shirley wrote much in the spirit later
cultivated in Italy by Goldoni. The sudden glory of an
age perished.

The drama of the period affords an ideal ground for
study in the continuity and evolution of literary and theatrical tradition. It is continuous because the playwrights
and theatrical companies for half a century formed a closely
knit society. Many plays were written in collaboration. A
group of eminent actors and theatrical leaders stamped
their impression upon the stage, so that a large number
of well-defined theatrical conventions were established.
Although such circumstances as the pestilence or a quiet
season in London led the theatrical companies to take to
the road, the plays were primarily for a relatively small
London audience, long accustomed to seeing and criticizing
performances. Some of the earliest of the famous dramas,
as Marlowe's *Jew of Malta* and *Doctor Faustus*, Shakespeare's *Romeo and Juliet* and *Midsummer-Night's
Dream*, were acted and printed even at the close of the

period. *The Jew of Malta*, indeed, survives only in a quarto of 1633. The latest of the playwrights, as James Shirley, were writing plays in 1640 clearly based upon ideas of plot, character, and dramatic language inaugurated in Elizabethan times.

But innovation is just as powerful as conservatism. Plays were being repeatedly revised to keep up with the changing taste. The age, the theatre, and the literary spirit were far too dynamic to remain in any respect static. Our studies will show both the unity of the drama and its own most dramatic development. The evolution will be repeatedly apparent as we contrast the earlier with the later works and the first generation of playwrights with the second. The chief distinction, as already indicated, is between what we may call the school of Marlowe and Shakespeare and that of Beaumont and Fletcher. Almost all plays produced by the earlier group possess a vitality and freshness lacking in plays by the later. The first excels in strength and imagination, the second in suavity and grace. As the earliest historians of English dramatic literature observed, the appeal of the former is national, that of the latter chiefly aristocratic. It is a primary object of the present study to show that the earlier group keeps a restless and exciting balance between medieval and Renaissance influences while the later group rapidly loses firm hold upon the medieval heritage, turns slowly from a Renaissance to an Augustan temper, and repeatedly foreshadows the tragedy and comedy of the Restoration. The last chapter summarizes this development in some detail.

Even the secondary influences throughout this entire period aided the brilliant and dynamic theatrical life. The English of the age, for example, were great lovers of music and dress. Many of their plays verge upon the operatic, so prominent are the musical elements. They contain delightful songs, and the original performances were accompanied by much instrumental music before and during the acts. Again, since the age was infatuated with dress, the theatrical spectacles, relatively bare in setting, exploited costume to an extraordinary degree. A large part of the wealth of the theatrical companies lay in their gorgeous wardrobes, to which the Court itself made loans and gifts. A notorious case is in the records of a play which might be supposed to have been one of the most simply and soberly produced, Thomas Heywood's bourgeois and sentimental drama, *A Woman Killed with Kindness*. For writing the play Heywood received only a fraction of the sum spent on the heroine's dress. In short, from the Elizabethans' love of music came naturally their lyrical drama, and from their passion for costume and spectacle their brilliant stage pictures.

London was the city where all the dramatists lived and many had been born. It was an ideal seat for intellectual and artistic stimulus. Here was the Court with its brilliant life and a patronage neither to be blindly trusted nor despised. Here, too, were the Inns of Court, the sanctuaries of the lawyers, who enjoyed a notable renaissance in their own right and enthusiastically supported the performance of plays. Between the lawyers and the actors a bond naturally arose, each being employed in voluble and vehement contests of words. Here, too, were many prosperous citizens eager for entertainment. The town was small, snug, and sociable, exactly the condition to incubate a robust theatre. Houses were relatively small and simply furnished, the scenes of busy family and commercial life. From them in happy hour the citizens issued forth to amuse each other as they could hardly be amused in their busy homes, too narrow and too much like workshops to harbor much varied entertainment. Tavern life was certainly gayer and

more popular than the life in the public houses and res-
taurants of any Anglo-Saxon city today. In the taverns
many of the plays were begotten and some apparently
written. There the wits met and talk flowed. This most
gregarious and sociable people passed in a step from their
intimate taverns and ordinaries to their small and tightly
packed theatres, numerous, busy, competitive, and thriv-
ing. There humanity crowded together upon the floor and
against the walls, leaving only the opening for the heavens
and for the fourth wall, which must of necessity become
the background for an eminently human though poetic
performance. Nursed under such circumstances, the Elizabethan drama was fated to become one of the most brilliant
creations of the Western World.

CHAPTER TWO

THE TRAGEDY OF EVIL

When the bad bleed, then is the tragedy good.
—TOURNEUR

IF THE BEST tragedies of the lesser Elizabethans are assumed to resemble the poorer works ascribed to Shakespeare, then that prodigy of horrors, his *Titus Andronicus,* becomes a measuring-stick for the serious drama of the age. Certainly many persons superficially acquainted with Elizabethan plays do have a conception of Elizabethan tragedy, apart from Shakespeare, as unrelieved melodrama. Turgid in style, bloody in action, and crude in all things, this drama has been described as the primitive darkness from which Shakespeare at length arose to realms of pure poetry. Such darkness William Archer found in the tragic scenes of Marlowe, Massinger, Middleton, Webster, and Ford. One associates an early and non-Shakespearean version of the Hamlet story with Thomas Kyd's *Spanish Tragedy* and sadly reflects on the rudeness of these barbaric authors. And there are Jacobean plays hardly less savage than the Elizabethan. Yet if the thoroughness of historical research teaches anything, it tells us that the highest genius rises only by degrees above his neighbors, that the finest fruit grows on the limbs of a tree already laden with rich and ripened productions. A great artist is unthinkable without distinguished contemporaries. The summarily unfavorable view of this tragic poetry is thus at best only a half truth. Although the finest dramas of the Elizabethan age, not even excluding Shakespeare's, are at times marred by melodramatic violence, a considerable number of the playwrights in only a less degree than

Shakespeare reconcile violent action with a deep and true vein of poetry. On the one hand it must be confessed that a too mordant note debars many of their chief works from the deep humanity of the ideal tragedy, while on the other hand it should be conceded that they do frequently achieve a hybrid form of satirical tragedy that is legitimate, moving, and poetic.

The conventional ideal of tragedy—at times referred to in this book as pure tragedy—marks a point of departure from which to trace the sturdy vein in Elizabethan drama that may be described as the tragedy of evil. Ideal tragedy evokes sadness rather than hate, sympathy rather than unmixed horror. Such art becomes universal in that it brings home to the spectators tragic elements ever present in their own lives. It reminds us that we are forever in the hands of forces threatening or attacking our welfare and our life, that we carry at all times within us the germs of unhappiness and of death. It appeals to an intelligent awareness of the tragic destiny of mankind. Evoking the feeling of a hostile and universally oppressive fate, it also evokes a sense of the nobility of man's resistance. Heroism, compassion, and fortitude arise in proportion to the pressure of misfortunes. In tragic life, we have been told, no villain need be; but it would be a bold thinker who would deny a need in tragedy for heroic suffering. The tragedy which we have come most to admire presents a sufferer who is fallible but who enlists our sympathy because of a greatness of heart. We associate ourselves with the tragic victim, are ourselves offered by vicarious sacrifice upon the altar of the stage, and find our hearts redeemed and our fears softened by awareness of the majesty of this atonement. As an Anglo-Saxon poet once wrote: *Thaes ofereode, thisses swa maeg*—that ill has passed, this may pass also. The finality and awe of ideal tragedy, the hushed calm of its conclusion, the sense at once of completion, of sadness, and of exaltation are cherished as among the most rewarding of aesthetic experiences. This effect is obtained in all the chief tragedies of Shakespeare and, as we shall see, in a few of the more impressive works of his contemporaries. But it is not fully or commonly attained by the lesser Elizabethans, and for this condition it becomes quite possible to account.

With all his theatrical and poetic genius, the Elizabethan dramatist is too often limited and partial in his vision. The universal escapes him because of his definite and pragmatic interest in lesser values. He is occupied with some more finite theme, as a thirst for revenge, a disgust with a corrupted court circle, an infatuation with physical brutality, or a horror of some heinous and unnatural sin. The Elizabethan drama becomes only too frequently the tragedy of colossal sinners. Hieronimo of *The Spanish Tragedy* is a less sympathetic figure than Hamlet; Doctor Faustus and Old Fortunatus have sold themselves wholly to the devil. The dramatist Marston habitually dwells with a preacher's zeal upon the horrible corruptions of a court; Tourneur depicts a society almost wholly depraved or centers his drama in the soul of a damned atheist; Middleton pries into the heart of lust, madness, and immorality; Webster depicts the disillusionment of depraved spirits, without actually asserting that through such disillusionment lies a solution of one of life's problems; Ben Jonson writes tragedy which virtually becomes satire on the disintegration of Roman morals. We look in vain among such works for tragic figures comparable with Romeo, Hamlet, Lear, Othello, Antony, or Coriolanus. Even Shakespeare's portraits of Macbeth and his wife had a heroic stature and sympathetic warmth lacking in the lesser plays. We are less impressed in *Macbeth* with any narrow or didactic in-

tention than with the tragic awareness that the most promising of men may fall into a chaos of madness or into a
state wherein all life appears inane. As a further measure
of the Elizabethan conception of sin restricting the lumi-
nosity and power of their plays, one may contrast the view
of incest in the more poetic tragedy of Sophocles and in
the more realistic drama of John Ford. The uncertainty
of fate overshadowing mankind lies at the heart of the
Greek drama, while the English play becomes principally
a study in a particular vice. There is a constricting power
in the bitterness of the Elizabethan vein of melodrama
from Kyd to Ford which the dramatists only partially and
occasionally escape. The Greek drama comes to us robed
in colors various as the world itself, while an Elizabethan
tragedy is too often swathed in a cloak of penitential black.
A medieval figure stalks through nearly half the serious
plays of the age. A misanthropic hero, skull in hand,
broods upon vice and cries out for revenge. Hieronimo is
speaking in Kyd's *Spanish Tragedy*:

> O eyes! no eyes, but fountains fraught with tears;
> O life! no life, but lively form of death;
> O world! no world, but mass of public wrongs,
> Confus'd and fill'd with murder and misdeeds!

So run some of the most popular lines spoken on the
Elizabethan stage, which well epitomize the spirit of this
darkly satirical drama. Nothing can be more tense and
sinister than such an Elizabethan tragedy, nothing more
relaxed and gay than a comedy proceeding from the same
mind.

Since a bloody revenge for murder or for love is a
theme in one or more of the chief tragedies of all the
principal playwrights of the age, historians have written
at length of a type of drama discovered by themselves

and dubbed "the revenge play." Of this type *Hamlet* is the most conspicuous example. But the true, poetic flavor of *Hamlet* is owing less to revenge than to cynicism. It is less a drama of blood than a tragedy of evil. A sinister and satirical spirit gives poetical wings to tragic work of all this line of dramatists from Kyd to Ford. The Renaissance mind was now wholly carefree, pleasure-loving, and amoral and now burdened with the sternest consciousness of sin, fired with the zeal of a Savonarola or a Luther. The imaginative genius of the age realized in fancy, if it did not practice in actuality, the darkest of possible crimes. It delighted to conceive either an individual or a social group sold to the devil. English poets freely evoked the Puritan spirit to express themselves sincerely, to thrill their audience or reader, and to attain more purely aesthetic ends. The old Catholic conscience was hyper-sensitized by the Reformation. The conception possessed great vitality for Elizabethan times and still retains a certain meaning for our own. Nevertheless some trace of forced or affected sentiment appears in the old melodramas, and this infection works still further to the detriment of our present appreciation. We recognize that the Elizabethan moralists fail to throw themselves wholeheartedly into their tasks, that they are not quite so persuaded of the weight or validity of their moral code as they profess to be. Their heroes, as Marlowe's Faustus, are half villains; their villains, as his Jew of Malta, half heroes.

Acutely sensitive to the piquancy of sin, the English children of the Renaissance turned to the sinister for their dramatic themes. Magicians like Faustus or Bacon, who had renounced their salvation, fascinated both author and audience. As Marlowe perceived when writing his Prologue to *The Jew of Malta*, Machiavelli, popularly conceived as Satan incarnate, was an ideal character to introduce a popular play. Lust and murder became alluring for their own sakes; hence the large number of plays based upon contemporary crimes. The dramatist wrote in the spirit of the criminals who made public acknowledgment of their sins on the scaffold before their execution. The stage became, as it were, the booth of the Catholic confessional abruptly exposed to the public eye. Satirical comedies disclosed the venial, satirical tragedies the deadly, sins of the community. The typical revenger, half hero and half villain, was scarcely a character to embody the fears and aspirations of the audience. So of all the notable figures in the revenge plays only Hamlet indisputably succeeds in reaching the eminence of pure tragedy. The audiences sought primarily excitement and thereafter satisfaction of their own strongly didactic natures. They delighted to find upon the stage the atmosphere of moral austerity and moral terror to which the eloquence of the pulpit had long accustomed them. The lesser Elizabethan playwrights are thus often satirists, while Shakespeare's more generous and humane nature distinguishes most of his tragedies from the corresponding works of his fellow playwrights. Life broadly envisaged, rather than the narrow provinces of lust, sin, murder, and corruption, becomes the subject matter of the Shakespearean plays.

Always in the background of the memorable tragedies stands the considerable body of popular but relatively mediocre work in which public taste for sensational evil and violence on the stage was gratified. The once beloved *Titus Andronicus* is such a play. Although it has elements of real tragic dignity and power, of poetic energy and validity, the drama as a whole from the point of view of posterity is greatly vitiated by fustian language and brutal action. One sees here the ground from which in their happier moments the dramatists emerged to light and air.

Henry Chettle, a hack writer, is the reputed author of another typical tragedy of revenge which has been quite forgotten by all but students of the period; nevertheless it epitomizes the true energy and vulgar limitations of the average Elizabethan mind. His *Hoffman, or A Revenge for a Father*, has some merit both as poetry and as drama. Often eloquent in expression and happily ingenious in plot, it seems a strangely animated work to be from one point of view dead and buried. Opening with a really poetic soliloquy, it proceeds through moving accidents by flood and field. The plot is a fantastic extravaganza. The villain-hero, not content with a solitary revenge, mows down a whole household of enemies. No dramatic criticism which approves singleness of action could approve of this play. Such an unrestrained work must inevitably be pushed to the wall, where over a score of inspired plays in approximately the same field survives. The glory of the really delightful Elizabethan tragedies of darkness is that they prove superior to these numerous commonplace specimens. Whatever may be the melodramatic elements which they contain, the better plays are something more than melodrama.

Artistic work is of course always to be recognized and understood not by its outward appearance but by its flavor. The series of Elizabethan plays exploiting the theme of evil should be remembered chiefly, as already urged, neither by the narrower feature of the prevalent theme of revenge nor by the horror of bloody scenes, but by the tang of moral tartness. More horrible than the physical odor of blood, so obnoxious in *Titus Andronicus*, is the spiritual sense of sin and damnation. The malcontent characters, we know, commonly appeared on the stage dressed in black, mourning for sin rather than for death. It is the accompanying sinister tone which points to the genuine poetic inspiration of Kyd, of the Marlowe of *Doctor Faustus* and *The Jew of Malta*, of Marston, Middleton, and their followers. In a group of distinguished plays this tone prevails. Indeed, how could it be otherwise, when the theatres, themselves in terror of the Puritans, cowered outside the city walls with the bawdyhouses, the beer gardens, and other resorts of pleasure and when the intellectual life of the age was so profoundly occupied with ideas of virtue and vice, the Christian and stoical moralists on the one side, the pagan mythology and man's immemorial practice upon the other?

The ancestor of all this long line of satirical and moralizing melodramas of revenge is Kyd's celebrated *Spanish Tragedy*, printed in 1594, one of the most successful of all English plays upon the stage and one of the most influential in the history of the theatre. It is probably the only original play by Kyd which has survived. While it cannot be held equal to the mature work of Webster, Jonson, and the playwrights of the golden age of the theatre, it has no place in the ranks of mediocrity. For at least a quarter of a century it was frequently played and continually revised. For the first time with complete success it introduced to the English stage love, lust, honor, murder, madness, and revenge as themes for tragedy. Far more rapid and lively and essentially medieval in its theatrical style and tempo than the French, Italian, or earlier English plays based on the poetic or declamatory works of Seneca, it set the most popular model for the serious Elizabethan drama. Marlowe's poetry could be parodied but not imitated; Shakespeare was destined for achievements too subtle for reduplication; but Kyd in one stroke determined the technique and the temper of most of the representative tragedies of the period.

The considerable merits of the work are unescapable.

It is both a better constructed and more dignified drama than *Titus Andronicus* or *Hoffman*. The chorus of Ghost and Revenge brilliantly focuses the attitude of reader or audience. The impressive antecedent action gives depth to the theatrical perspective. Major and minor plots are artfully drawn together. Thus at the same moment that the Viceroy of Portugal discovers that he has not, as he has believed, lost a beloved son, Hieronimo finds himself a wrongfully bereaved father. A network of relations between the various characters is firmly knit. Almost all the persons are of some interest, as may be instanced in such secondary figures as Pedringano, who jests so diabolically at death, and Hieronimo's wife, who cries in vain for justice. The relation of brother and sister is successfully studied in the roles of Bel-Imperia and Lorenzo, affording a suggestion for Ophelia and Laertes. Lorenzo and Balthazar, seeking love through secret murder and wealth through conspiracy, are perfect types of the theatrical villain. Hieronimo madly crying for justice in an unjust world and attaining his end only by wide-embracing and bloody murders becomes a type for one of the most important characters repeated throughout Elizabethan drama. He is conceived of as both hero and villain: an unjustly injured man seeking retaliation and a bold individualist breaking the laws of society to effect his primitive and violent justice. Revenge is an even sweeter sin than lust. A much more sinister and less idealized figure than Hamlet, Hieronimo stands somewhere between Shakespeare's noble prince and Tourneur's too savage Vendice in *The Revenger's Tragedy*. Repeatedly the play points the way to later, more mature and more brilliant work. We have foreshadowings of characters and situations, of thoughts and words, in *Hamlet, King Lear,* and *Macbeth*. The use of a play within the play to end the tragedy and serve

THE TRAGEDY OF EVIL 23

the conspirators as a cloak for murder gives a stately conclusion not only to this tragedy but to nearly a score of
notable plays to follow.

The verse has the quality of an art movement in its
lusty youth, the strength and glamour which connoisseurs
commonly term "primitive." Though stiff, over-formal,
and derivative from earlier English neo-Senecan drama,
it is nervous, vigorous, and expressive. Kyd's language
seems entirely adequate to voice the sturdy and elementary
feelings which he seeks to convey. The unknown hands
who contributed the additional passages found in the later
quartos enriched the play without marring Kyd's original
spirit and design. He obviously writes as a brilliant apprentice in his craft, not as yet free from verbal imitation.
Thus he freely quotes or translates passages from Seneca,
especially the *Thyestes*, and uses those rhetorical devices
which Lyly and his Elizabethan contemporaries loved and
which Jonson and the Jacobeans shortly put to tireless
ridicule. "O eyes, no eyes" is neither the worst nor the
purest style. But the writing becomes an integral part of
Kyd's feeling for his art and of the design and sinews of
his play. He gives us that first pleasure which we derive
from any work aesthetically sound: the joy of encountering
a mind which knows thoroughly where it is going. So
however we may value his work, we must at least acknowledge it to be unfaltering. His dialogue, based on end-
stopped lines, balanced phrases, and frequent rhyme, lacks
the flexibility and ease of verse-conversations in the later
playwrights and yet has the measured firmness of a truly
lyrical and artificial style. The famous opening speech of
the Ghost, the soliloquies of Hieronimo, and the last love
scene between Bel-Imperia and Horatio exhibit his style
at its typical best. It sounds like clear bells booming over
water. Poetry in a measure it undeniably is, though it never

reaches the heights attained by any of Kyd's greater successors. Even Ben Jonson in the last stages of his career spoke with apparent sympathy for the old play which he had so often parodied yet to which he had himself made repeated additions.

So far was Kyd in advance of his age that the most faithful and distinguished of his followers in the drama wrote a considerable time after he had come to his own tragic end. Nearly a score of years had passed before it became apparent that Kyd had discovered the richest single vein in the drama of the period. A bloody revenge in which honor exacts the price of lust became the formula for many an Elizabethan masterpiece. Especially the austere satirical elements in *The Spanish Tragedy* were destined to a long course of development. The strong moral flavor of all the serious drama of the age and its preoccupation with sin and evil appear in notable works representative of English tragedy at the close of the sixteenth century. A theatrical vogue springs from a serious and tragic conviction. Two of the most poetic and theatrically successful tragedies of this period are singularly eloquent in expressing the stringent Christian view of sin. In the gift for sheer poetry Shakespeare had in the early part of his career no more eminent competitors than Marlowe and Dekker. The former never wrote more powerfully than in his *Doctor Faustus,* and *Old Fortunatus* proved the chief tragedy of the latter. These plays resemble each other in being more than half medieval in both thought and imagery. Each depicts the seductive power of sin over mankind. The playwrights paint evil in its brightest allurements and in its darkest consequences. Faustus sees Helen in her splendor before he meets Satan in his horror. Fortunatus and his evil son revel in the pleasures of the world and the flesh before they fall into the hands of the devil.

Dekker's play has an impressive choral apparatus, arranged in two choirs; that of Fortune stands for the world, the flesh, and the devil, that of Virtue impersonates honor, truth, and goodness. In these intensely moral works the avowed subject is always the war of good and evil, and even here the dramatists give to evil the greater share of their attention. The drama of the sixteenth century, to be sure, seems generally lighter and more cheerful than that of the austere Jacobean period; yet even so, a moral earnestness prevails. Two other of Shakespeare's chief early contemporaries use highly moral and even Biblical subjects in the most effective of their serious works: George Peele in *David and Bethsabe* and Robert Greene in *A Looking Glass for London*. One of these plays depicts the sins of David, the other the prophetic fulmination of Jonah over Nineveh.

The long line of distinguished plays following the tradition inaugurated by Kyd of a darkly satirical drama rich in irony and deviltry assumes its full swing in the serious works of John Marston. Like a number of his fellow dramatists, this highly interesting author began his literary career by writing satires, his own appearing in 1598, and proceeded to a number of comedies and tragedies with considerable asperity and originality until his early retirement. He was in prison in 1608 and in holy orders shortly thereafter. Marston delights in showing a court in which lust and murder prevail, where diabolical trains are laid alike for the innocent and the guilty and virtue scarcely draws breath in the foul atmosphere. There is a good deal of repetition in Marston's writing. The macabre tragedy *Sophonisba* bears close resemblance to bitter *Antonio and Mellida*, while *Parasitaster, or The Fawn*, like *The Malcontent*, deals with a disguised Duke who pries into dark corners. Indeed, one temper prevails in all. That *Antonio and Mellida* becomes by virtue of its second part a tragedy while technically *The Malcontent* is a tragicomedy, or serious play with a happy ending, indicates no fundamental difference between the two works, the most interesting of their author's serious plays. Each has the same sinister outlook upon life and eloquent and trenchant though slightly grandiloquent expression. Without ever attaining complete surety of touch, Marston becomes a really distinguished poet in his favorite blending of tragedy and satire. Although his works tend to be episodic and imperfectly composed, they have a striking validity. Like Hamlet, he broods over the crimes, the vices, and the follies of court life.

The plays on Antonio and Mellida give good instances of the strength and the weakness of the mordant strain in Elizabethan drama, especially in the so-called tragedies of revenge. The first part of this bisected play sets the mood and sketches the characters, giving only a minimum of action. The one milestone in the action, the discovery of Antonio's letter, is slobbered over with an apparently humorous distaste for mere deeds. Marston is concerned primarily with the spirit. His interest is in the Machiavellian hypocrisy of the usurping Duke Piero, in the stoical fortitude of the banished Duke Andrugio and his brave and super-emotional son, Antonio. The best of his play is conversation, not especially dramatic but lively and at times highly poetic. The second part of his tragedy, on the other hand, abounds in violent, improbable, and bloody actions, rivaling those of *Titus Andronicus*. Antonio, the hero, kills almost from a wanton joy of killing, butchering the innocent son of Piero in a church. One murder treads on another's heels and the final slaughter, with the dissevered tongue and the needless torments, accords with the more barbarous taste and manners of the age. The sequel proves, indeed, closer to theatrical claptrap than to true dramatic poetry. The first part shows the spiritual heights of which the Elizabethans are capable; the second part, despite some brilliant bits of detail, their physical brutality and cultural immaturity.

One of the brighter passages in Part Two deserves, nevertheless, a special notice as typical of its author's reflective and satirical tendencies. Pandulfo, the venerable and virtuous courtier, has long preached and exemplified the stoical ideal. Yet in time his heart breaks, his ideal vanishes, and he confesses, "Nature will out, despite philosophy." Marston characteristically likes to remind us that Seneca, the arch stoic, was himself a man of strong doctrines and weak deeds. Neither he nor anyone else, it is cynically assumed, can practice such teachings. Marston is disillusioned with the very moralist whom he and his fellow playwrights are in the habit of citing with the most favor.

The sophistication of Marston's mind at its best is exhibited in his habit of critical commentary upon himself. So, in the chief love scene between Antonio and Mellida where both are disguised, each on recognizing the other commences to speak in Italian. After the ecstatic speakers return to English, a minor character coolly soliloquizes over the matter, apologizing to the audience, "if I should sit in judgment, 'tis an error easier to be pardoned by the auditors, than excused by the authors; and yet some private respect may rebate the edge of the keener censure." A good apology can indeed be made for the "authors." Marston used a bold but artful device in an eminently artificial play to express a moment of ecstasy. Further evidence of his self-consciousness, which has at times an air of adolescent smartness, appears in the valuable "Induction" where the various actors comment on the conventionality of their respective roles. One plays the arrogant duke, and others play the gallant, the parasite, the fool, the fop, the braggart, the stoic, and so forth to the end of the list. Such writing shows how consciously Marston realized the prevailing conventions in the roles of Elizabethan drama and fiction. His satirical bent is much strengthened by his intellectual attitude.

The strongly reflective element in his best work associates it with the writing of Kyd, Webster, Tourneur, and other authors of plays dealing with revengers and malcontents. Some of these plays are more disillusioned than others, but all are alike bitter. It also distinguishes his work from the paler tragedies with which the first great period of modern drama drew to a close. The earlier dramatists, with an essentially Elizabethan inspiration, are medieval, intense, and almost savage in their morality, while the later playwrights of Jacobean inspiration are rhetorical, sentimental, and superficial. The difference is essentially that between John Donne, the Elizabethan, and Robert Herrick, the Cavalier. The school of Fletcher was not as a rule happy in its reflective mood. Massinger, the most meditative of the group, is usually ineffectual as a thinker; their tragedies contain little to arrest the mind. Shirley, the last of these dramatists to linger upon the scene, is particularly incapable of a philosophical style. With a superficial and apparently happy and normally adjusted life, he was one of the last persons in the world to carry on the spirit inherent in *Antonio and Mellida* or *Hamlet*. If there is something adolescent in Marston's brooding over discrepancies between life and the Senecan ideal, there is something almost senile in the vacuity of Shirley's inner life. Not merely violent events but inner problems make poetic tragedy, and of such problems the gifted and witty Cavalier playwright knew little. Assiduously imitating the letter, he never captured the graver spirit of his predecessors. With the stronger power to think there goes also in the case of Marston a stronger power to feel. Excessive violence, as in *Antonio's Revenge*, may defeat the better genius of the playwright; but when he writes at his best we enjoy both a sincerity of emotion and a critical spirit.

The major action of *Antonio and Mellida*, Part One, provides the best specimens of its author's passionate manner. Thus Charles Lamb turned with special enthusiasm to the dignified and stirring passages that depict the sorrows of the exiled Andrugio in the Venetian marshes. As in the case of Hieronimo, we are inevitably reminded of the aged Lear upon the heath. The slightly affected and self-conscious manner of the young poet by no means prevents genuine emotions from lively expression. Some delicate touches also accompany the story of the fortunes of the deposed and faithful Duchess Maria in *The Malcontent*. But the best of Marston is in the fusion of thought and feeling as contained in the satirical roles of his own malcontents. The disguised Duke in his famous tragicomedy is melancholy and surly as Jaques, misanthropic as Hamlet, and austere as his spiritual brother in *Measure for Measure*. Marston in this work began a fashion not only for himself but for several others. The cynical duke in disguise testing the morals of his corrupt subjects becomes a stock figure in the drama of the age. Yet none of the roles exceeds in interest that of Marston's Malevole. Of the earlier malcontents it owed most to Ben Jonson's fine satirical figure of Macilente in *Every Man Out of His Humour*. Marston's play, significantly enough, is dedicated to Ben Jonson. The great Burbage acted the leading role in each work.

The relation of the first to the second half of *The*

Malcontent seems deliberately to parallel that between the two plays on Antonio and Mellida, although the tragicomedy is throughout the more mature and polished drama. The first two or three acts of the tragicomedy are sparing in action and profuse in the exposition of character and philosophical ideas. Malevole enters solely as malcontent. Only when the plot passes into that period of complication which Jonson learnedly termed the *epitasis*, does the hero appear as a dethroned Duke conspiring to repossess his former power. As usual in such cases, the early scenes prove more literary and intellectual, the later more theatrical and stirring. Despite the Machiavellian plots and counterplots, the later scenes retain a surprising amount of dignity and genuine feeling.

Both of Marston's notable dramas in addition to their major characters contain a considerable number of minor figures of little or no value to the story but of the utmost importance in producing the satirical atmosphere. Marston is usually disdainful and highhanded in multiplying such characters in defiance of the easier art of stage plotting, which he commands quite as readily as most of his contemporaries. Those who immediately followed his lead, as Middleton and Ford, retain the same types of characters worked more conscientiously and, if one insists, more skillfully into the action. But it will be recalled that one of the finest of all the characters in Elizabethan tragedy, Flamineo in Webster's *White Devil*, takes no great part in the action, providing primarily a chorus of satirical comment. Such, too, is the important role of Thersites in Shakespeare's *Troilus and Cressida*. It is in sketching the atmosphere of a fatuous and immoral court life that Marston chiefly excels. The fools, parasites, flatterers, and braggarts, frail women and aged procuresses, he paints in vivid strokes, setting all against the contemptuous comments of a Malevole, a Pandulfo, or a Falice. This gives his plays their tang, the quality for which they are most admired and which places them with the most prolific vein in the tragedy of the age.

At approximately the time that Marston ceased writing plays, or about 1606, Cyril Tourneur began to write for the stage, carrying on the vein opened by Kyd and so profitably followed by the author of *The Malcontent*. The dramatic works of Tourneur are equally few and disputable from the bibliographical point of view. *The Atheist's Tragedy* is regarded as certainly, *The Revenger's Tragedy* as questionably, his. Into the doubts regarding authorship it is irrelevant to go here, since the chief burden of this, as of other chapters in the present book, is that the plays are even more clearly typified by theatrical convention than by the individuality of their authors. So it is equally insignificant that John Webster wrote passages for the second version of *The Malcontent* and that some good grounds have been given for assigning the authorship of *The Revenger's Tragedy* in whole or in part to Thomas Middleton. The style minutely resembles neither that of any known work by Middleton nor that of the one play universally (though perhaps wrongly) assigned to Tourneur, *The Atheist's Tragedy*. For the average reader the essential point is that all the tragedies in this group have many notable features in common: all are dark and passionate flowers springing from a single stem.

The full title, *The Atheist's Tragedy, or The Honest Man's Revenge,* indicates its somewhat paradoxical relation to the so-called revenge plays. Charlemont receives from the ghost of his murdered father counsel similar to that which Hamlet receives regarding his mother. He himself is enjoined to eschew vengeance. Vengeance, a delicious vice among men, though a virtue in heaven, is to be left in those hands in which by Scriptural warrant it rightly belongs—with God. The inference here is that the sins of the atheist are such as only God's wrath can justly punish. At the end of the play by a miracle the atheist in his attempt to behead Charlemont stumbles and kills himself. This is therefore the drama of God's revenge upon murder and impiety.

Conforming in general to the favorite pattern of the age for dark, melodramatic tragedy, the play nevertheless proves in some respects exceptional. It becomes one of the most philosophical of Elizabethan dramas, dealing as it does so frequently with the problem of atheism. D'Amville denies both the moral law and the Supreme Being, pursuing his own welfare and that of his sons by murder and rape. Felicity he places in wealth. But God defeats him in the end; his sons die leaving no heirs; their loss and the pricks of conscience drive him to distraction; and in the moment when his triumph seems assured the vengeance of heaven brings sudden death.

Still in the tradition of the Senecan play grounded on moralized horrors, this drama makes much use of ghosts. The spirit of Montferrers appears several times, and the dread of it haunts the larger part of the fourth act, which takes place at night in a graveyard. Machiavellian plotting on the part of the atheist follows the witty tradition of English stage intrigue. Like all dramas of its class it lacks the elements of the purest tragedy. D'Amville is a villain unredeemed by any qualities sympathetic to the audience. He is not "one of us" but, on the contrary, a monster, sufficiently typical of human nature, perhaps, in some of his immorality, but abnormal in his brutality and in his inveterate contempt for theism. His victims, on the other hand, are so perfect in stoicism as to be equally beyond our sympathy. The play has its sad or its terrifying moments, but its atmosphere as a rule remains that of bustling tragicomedy rather than that of true tragedy.

One pleasing aspect of the work is the unusual interest attaching to some of the minor roles. In Sebastian, of the family of Mercutio and Mirabel, we have an excellent example of the type best loved by John Fletcher: the cavalier hero, generous, courageous to the degree of recklessness, humorous, carefree, and profligate with women. The antithetical part of the puritan, Languebeau Snuff, is likewise well conceived:

> Verily
> Your gravity becomes your perished soul
> As hoary mouldiness does rotten fruit.

The scandalous affairs of the two loose women, Levidulcia and Cataplasma, the bawd, though very licentious, are realistically convincing. Sebastian's sickly brother must have presented an unusual and striking figure upon the scene. The old Montferrers possesses the dignity of some of the old men in Shakespeare. Charlemont, the hero, becomes exceptionally eloquent in the episode of his military adventure and in his grief for his murdered parent. The play affords a good instance of that theory of Christian or chivalrous ethics which declares that a good woman is without sexual desires—an idea later to be developed even more extravagantly by Fletcher and most of all by Massinger. There is much emphasis on Castabella's physical purity. Addressing Charlemont in her last speech she exclaims:

> ... Now at last,
> Enjoy the full possession of my love,
> As clear and pure as my first chastity.

To which Charlemont replies:

> The crown of all my blessings.

Of interest, too, are the macabre speeches in the grave-yard scene, reminiscent of *Hamlet*. One of the clearest tests of the worth of Tourneur's play is that even in the midst of the fantastic incidents in the graveyard episode, with its multiplicity of artificial meetings and disguises and its sadly strained idealism, the dignity of the drama remains scarcely impaired. While the verse is not always distinguished or euphonious, the style at times becomes powerful and is generally a flexible vehicle for dramatic expression. The playwright succeeds at all times in embodying his eminently moral theme in lively word and act.

If *The Atheist's Tragedy* is a picture in several colors, *The Revenger's Tragedy* becomes a study in black. Only a frail white line of virtue edges and defines this work carved out of ebony or the heart of midnight. The ruthlessness of the avengers renders them more than half villains. The chaste and virtuous Vendice is no less brutal than his wholly depraved enemies. Once more the heroes are merely the scavengers of sin, subdued by the element they work in. The scenes in which Vendice first tests the honor of his mother and his sister and then frightens the former into repentance prove as savage and repellant as any representation of evil itself. The play, which has never been surpassed for logical consistency, carries to its inevitable conclusion the dramatic tradition of the tragedy of evil. It represents a world of virtually unmixed evil, every line dyed in the consciousness of sin. Drunkenness, for example, is called "liquid damnation." Much is made of the crime of bribery and of the horror of impenitent dying. Such a community of the damned as Tourneur imagines could exist only in hell; in the state of nature its constituent parts would immediately destroy one another. Thus the tragedy has the absolute qualities of a mathematical axiom or religious belief. It is neither realistic nor in the finest sense of the word tragic. Yet as an intellectual achievement and even as a poem this black serpent among Elizabethan tragedies obviously has merit and fascination.

The well-deliberated artificiality of the work is indicated even in the naming of the characters, Tourneur carrying further a device tentatively employed in *The Atheist's Tragedy*. The characters all bear abstract names, such as Lussurioso, Spurio, Ambitioso, Supervacuo, Vendice, Castiza, and Gratiana. Such technique had long been employed in comedy, deriving partially from the allegorical drama of the Middle Ages. Faithful to the same spirit of abstraction, the playwright lays his scene in no particular city or period of history. The drama remains almost devoid of historical allusions, only an uncertain reference indicating that the scene lies somewhere in drug-damned Italy. Tourneur evidently knew well enough that his play was in fact a "morality" and no realistic representation of any time or place. Some of its critics, however, confusing modern realism with Elizabethan artificiality, have sentimentally reviewed it as though its scenes were intended to reproduce actuality.

The high degree of artificiality and the manner of naming the characters are only two of the qualities relating this sinister work to comedy. With this play Tourneur brings the picaresque drama to its climax. Quite as intellectual as emotional, it stresses the cleverness of the intriguers as much as the horror of their crimes. Bitter irony turns to sardonic humor. Thus Tourneur develops to the full the type of writing in the mad scenes depicting Hieronimo and in the death of that memorable humorist, Pedringano. Infernal laughter reaches its height in the central episodes. Two characters, who may be called sons of the Duke, are in prison, one his bastard and the other the youngest offspring of his Duchess by a former husband. The envious elder sons of the Duchess beseech the Duke to pardon the bastard, while by intimation they suggest his execution. The Duke decides to trick his petitioners. Secretly he sends a message releasing the bastard, while he gives the two sons of the Duchess an order for the execution of his legitimate son. This message they joyfully deliver to the jailor, but are unaware that the letter refers actually to their own brother. So they become the unwitting means of accomplishing what they least desire. While they rejoice over their triumph, the man whom they believe slain enters the room, and the truth of their action dawns upon them. The two knavish companions are depicted as bound in alliance only by self-interest and, when occasion arises, as exchanging their disguise of friendship for irascible hatred and contempt. This humorous theme Spenser employs in his Legend of Friendship in *The Faerie Queene*, nor is it uncommon in the dramatists. Ben Jonson uses it in his *Alchemist* and elsewhere. Tourneur's macabre humor also appears to advantage in the scene in which Vendice is employed to murder himself.

Despite its knavish wit, *The Revenger's Tragedy* is the most mortifying of all Elizabethan plays. Hamlet, to be sure, meditates upon bones dug up in a graveyard, and many a scene in Kyd, Marston, Webster, and Middleton carries us back to the old dance of death. But it remains a large part of the conception of sin as presented in *The Revenger's Tragedy* to recall the change from sensual pleasure and luxury to the bleakness of the grave. The joys of this world are material pleasures that vanish into dust: only the actions of the just are preserved in immortality. Hence the tragedy abounds in penitential imagery resembling that of an Elizabethan sermon. Tourneur's imagination, like Donne's, flourishes in the tomb. The finest poetical passage in the play is the address of Vendice to the skull of his mistress while he rubs its jaws with the poison presently to prove fatal to the Duke. Admirably setting the key, a similar passage with a grimace of dry bones about it begins the play. As in *Macbeth* and other Jacobean plays of a semi-melodramatic type, thunder and lightning punctuate the action. The play begins and ends with funereal grief. How well the author knew the conventional vein in his art appears in a number of theatrical metaphors. While tormenting the Duke with the poisoned skull of his mistress and the spectacle of his bastard son corrupting the Duchess, Vendice exclaims:

> Brother, if he but wink, not brooking the foul object,
> Let our two hands tear up his lids,
> And make his eyes like comets shine through blood.
> When the bad bleeds, then is the tragedy good.

To this Hippolito adds:

> Whist, brother! the music's at our ear; they come.

Evidently Tourneur liked the theatrical figure, for he repeats it with small variation in the last moments of the play. Here Vendice cries:

> No power is angry when the lustful die;
> When thunder claps, heaven likes the tragedy.

Because of its extreme artificiality and exaggeration *The Revenger's Tragedy* lacks the warmth and humanity of *The Atheist's Tragedy*. It lacks, too, variety and scope. Nevertheless within its narrow and eminently logical confines *The Revenger's Tragedy* proves the more mature, consistent, and accomplished work. Entirely of a piece, each page is written in a terse and bitter style admirably sustaining the theme. A consistent vein of imagery, like the unpleasant tang of cold metal on the tongue, runs through the whole. Even more than in *The Atheist's Tragedy*, Tourneur employs a mixture of frequently contrasted verse and prose. Broken rhythms express the disharmony of tortured souls. In brief, *The Revenger's Tragedy* is a distinguished play, short only of the greatness of the masterpieces of Webster and Jonson because it lacks their ampler humanity.

Turning from the two masterpieces of Tourneur to those of Thomas Middleton, one passes from the more abstract and poetic work in the tragedy of evil to the more realistic and human. In a mordant, witty, and disillusioned vein Middleton composed many popular plays, chiefly comedies, from about 1600 to his death in 1627, collaborating with Rowley, Dekker, Fletcher, Massinger, and others. In place of the poetical elevation of *The Revenger's Tragedy* we find in his tragedies the sharp scrutiny of an accomplished painter of character. Less the preacher proceeding from *a priori* notions of sin than the keenly deductive observer of life, Middleton writes the tragedy of evil with a more convincing sense for actuality. While Tourneur wrote from the point of view of the Elizabethan conservative opinion regarding Machiavelli's philosophy, Middleton writes from the Elizabethan outlook on the supposed depravity of Italian life. He minimizes the literary or Senecan ghost, though he is not averse to the popular notions of witchcraft. His own genius for comedy, as well as the assistance of his collaborator Rowley, helps him to introduce into tragedy an unusually large number of the dryly satirical and harshly humorous scenes based on the follies of shallow-brained men. A dry scorn instead of a moist-eyed pity characterizes his tragic mood. He prefers unpleasant and ignoble figures, a harsh literary style, an absence of the heroic, and above all a most mordant temper. The least sentimental of all the playwrights of his age, excepting only Jonson, he relishes a thorny and juiceless language. If he generally lacks the vein of romantic poetry to be found in Marlowe and Fletcher, he has a tart manner and a wealth of observation. Artful in economy and design, he can afford to dispense with the eloquence that now soars into heroic poetry and now descends to fustian. The exaggerated type of stage villain with a snatch of the heroic proves relatively inconspicuous in his work. His instinctive fondness for theatrical situations dissuades him also from the more subjective type of biographical tragedy cultivated by Marlowe, Shakespeare, and Chapman. But no less than his predecessors he bases his conception of tragedy on the law that the wages of sin is death. None better than he shows the acidity so commonly found in Elizabethan drama.

Middleton's *Witch* is often remembered because certain passages in the play distantly resemble the witch scenes in *Macbeth*. *The Witch* might better be recalled as a rather second-rate drama affording an instance of Middleton's scorched and unpoetic manner, with his active fancy for intrigue. The scenes passing in rapid succession are sensational in theme and commonplace in dialogue, much like an average modern motion-picture play. Such journeyman's work does no real justice to Middleton's power as a tragic poet, though it does indicate certain of his lively qualities. All his best work has a macabre humor only intimated in the witch scenes. That *The Witch* is a tragicomedy itself hints that he is not here putting forth his full powers in tragedy.

Much more judiciously admired are his two fine tragedies, *The Changeling* (written with the aid of William Rowley) and *Women Beware Women*, both pictures of the unsavory fruits of the sins of lust and murder. Middleton's tragic muse is crowned not with the bays of Apollo but with such ashen fruits as grow upon the evil trees in Dante's Inferno. Although more objective in his unpleasant view of life than Webster, he proves even more consistent. The plots of the plays themselves well express his mood.

The central story in *The Changeling* relates how a noble lady named Beatrice, to avoid an unpleasing marriage, employs a rough and unsightly servant, De Flores, to kill her betrothed and thereby compromises herself so far that she cannot avoid his loathed embraces. As she perceives the diligence and energy of De Flores, however, her hate for him turns almost to admiration. Meanwhile she marries Alsemero, the man whom she has originally loved. To deceive him as to her lost virginity, she arranges that Alsemero shall lie on the wedding night in the dark with her servant, Diaphanta. Alsemero's suspicions are allayed and the plot is successfully executed. To avoid betrayal, De Flores cunningly murders the maidservant. But eavesdropping spies report to Alsemero an intimacy between Beatrice and De Flores. She protests herself innocent of adultery, but in a moment of weakness and misjudgment admits the murder and so betrays De Flores. He then revenges himself upon her by confirming their amorous relationship and secures her death beside him, since the two escape justice and torture by killing themselves together. Of some further interest is the brother of the man to whom Beatrice was first betrothed. Through him the note of revenge is introduced as an undertone. Elaborate humorous scenes laid in a madhouse give the authors an opportunity to exploit their love of the grotesque and this device apparently attained considerable popularity among Jacobean audiences.

Although some dignity is lost by the motion-picturelike rapidity and implausibility of the fourth and fifth acts, the play as a whole is strikingly lifelike and sincere. The irony of the relations between Beatrice and De Flores, especially as her disgust yields to admiration, becomes the core of the play. The brutality of De Flores' passion must have seemed to the spectators a supreme instance of lust. The two leading characters are admirably contrasted, the woman criminal almost by accident, the man by nature.

The dialogue, especially in the first three acts, becomes amazingly real and convincing. True poetry is achieved in an almost colloquial idiom. In the rapid and unrhetorical manner here employed, a single word or gesture carries immense weight. The play, it seems, stands midway between Shakespearean poetry and a modern melodrama upon the screen.

How far its spirit depends upon a Christian sense of sin may fairly be judged by a few unpleasant words spoken by the jealous husband to his rival:

> I'll be your pander now; rehearse again
> Your scene of lust, that you may be perfect
> When you shall come to act it to the black audience,
> Where howls and gnashings shall be music to you:
> Clip your adulteress freely, 'tis the pilot
> Will guide you to the *mare mortuum*,
> Where you shall sink to fathoms bottomless.

A similarly sinister and ironic story inspired with the dread of sin occurs in the tragedy bitterly entitled *Women Beware Women*. As usual, Middleton is leisurely in getting the story under way and rapid to a degree of haste in the conclusion. True also to the technique used in his comedies and other tragedies, major and minor plots are employed. The Duke of Florence sees in a balcony a woman of unusual beauty named Bianca, who has recently been married to Leantio, a poor clerk. Livia, a great lady, arranges the girl's seduction by inviting to her mansion first the mother-in-law and then the girl herself. While the two older women play chess, Bianca is shown over the house and betrayed. Livia, however, inconveniently falls in love with Leantio. When the latter rudely boasts to his wife, Bianca, of his new fortunes, Bianca complains to the Duke. At this juncture a minor plot is drawn into the major one. Isabella, a Florentine, and her uncle Hippolito, brother of Livia, are in love. Livia, to favor her brother and satisfy her thirst for intrigue, pretends to Isabella that the latter is really an illegitimate child. Thereupon Isabella marries a foolish young man known to us merely as the Ward, to shield illicit relations with her uncle Hippolito. It is to him as a kinsman and therefore as a becoming avenger of Livia's honor that the Duke appeals. Angered at his sister's relations with so humble a civilian as Leantio, Hippolito kills Leantio. Livia is now incensed against Hippolito and truthfully charges him and Isabella with incest. The two factions plot the destruction of each other during a masque at court. All their plots prove only too effectual. Bianca seeks to poison a Cardinal, the Duke's brother, who has rebuked their marriage. By an accident reminiscent of *Hamlet* the Duke receives the poison, and thus the play ends with the deaths of six of the most prominent characters, the Cardinal remaining to pronounce the pointed moral:

> Sin, what thou art, these ruins show too piteously;
> Two kings on one throne cannot sit together,
> But one must needs down, for his title's wrong;
> So where lust reigns, that prince cannot reign long.

As Hippolito has said more poetically a few moments before:

> Lust and forgetfulness has been among us,
> And we are brought to nothing.

Although several critics hold that the complicated intrigues with which the tragedy closes mark a notable falling off from the brilliant character-studies of the earlier acts, it would be too harsh to describe the conclusion as a failure. The poetry and pomp of the masque are well managed, and the relations of Livia to Isabella and of Bianca to the Duke remain of interest to the last. One of the finest figures in the play, Leantio's equivocally minded mother, unhappily drops out in the second half, but at least some recompense is made in Act Three by the introduction for the first time as a speaker of the impressive Cardinal, the Tiresias of the play, whose voice sounds a prophetic warning of the denouement. All the characters except the Cardinal are essentially evil. He remains to pronounce their damnation.

The power of this tragedy is in the characterizations and the style. The conventional plot resembles that of dozens of pieces by Fletcher, Ford, Massinger, Shirley, and the school of Cavalier playwrights. In its story a recital of sordid intrigue, such a play can indeed become a work of the imagination only by virtue of its execution. Although it comes nearer to pure tragedy than several of the plays considered in this chapter, it everywhere leans heavily upon satire. The dry and bitter wit of Livia, Bianca, and the Duke at the expense of Leantio and his mother represents the spirit of the piece. Middleton makes superb use of contrasts, notably in the roles of the tradesman Leantio and the aristocratic Livia. The dialogue crackles with irony and contempt. For once he uses speeches as long and eloquent as those of Fletcher or Massinger, but his style remains his own—homely in imagery, abrupt in rhythm. A fair specimen of it might be plucked from Bianca's acid rejection of her bourgeois husband when she has just become the Duke's mistress:

Is there no kindness betwixt man and wife
Unless they make a pigeon-house of friendship
And be still billing? 'tis the idlest fondness
That ever was invented, and 'tis pity
It's grown a fashion for poor gentlemen;
There's many a disease kissed in a year by't,
And a French curtsy made to't; alas, sir,
Think of the world, how we shall live; grow serious;
We have been married a whole fortnight now.

The most direct way to realize where the true spirit of his work lies is to examine the characterization. Lamb made an almost inevitable comparison when he likened the delineation to Chaucer's, although when he described Livia as "such another jolly housewife as the Wife of Bath" he singularly neglected the tragic seriousness and sharp satirical venom of Middleton's portrait. The weak-willed mother is the most lifelike and original of the figures. But a vivid imagination created also the vivacious Bianca, the infatuated Leantio, the formidable Livia, yes, even the detestable Guardian and his foolish Ward. Duke and Cardinal prove excellent as characters of "state." And skill appears also in the secondary plot, finally so well united with the major action. Middleton, like his friend and collaborator Rowley, was a man to relish the sinister flavor of the story of Isabella's incest and the grotesque and ironical humor in the clumsy antics of the fool. With less philosophical amplitude and poetic elevation than Webster, Middleton has a more flexible and humane mind. He is almost as poetic as it is possible to become without a more metaphysical cast of imagination. By virtue of his two masterpieces he proves himself among the most distinguished authors of works falling into Bernard Shaw's category of "plays unpleasant." The earlier acts of *Women Beware Women* cannot readily be equaled in their kind.

But the most enduring fame won by the "unpleasant" or satirical tragedies of the Jacobean age has fallen to the two masterpieces of John Webster. This playwright was active during almost exactly the same years as Middleton and likewise wrote realistic comedy more often, though less well, than sober tragedy. He was more closely associated than Middleton with the group of scholarly poets led by Jonson and Chapman. Gifted in the vein of melancholy melodrama as his predecessors had been, Webster surpassed them all. More poet and philosopher than they, he writes with greater maturity. In the depths of passion with which these sensational tragedies profess to deal, he shows himself the most deeply versed. More clearly than his immediate rivals he redeems the sensational by touches of imagination. As an artist he stands midway between Kyd and Shakespeare. After him the more robust elements in the tradition rapidly decline, till the form is thinned out in the relatively prosaic tragedies of Shirley.

It is hardly necessary to remind the reader of the plots and characters of *The White Devil* and *The Duchess of Malfi,* excepting Shakespeare's the most familiar of all Elizabethan plays today. That there is much repetition of situation is at once apparent, since each tragedy presents an Italian scene with two brothers, one a Cardinal, savagely avenging the honor of a sister. Each play is nominally based upon history. Each celebrates the bravery of a defiant woman and depicts the Machiavellian intrigues of subordinate courtiers. Each is bitter and strong, a moral darkness illumined by quick cross-lightnings of trenchant poetry. Vittoria and the Duchess of Malfi, Flamineo and Bosola, Brachiano and Antonio, Francisco and Ferdinand need at least no introduction to readers of English poetry and drama.

How Webster's Italian tragedies blossomed on the

rugged stem of the neo-Senecan tragedy of revenge is a
story somewhat monotonously repeated by literary historians. Despite much that is new or greatly altered, the old
design undeniably remains. Thus *The White Devil* and
The Duchess of Malfi resemble *The Spanish Tragedy* in
being plays of revenge for domestic honor, bloody and
spectacular, fierce and passionate. Madness is treated in all
the plays, and Webster even preserves some traces of the
Senecan Ghost. To supernatural horrors are added those
of the Renaissance torture chamber. Women vie with men
in boldness and sin. The occasional introduction of pity or
compassion relieves the otherwise dense criminal darkness.
So far the pattern is a familiar one, and Webster introduces nothing new.

But even his indebtedness to tradition goes much farther
than this, farther than his brilliant editor, F. L. Lucas, has
shown. The moral and satirical temper of the plays is their
most vital quality. In writing another scourge of villainy
Webster is merely developing with new variations a theme
cultivated by the bitter Kyd, the morose Marston, the savage Tourneur, the sardonic Middleton. Ben Jonson had
disclosed the crimes of ancient Rome in serious plays much
like Webster's satirical tragedies of modern Italy. Webster, in short, uncovers a nest of villains in the spirit of his
predecessors and in the severest tradition of Christian morality. His plays come nearer to pure tragedy than theirs
because of his ampler share of poetry, nobility, and sympathy and because by virtue of this sympathy they contain
fine strokes of characterization, yet they miss the perfection
attained by his master Shakespeare largely because they
remain on the whole satirical essays and moral onslaughts
upon mankind rather than impartial tokens of human fate.

Although Webster does not reveal himself as a pessi-
mist, the ripeness of his mind shows in the degree to which

his dramatic satire has in many points mellowed into pessimism. With high imagination in his poetic designs, he contrives that the two most original characters in his plays are virtually choral figures set forth to promulgate their doctrine of disillusionment. Flamineo and Bosola cast a mist of melancholy over the two tragedies. They speak a remarkably large proportion of the lines which are the most poetic, although frequently in prose. The Greeks wrote lyrical choruses for their plays, otherwise in epic verse; Webster writes, as it were, prose choruses for his tragedies in blank verse. Although pity and horror are both important in his works, disillusionment and pessimism are more notable still. The chief horror of *The White Devil* is, in fact, that so many persons make "a bad end"; while the real catastrophe of *The Duchess of Malfi* is not the moving spectacle of the Duchess' heroic death but those remarkable scenes in which one knave after another goes out like a candle in a fog. Webster's appeal to the mind of the twentieth century has been chiefly due to this melancholy strain.

While analyzing his art, something may be said in behalf of *The White Devil*, which is usually described as markedly inferior to *The Duchess*. To be sure Mr. Lucas, who knows better, reverses the familiar judgment, but with no more than an expression of personal preference. The latter play is closer to the Caroline than to the Elizabethan spirit. In it Webster composes an exceptionally smooth piece of art with few sharp excrescences, a polished work somewhat in the manner of the school of Beaumont and Massinger. Compared with its predecessor it is simpler and more classical, less prodigal and abundant. The Duchess is a more sympathetic figure than Vittoria, but so sympathetic as to become more pathetic than tragic. Typical of the Cavalier drama are the pathetic moments, far more

numerous than in *The White Devil*. There is something
almost sentimental in *The Duchess of Malfi*, especially in
the role of Antonio, a quality which rendered the play the
more admired and imitated from the time of Shelley and
Lamb to that of Swinburne and Browning. One play suggests the harsh masculine realism of Jonson, the other the
romantic and effeminate sentimentalism of Ford. As a
well-made play the earlier cannot compare with the later.
But as a document of human interest *The White Devil* is
ultimately the more remarkable. Although less coherent in
plot, it proves no less unified in poetic mood. And its characters are more sharply drawn. Flamineo is more powerful
than Bosola, Vittoria than the Duchess, Francisco and
Monticelso than Ferdinand and his brother. Certainly
Brachiano is superior to Antonio. And there can be no
group of minor figures more effectively conceived than
the sorrowing mother Cornelia, the innocent brothers
Marcello and Giovanni, the brigand Lodovico, the Moor
Zanche, and the faithful Isabella. In the end men and
women must be fascinated by Webster because he himself
was fascinated by them. His regard for personality approaches Shakespeare's. The brazen and defiant characters
of his first play may seem less suavely delineated than
their less intense successors in his second, but as Elizabethan vigor surpasses Caroline sentiment and preciosity,
his first masterpiece surpasses its fainter and more delicate
echo. With *The Duchess of Malfi* we see the long tradition of the satirical tragedy already tending toward its
decline.

Webster's style is the perfect medium for the rugged
and dramatic satirist. His verse was formerly accused of
harshness and unmusical movement. Similar criticism was
once universally leveled against Donne and now is in that
instance universally discredited. The playwright merely

employs in his own idiom a tendency strongly marked in
Tourneur, Middleton, Jonson, and other of the satirically
minded poets. He composes a jagged verse to express his
scorn for the barbarity of life itself. Prose mingles subtly
with verse to the same end. His famous figures of speech
remain in perfect harmony with his unharmonious versification. Webster believes in "stabbing metaphors," sudden
thrusts of the imagination, enabling us to read his dark
philosophy as if by lightning flashes at midnight. On the
point of death Flamineo reflects:

> My life was a black charnel. I have caught
> An everlasting cold; I have lost my voice
> Most irrecoverably.

Nervous and abrupt in their style, these images must have
seemed frightfully uncouth to the taste of the Restoration
and of the eighteenth century, but from a more catholic
point of view constitute a large part of the strength of
Webster's art. As the foregoing citation shows, he is the
absolute master of the terse and imaginative dramatic
phrase. Such a poet is indubitably a conspicuous figure on
England's Parnassus, standing among the dramatists as
Donne stands among the lyrical poets.

One of the most celebrated tragedies by John Ford,
whose eminently poetic dramas were written about 1630,
carries on with considerable fidelity this tradition of the
melodrama married to morality or, in other words, of the
tragedy of violence haunted by the sense of sin. '*Tis Pity
She's a Whore* is not only a Senecan tragedy of horrors
perfect in all except its want of a ghost; a tragedy of evil,
it presents a group of characters almost without exception
sinful or despicable. Once more, as in Marston, Webster,
and Tourneur, the Italian setting is used as appropriate to
a tale of lust and murder, English playwrights comfort-

ably assuming the land of Machiavelli and the Pope to be the home of vice and crime. Again we have the familiar brevity and terseness of scenes, rapidity of action, complication of plot, intrigues at cross-purposes, and ceremonious conclusion. Even the same Cardinal, whose robes seem symbolical of crimson murder, adorns the spectacle, as in Webster and Middleton. Society in general is pictured as fallen into depravity. The Papal Court is corrupt; incest and equally dark crimes possess the more intellectual and forcible characters, ignorance and folly make the remainder contemptible. Here is a nest of snakes in human form; Ford's Parma rivals Webster's Malfi and Ursini or Middleton's Florence and Alicant.

To understand the spirit of this work, it is well to review the persons whom the play unrolls before us. Here is an honest friar, almost the sole figure of any consequence who is not morally culpable, yet whose counsel no man heeds. At the end of the play he leaves the cursed walls of Florence forever. The Cardinal is protector of the swordsman and murderer, Grimaldi. After his rape upon justice a voice is heard to question:

> Is this a churchman's voice? dwells justice here?

To which the reply follows:

> Justice is fled to Heaven, and comes no nearer.
> Soranzo!—was't for him? O, impudence!
> Had he the face to speak it, and not blush?
> Come, come, Donado, there's no help in this,
> When cardinals think murder's not amiss.
> Great men may do their wills, we must obey;
> But Heaven will judge them for't another day.

This Soranzo is a brutal and impetuous creature, whose most memorable act is to drag his wife furiously about by the hair. Hippolita, his lover, is a woman carried headlong by unrestrained sensual desire, a fury in a woman's form. Vasques, the villain of the piece, surpasses most of his rivals in drama in his absorbing interest in bloodcurdling crime. His plots to poison Hippolita, torture Putana, and avenge his master are almost without an equal in brutality. He amusingly aspires to prove that a Spaniard can outgo even an Italian in revenge. Putana herself multiplies tenfold the cynical note of Shakespeare's Nurse in *Romeo and Juliet* and wholly lacks the Nurse's amiability. Richardetto, supposed to be dead but disguised as a physician in order to pursue his unfaithful wife, presents a sinister picture of a man caught in a dark net of falsehood. Finally, the leading characters are an impious brother, Giovanni, and a frail-willed though impetuous sister, Annabella, caught in the deadly sin of incest.

It is true that in certain respects the play proves less sinister than its still more melodramatic predecessors. Ford treats the sins of his two chief lovers more gently than might have been expected. Though presumably, like the audience of his play, still believing in God and in the Christian conception of sin and morals, he by no means takes so uncompromising a view of Giovanni's impiety and skepticism as Tourneur takes of the atheism of D'Amville. Although he evidently holds most of Giovanni's arguments in defense of incest to be sophistical, with Cavalier slipperiness as much as with tragic insight he ascribes some nobility to Giovanni's character and even introduces a note of pure tragedy into his speeches addressed to Annabella just before her death. Ford understood the true spirit of tragedy perhaps as well as any of the Elizabethans except Shakespeare, as three or four of his other dramas sufficiently show. But with the momentum of so long a line of successful and really poetic melodramas behind him, in *'Tis Pity She's a Whore* he makes only these tentative departures from the more generally accepted tradition. The most hasty comparison of the pessimistic elements in *Macbeth* and in Ford's play reveals how much more truly Shakespeare is the tragic artist even in the most sensational of his later tragedies. Clearly Macbeth and his Queen are incomparably stronger figures than Giovanni and Annabella.

Ford handles the intrigue in *'Tis Pity* with considerable success, leading us to ever stronger and stronger moral thrills. When the play begins, the incestuous passion has already reached an advanced stage. The lovers yield to each other in the first act. In this act, too, their peril becomes acute. As they grow more and more deeply involved, the catastrophe is postponed by abrupt turns in the action. The various possibilities raised by the suit of the foolish and wealthy heir, Berghetto, are forever removed when he dies by accident on the poisoned sword of Grimaldi. The perilous marriage with Soranzo hangs upon a hair, till Hippolita's plot ends in her own death instead of his. Soranzo's life has twice been saved as if by miracle. The violence and physical brutality of the last two acts has scarcely an equal in the entire range of English drama. These scenes, it should be remembered, mark a culmination not only in the horror of blood but in the horror of sin. The spiritual terror is even greater than the physical, and the drama is no more remarkable for its melodramatic shudders than for its play upon moralized emotions.

But an even more eminent figure than Webster or Ford enters into the group of playwrights who cultivate this essentially satirical vein of tragedy. Ben Jonson, like Shakespeare, stood at the same time in his age and above it. Stubbornly protesting his own independence, he wrote in an idiom partly his own as he both guided and followed his contemporaries. In his most popular works he achieved a harmony of comedy and satire, of farce and earnestness, not precisely duplicated elsewhere. Similarly in his trage-dies he carried to a unique development the satirical vein first opened successfully by Kyd and cultivated by a group of distinguished successors. He frowned upon the popular Italianate melodrama of revenge. Pure tragedy he never so much as approaches, for he has no conception of the true tragic character. His stoical figures are incapable of deep suffering; he is more interested in morals than in men; his virtuous characters are prigs; and his numerous knaves are, of course, depicted altogether unsympathetically. Hon-est and uncompromising moralist that he is in his tragedies, he never allows his criminals, as Ford, Shakespeare, and even Webster do, for moments at least to insinuate them-selves into our favor. In *Sejanus* all the chief persons are rascals, virtue being reserved for a few minor personages who constitute a satirical chorus. In *Catiline* the conspira-tors are more conspicuous than the just men. The play deals with Catiline's fall and Cicero's triumph. But the fall of so unqualified a villain cannot constitute tragedy, and certainly no tragic feeling is evoked at the sight of Cicero in his hour of triumph licking his eloquent lips like a cat.

Even the texture of Jonson's language precludes a tragic effect. His intellect is in advance of his intuitions and his emotions. Warmth and coloring are lacking in the ample blocks of whitely gleaming marble that constitute his dramatic paragraphs. A true son of the classical Renais-sance, he has a vastly more rhetorical and expansive style than Middleton or Webster. More gifted with the histo-rian's or the scholar's feeling for detail than with the romantic poet's instinct for the climatical changes of human moods, he remains everywhere heavy, realistic, and, from one point of view, prosaic. Like the Bellman, he believes that "what I tell you three times is true." Each of his two tragedies contains several important scenes of senatorial debate; indeed in their most private intercourse his characters are likely to be forensic. The most sustained passage in the colloquial spirit is the scene in Fulvia's chamber, which constitutes the second act of *Catiline*. This passage T. S. Eliot refers to as the best scene in the two plays. It is certainly the most Shakespearean passage and probably, from one standpoint, in the best poetical tradition. But the leading English master of Renaissance rhetoric should be remembered for what he chiefly is rather than for what he generally is not. Jonson is the greatest Roman historian in England before Gibbon. He possesses a style in verse as nobly modulated and as musical, as ample and as eloquent, as Gibbon can boast in prose. There is no more manly eloquence than Jonson's Roman plays. As an artist in the iambic pentameter line he equals his friend John Donne. Although moments of splendid dramatic action frequently enliven the periods of sonorous debate, Jonson's style, whether in comedy or tragedy, is based upon oratory. One recalls that his first advice to an aspiring poet is the devoted study of Quintilian. Perfect in all his tropes and figures, never merely ornamental as the effeminate euphuists or denuded and bare as the flaccid realists, he preserves a superb strength of diction. The time intervening between the Elizabethans and ourselves is divided almost equally between the neoclassical era, which on the whole preferred Jonson's style to Shakespeare's, and the romantic and modern eras, which definitely prefer Shakespeare's to Jonson's. Whether the public taste will ever return to Jonson's Augustan eloquence is indeed doubtful; but readers of moderate education must from time to time envisage the robust joys of Jonsonian expression.

His two great tragedies, *Sejanus* and *Catiline,* are alike studies in statecraft, the first somewhat dryer and more cynical, the later more epic and poetical. *Sejanus* relates the intrigues by which this favorite of the Emperor Tiberius brought about the downfall of a series of potential heirs to the throne, brushing his enemies ruthlessly aside, till he was himself destroyed by the elaborately concealed treachery of the Emperor. The second play has a simpler and more concentrated action. It relates, with some of the artifice of compression which Shakespeare practiced in dramatizing Plutarch, the Catilinean story, chiefly out of Sallust. The plans which the conspirators concoct in secret are repeatedly discovered. Catiline is defeated in the election of the consuls. A desperate band attacks Cicero's house. He delivers the great oration which drives Catiline from Rome. The conspirators who remain at home are executed. While the Senate debates the punishment fit for the rebels, Caesar underhandedly giving them aid and Cato advocating the utmost severity, news comes that Catiline and all his army have fallen beneath the sword.

Some qualities which deprive these plays of the wide popularity enjoyed by the usual melodrama may be observed. Each tragedy, especially *Catiline,* gives a greater scope for oratory than is generally relished either by English audiences or actors. Jonson's drama is not nearly so rhetorical as that which has flourished lustily on the stage in Latin countries, but the English have always been lovers of action. Shakespeare proved far more faithful to the national tradition. Jonson's tragedies always read like translations from Cicero, which, indeed, they occasionally are. Again, in certain of his plays he has little interest in sustained narrative value. While he never wanders from his subject, a more intellectual task than storytelling arrests him, even in such works as *Every Man Out of His Hu-*

mour and *Bartholomew Fair* as well as in *Sejanus* and *Catiline*. Such a course is not followed because he is incapable of a good plot, as *Epicoene, or The Silent Woman*, and *The Alchemist* show, but through choice. He invites the educated reader or audience to follow the almost invisible threads which Sejanus and Tiberius, Catiline and Cicero weave for each other's undoing. But Sejanus' goal is always remote. The action grows episodic. Characters disappear altogether or abruptly come into view in a manner highly disconcerting, unless one holds firmly in mind the totality of the intrigue. The principal figures are often absent for long periods from the stage, their power being shown only in its effect upon others. In the midst of *Sejanus* Tiberius drops out of the scene or, one might say, becomes invisible, while Macro arises. Sejanus is seen only through his puppets in the fourth act. When considered as a story *Catiline* proves even more disjointed. The characters in the second act are barely mentioned in the first. The protagonist has been seldom spoken of in the first two acts; he appears first in Act Three, and he meets his antagonist only once in the play, namely in Act Four. Even then they have no real dialogue or action together, since Cicero delivers an oration interrupted only by the muttered curses of his opponent. In the last act the scenes fluctuate between Rome and the mountains where Catiline is fighting. Jonson takes an intellectual rather than a dramatic view of the subject. Although logically the act proves a beautiful piece of architectural symmetry, the playwright indisputably sacrifices theatrical suspense. Finally, among the limitations to the popular reception of the plays is Jonson's inability to draw any woman who is not at heart a man. Agrippina and Sempronia attempt to outdo men in mannishness. Entirely devoid of the romantic or sentimental points of view, Jonson differs here almost as far as possible not only from Shakespeare but from Beaumont and Fletcher, Ford, Dekker, Shirley, and other contemporaries. His Roman matrons seem more masculine than even a history of Roman culture will concede. Jonson's art is a rugged mountain whose summit reaches far above the slopes shrouded in the graceful drapery of trees. His words are quarried out of marble and are not growing things. From a variety of causes, then, his austere and fiercely satirical tragedies please only a limited number of readers. Discarding the somewhat savage tradition of the tragedy of revenge, he retains the profounder tradition of satire which robs tragedy of its exaltation but by no means deprives it of substance and worth.

The two tragedies of Jonson, then, both by what they include and what they omit, point clearly to the central feature of this long line of notable English plays. Although for the most part tragedies of horror and revenge, all are knit still more firmly together because all are satirical plays exemplifying the tragedy of evil. Each, in Marston's words, is a scourge of villainy. Conceived and animated in the severest tradition of Elizabethan morality, they owe to it their most distinctive flavor. From this source flows the poetic energy which in no small measure they possess. The end which they achieve is by most critics today deemed inferior to that pursued by Shakespeare, the purer poet and ultimate master of both comedy and tragedy. But it is no small matter to do the second-best thing well. The chief Elizabethan tragedies of evil, truly imaginative and humanly moving, are far better poems and plays than such monstrosities of horror as *Titus Andronicus*. They are tragedies of thought as well as of blood. Although of neither variety, they stand nearer to true tragedy than to vulgar melodrama.

This description, though not quite like previous accounts, represents in a broad way a generally received opinion. It is, of course, always easier to describe than to explain. As already indicated in this chapter, the causes for the emergence of such a tragic tradition are so complex as to lie beyond the reach of satisfactory statement. Such a drama developed because it could not be otherwise. Elizabethan tragedy originally sprang from Seneca, himself a moralist. It accorded with the Christian and largely medieval sentiments of its authors and audience and, incidentally, justified itself before the formidable Puritan censor by its moral tone. No subject was more thrilling to the Elizabethan soul than sin. The attitude of the preachers too often controlled the playwrights. Pessimism and disillusionment followed horror and dismay as the typical English reaction to Machiavelli and the new materialism of the Renaissance philosophers. English tragedy reflects a sixteenth-century British prejudice regarding Italy. It reflects also the remarkable revival of satire at the hands of Jonson, Donne, Marston, Hall, Nash, and a throng of others at the close of the century. It reflects the actual disaffection in court life. In varying degrees all these factors, with many others, combine to bring about the type of somber play which ranges from Kyd and Marston to Webster and Ford.

CHAPTER THREE

TRAGIC IRONY

O good Iago!
—SHAKESPEARE

IN THE PRECEDING CHAPTER we have seen how powerfully the impassioned Elizabethan conception of sin
dominates many of the tragedies of the age. Yet it would
be inaccurate to hold that the larger number of the serious
dramas conform to this melodramatic, satirical, and malcontent spirit. Though no single tradition becomes so conspicuous as the sinister tragedy, the fecundity of the
playwrights surpasses even their obsession with moral depravity. Some of their plays, though less powerful than
Shakespeare's, come close to the stricter ideal of tragedy.
Other serious works bear relatively little indebtedness to
the tradition early established by Kyd, Chettle, and Marston, but are dominated by other ideals, as the expression
of the Renaissance philosophy of the true prince and
courtier, the newly acquired historical objectivity, the
flourishing tradition of romance, or the mere extravaganzas
of fancy and hyperbole. Along all these lines admirable,
or at least memorable, work was produced. Instances in
which Shakespeare's fellow dramatists most nearly approached his own purer spirit of tragedy are strikingly
contrasted with the more usual conformity to melodramatic
play-writing.

In the mature period of his art Shakespeare wrote no
play conforming to the Elizabethan satirical tragedy which
exploits the sense of sin. The principal character is always
more sinned against than sinning. If there are exceptions
in his earlier work, as in *Richard the Third* or more nota-

bly in *Titus Andronicus,* a tragedy as certainly bespattered with blood as it is dubiously Shakespeare, these remind us of how rapidly he outgrew the cruder and more conservative art and morality of his contemporaries. With his imaginative mind and charitable heart he soon graduates from the rule of thumb dividing humanity into the good and the bad. While he remains to the last absorbed in ethical problems, he tends to make his immoral characters heroic or sympathetic, his upright characters both fallible and human. He never writes plays with the moral vehemence of the inspired Christian preacher nor does he allow, even in his most savage works, physical horror for long to dominate the scene. The Machiavellian monster fails to haunt his imagination, as it beset the mind of Marlowe; the bitter misanthropy of Marston similarly casts only a shadow upon his canvas. The hatred and horror of sin are absorbed in a larger unity. The moral and aesthetic purity distinguishing his major dramas forbids him to whitewash or blacken human life. He is no more taken in by his own Timon of Athens than by his own sentimental Duke in *As You Like It.* His serene impartiality is no denial of ethical values but simply a rare restraint from rude oversimplification. At no time does he descend, with Webster, Middleton, Ford, or Tourneur, to depict a world as almost totally depraved. Never with these playwrights does he depict an Italian court as a scene of unmitigated vice. He neither calls the persons of his plays to a last judgment nor lays undue stress upon the moral issues of which he remains so clearly aware. In short, he gives friendly credence to the conventional code of morality without making emphasis upon it a key to his thought.

It is well to glance still further at the plays in which Shakespeare leaves the Senecan tradition furthest behind, especially since in a few cases his moves in this direction were much imitated. The pessimism darkening the background of *Hamlet, Lear,* and *Macbeth* has little or no place in *Othello, Antony and Cleopatra,* or *Coriolanus.* The wise and judicious humanity of *Antony and Cleopatra,* though singularly engaging and beautiful, was not easily imitated, just as the one quality most difficult to produce in landscape painting is the sunlight in which a scene is bathed. The Cavalier dramatists proved singularly deficient in the type of character analysis brought to high perfection in *Coriolanus.* But the romantic narrative, the aristocratic setting, and above all the portrait of physical passion represented in *Othello* much attracted the Cavalier mind. Beaumont and Fletcher, Ford, Massinger, and Shirley, distinctly lacking the moral or philosophical earnestness of the Elizabethans, imitate this play far more often than any other work by the master dramatist. Infatuation and jealousy become favorite subjects, while court scenes in Mediterranean settings warmly allure them. In *Othello* more than in any other play Shakespeare bid fair to set up a dramatic model to rival the melodramatic and satirical tragedy inaugurated by Kyd. *Othello* is quite without misanthropy or social satire. It has none of the anti-Italian venom affected by so many Elizabethan playwrights. From a personal, rather than from a religious, motive Othello himself seeks Desdemona's death. Whatever the characters may do, the horror of sin is not a dominating thought. Nor is the work narrowly didactic, in the sense that Othello's stupidity, as this appears to Emilia, brings the whole play to its focus. We have simply the story of one flourishing villain and of a number of honorable souls, of whom Othello is one, all of whom come to desperate misfortune. Life is so constituted that disaster falls in terrifying measure upon Othello, Desdemona, Emilia, Brabantio, Cassio, and other honest spirits. Although they may be driven at times to madness or to some other weakness, they show much bravery in meeting and in withstanding their pain. The nobility of the tragic mood reaches its fitting climax in the words of the repentant Othello. Here more clearly than in many another equally pure tragedy the ancient ideal of this dramatic form is clarified. As Milton writes at the end of his great poetic tragedy:

> His servants He, with new acquist
> Of true experience from this great event,
> With peace and consolation hath dismissed,
> And calm of mind, all passion spent.

But there is in a true tragedy something above both the storm of the passion and the calm of the conclusion. The awareness of man's apparently unlimited capacity both to suffer sorrow and to conquer it, to pass through "a hell of a time" without losing either dignity of spirit or sanity of mind—this defines the worth and grandeur of the tragic experience. Not what the characters feel, but what we feel, determines the result. It is necessary but hardly more than incidental that at their last moments Shakespeare's tragic figures surmount their anguish or that Othello is more clearly the master of his grief than the distraught and illusion-haunted Lear. The drama itself becomes the symbol for the sacrament of art whereby the audience experiences its own purgation. So Aristotle had written; and the world has long experienced the truth of the observation. The purgation is effected through sympathy. We discover the tragic resolution of the difficulties of life. Perhaps death itself contributes a part of this resolution. Certainly it belongs rather to the psychic than to the aesthetic significance of tragedy. In any case it is that experience which all the turmoil and grief of the satirical melodramas from

The Spanish Tragedy to *The White Devil* do not give, but which *Othello* does give, and the other masterpieces of Shakespeare as well. In certain cases he uses the formula of Kyd and transforms it into pure tragedy; in other cases he discards most of the melodramatic tradition and attains pure tragedy by other and less sensational means.

The outstanding quality of the purer tragedy is irony. This is the quality which has been frequently called tragic irony both to distinguish it from less august manifestations of the ironical and to emphasize its high place in tragedy itself. One cannot think of Greek tragedy (our loftiest school of tragic drama) without thinking also of the irony pervading it in the tales of Thebes and of Troy, of Oedipus and of Agamemnon. Irony lies in the sinister whims of chance, in the inveterate persistence of bad luck, in the yawning discrepancy between expectation and fulfillment, between the ideal and the actuality. It lies rooted in the malicious antagonism between the elements of human nature and of the universe. Winter is the irony of summer, frost of running water, sorrow of joy, and death of life.

> ... Indeed this counsellor
> Is now most still, most secret and most grave,
> Who was in life a foolish prating knave.
>
> .   .   .   .
>
> When that this body did contain a spirit,
> A kingdom for it was too small a bound;
> But now two paces of the vilest earth
> Is room enough.
>
> .   .   .   .
>
> But yesterday the word of Caesar might
> Have stood against the world: now lies he there,
> And none so poor to do him reverence.

Tragedy presents a change for the worse, indeed many such changes, and these are presumably ironical. Nobility

turns to folly, and happiness to sorrow. The crowning irony
of a tragedy occurs when truth is discovered too late. So
Oedipus recognizes his spiritual blindness, and Othello his
criminal mistrust. But the irony inspiring typical English
plays can better be considered in specific instances than in
further definition of what is after all a sufficiently simple,
although broad, general idea.

The moral earnestness and extravagance of Shakespeare's
contemporaries render them less fertile in the subtler
moods of ironical tragedy than the slightly younger playwrights of the Cavalier period. Beaumont and Fletcher
are on the whole too fantastic and mercurial to achieve a
mood which is rarely attained without a depth of spiritual
quietness. Inferior poet as he was, Philip Massinger, active
from about 1616 to 1640, had a surer instinct for tragedy
than his more brilliant companions, and the rare genius of
John Ford, when not overcommitted to pathos or to melodrama, at times touched the classical ideal even more
nearly. In happy moments these playwrights, freed at once
from both sentimentalism and sensationalism, envisaged
essentially noble or well-meaning men or women who come
to grief through external forces or an inner want. We feel
in the face of their characters, "O, the pity of it"—a feeling too seldom appropriate to the harsher scenes of dramatists whose disposition is less often to pity than to condemn.
We discover that Massinger and Ford are here less concerned with images of passion created for their own exuberance than with images of grief that in their beauty
bring their own balm. This tragic mood is certainly touched
upon by Kyd, Middleton, and especially Webster, but it is
not so fully sustained as in plays by their successors. In
selecting examples of this achievement from the later
dramatists there is no intention to point to the best of the
plays, but only to the instances in which this particular

tragic mood has been most clearly reached and adequately
sustained. Ideally speaking it should be an aroma surrounding the entire play. In fact it is more often achieved
unmistakably only in the last scenes. Since the tragic feeling arises quite as much from situation as from language
and is the almost inevitable consequence of situation, a
summary of the story of a play with little or no further
insistence upon definitions of tragedy and irony readily
explains itself in these terms.

The Duke of Milan is commonly regarded as the most
moving of Massinger's tragedies. By temperament much
more given to tragedy than to comedy, this author spent
most of his powers in sober dramatic romancing. His ex-
cessively didactic inclinations, to be sure, mar several of
his tragedies, as in his frigid work, *The Roman Actor*—his
own favorite among his plays—while a lack of vitality reduces the dignity of many of his works, turning them from
tragedy to tragicomedy. Without slavish imitation he
attains in creditable manner, in at least *The Duke of
Milan*, what Shakespeare achieves supremely in *Othello*.
Beside the more moving drama the lesser work seems
more conspicuous for good intentions than for great
achievement. Nevertheless, like so many of its author's
plays, it tells a simple story uncommonly well. To a classical feeling for the tragic irony is added a classical feeling
for form. No superfluous intrigues burden the plot. Only
the incessant rhetorical language points unmistakably to
the baroque phase of Renaissance taste. In point of morality the play is also much of its age. Sexual pleasure enhanced by the idea of female purity is made the center on
which the tragedy turns.

The story tells of Lodovico Sforza, Duke of Milan,
infatuated with his own wife, Marcilia. When he hears
that Charles, the Emperor, has defeated Francis, his ally,

at Pavia, he hastens to acknowledge the sovereignty of Charles, leaving his wife and his dukedom in the protection of Francisco, his favorite. Fearing that he may not return alive, he leaves with Francisco a command to kill the Duchess in the event of his own death, sealing in advance a pardon for Francisco. The latter bears a secret resentment against the Duke for a long-past injury to his sister. Hence he attempts to seduce the Duchess and, on failing to accomplish this, secures her forgiveness by exhibiting evidence of the secret command which the Duke has laid upon him. The Duchess greets Sforza coldly on his return from the Emperor. Stung by her obstinacy and by the report, seconded by Francisco, that his wife has been unfaithful, he kills her. But the eloquence of her dying words convinces him of his error. Like Othello, he soon learns the truth of his crime and longs for forgiveness. So distracted is he that his courtiers find it impossible to admit to him the death of his wife. He imagines her to be merely unconscious. Francisco, disguised as a doctor, is employed to make the corpse appear alive. Serving his own ends, he rubs the lips with poison, and the Duke literally dies upon a kiss. Francisco, like Iago, is content with his revenge, although he is sentenced to death. In passing it may be worth note that since Francisco has actually been rebuffed by the Duchess, he is a more plausibly motivated character than his Shakespearean prototype. The central intrigue is further made more impressive by the addition of two women jealous of the Duchess, the Duke's mother and his sister, who is also the wife of Francisco. Counseling the Duke wisely is his high-minded friend, Pescara. Such is the simple and moving story.

An essential feature in the tragic irony of the play is the generally admirable character given to the chief persons in the action, the Duke and the Duchess. The former is represented as a heroic figure suffering from an excess of the virtue of affection and from the unavoidable pitfalls of an intriguing enemy. Exactly as in the case of Othello, we have a sympathetic figure, with a blind spot, made victim of a malicious deception. Although Massinger lacks the dynamic vitality to create a really powerful character, he can convey the impression of a certain nobility. While his chaste art has something of the dullness of all neoclassical tragedy, from Norton and Sackville's *Gorboduc* to Arnold's *Merope*, it achieves part of the awareness of human tragedy and warmth of human feeling found in Shakespeare.

Ford's *Love's Sacrifice* gives us an example of more spirited characters with whom we are sympathetic but who through their own errors and external forces come to great sorrow and to the mercy of death. Again by a cruel irony the husband murders the woman whom he loves. We are far removed from the astringent moralizing of the tragedy of evil. Passions are conceived in spacious and imaginative spirit as elemental forces sweeping through life. Universal, sad and tender, the thought at least accords well with the severest definition of tragedy. Some of the trappings, to be sure, reveal the superficiality and frivolity of the author and his age. Amorous intrigues are multipled in a manner that mars rather than enhances the dignity of the play. The Cavalier audience delighted in subsidiary episodes of backstairs whispering and deception, a pleasure to which Ford panders. Long before the period of his own dramatic activity, approximately from 1622 to 1638, the macabre humor of secondary scenes in the tragedies of Marlowe, Shakespeare, Middleton, Marston, and Tourneur had made a genuine contribution to their sardonic atmosphere. The lighter passages in Ford's own *'Tis Pity She's a Whore* harmonize sufficiently with the work as a whole. But ex-

ception may be taken to a few passages in the minor
scenes of *Love's Sacrifice*, which introduce moods as various
as horror and farce but never quite accord with the obviously tragic intention of the drama itself. Although not
wholeheartedly devoted to pure tragedy, when he does
strike this note he strikes it unfalteringly. Occasionally
negligent, his inspiration whenever called upon rises to the
heights.

Ford's story, developed with many reminiscences of
Othello, when seen more closely resembles Massinger's
Duke of Milan. Caraffa, Duke of Pavia, has married a
woman of humble rank but great beauty and high spirit.
Fernando, the Duke's favorite, is impelled against his will
by a passion for the Duchess. Twice he pays court to her
and is twice refused. The second time he admits his guilt,
swearing eternal purity in his future relations with her.
Now it becomes the woman's turn. She comes to him to
plead her own passion, declaring that if their love is once
sexually consummated she will end her life by self-
slaughter. Fernando keeps his oath. Envious courtiers tell
the Duke that the two have been unfaithful to him. At first
a disbeliever, he later overhears them in a private conference, is convinced of their guilt, and kills the Duchess.
While threatening to execute Fernando with his own hand,
he is persuaded by the force of his friend's eloquence that
he has been mistaken. The last scene is theatrically most
effective. The Abbot of Monaco, brother of the Duchess,
adds solemn dignity by his presence. When the monument
of the Duchess is opened in the presence of the Duke, Fernando is found entombed with the body. As the guard is
about to seize him, he drinks poison. Smitten by the loss
of wife and of friend, for whose deaths he must answer to
heaven, Caraffa kills himself, like other tragic lovers of
the Elizabethan stage, dying on the breast of his beloved.

In a heroic speech before his death he declares his abiding affection for the two who have preceded him and commands that all three be buried in one tomb.

Ford's tragic intensity, his gift for poetic and dramatic phrase, and his keen psychic realism and understanding of passion make his play superior to Massinger's suave and symmetrical *Duke of Milan*. The interviews between the principal characters are scarcely inferior to those in *'Tis Pity She's a Whore* and *The Broken Heart*. The sense of tragedy as a rule involves a consciousness of the prodigious waste of human feeling. Our hearts are like vessels broken by accident, whose contents are spilled idly upon the ground: "The expense of spirit in a waste of shame." Life, which should somehow be planned, is ironically the slave of chance. Notwithstanding the theatricality of his last scene, Ford overawes us with this tragic awareness. We are impressed less with the sinfulness of his major characters than with their misfortunes. None of them violates the moral code. They are not wicked, but mistaken. And even had Ford preferred to depict them as active rebels against moral standards, he might still have retained his stronger emphasis upon fate than upon evil. His play stems not from the tragical-satirical tradition of *The Spanish Tragedy* but from the more purely tragic example of *Othello*.

The perils of love are equaled by the instability of fortune. Dozens of Elizabethan plays attain a tragic effect in part at least through dramatic realization of the eternal slipperiness of political power. The walls of the theatres resounded with the falls of princes. Shakespeare makes insistent use of the theme in those historical tragedies that depict the winds of chance blowing now this way and now that among the rival factions in the Wars of the Roses. It was the old theme so delightful to the Christian Middle Ages, most impressively embodied in Boccaccio's *De casibus*

virorum illustrium and in that immensely popular Elizabethan collection of biographies, *The Mirror for Magis-
trates*. But it is difficult to cite any really brilliant play
produced on the popular stage during Shakespeare's lifetime that was actually dominated by this conception. The
fall of one aspirant to princely rule supplies, to be sure,
the catastrophe of one of Ford's most successful tragedies,
the realistic drama *The Chronicle History of Perkin
Warbeck*. Since that play will be discussed chiefly in connection with its historical objectivity, it need only be mentioned here in connection with its moving picture of the
ironic fate of princes.

A deep undercurrent of irony runs through a notable
tragedy that altogether departs from the rhetorical style
of Massinger and from the princely setting common alike
in Ford's serious works and in the Elizabethan chronicle-
history plays. Ford, who wrote a number of realistic tragedies now lost, had some share in a work largely by Dekker,
The Witch of Edmonton. William Rowley, another of
Middleton's collaborators, also had a hand in it. As the
title suggests, this drama belongs to that sturdy minority
of English plays of the period native in thought and expression and by no means guided by the princely spirit of
the Renaissance. It is almost devoid of the elaborate rhetoric of the age, deals with rustic instead of court life, and
reflects none of the ideas of the reigning aristocracy. Similar
tragedies are *Arden of Feversham*, a work of undeter-
mined authorship, the anonymous *Yorkshire Tragedy*,
with which Shakespeare is said to have been associated,
Heywood's *Woman Killed with Kindness*, and a score of
other plays. *The Witch of Edmonton* is perhaps the finest
specimen of this humble stock. Its products, for the con-
sumption of the rising middle class, grew from degraded
prose romances, such as those by Thomas Deloney, or from

broadside ballads concerning the latest and most-talked-of murder. The fruits are homely and picturesque but lacking in intellectual and artistic distinction. Had Elizabethan drama developed largely without foreign aid or without the resources of Renaissance thought, much more work of this nature might have been produced. It proves almost antithetical to the more literary tradition, for it offers simplicity instead of elegance and a background of English folkways instead of a spirit of cosmopolitan culture. It stands closer to the plays of Tolstoy than to the prose of Sir Philip Sidney. The best of Elizabethan drama is neither specifically for the vulgar nor for the aristocrats but for an audience of really national scope.

Many circumstances hinder these plebeian works from attaining with any frequency the traditional spirit of true tragedy. Addressed to the less cultivated of the Elizabethan audiences, they are as a rule by the less gifted playwrights. Their tendency to realism often results in an insufficiently organized poetic idea. The plebeian mind is more attentive to action than to feeling. No grand passion is likely to be evoked. The bourgeois intellect insufficiently grasps those larger imaginative ideas which give to tragedy its universal meaning. Thus *Arden of Feversham*, a representative play, more nearly resembles sensational journalism than tragic poetry; and *A Woman Killed with Kindness*, one of the most celebrated specimens of the type, distinctly lacks elevation of thought or feeling. An ever-popular sentimentality vitiates its scenes.

Some tragic power is attained within the confines of this genre, nevertheless, as appears in *The Witch of Edmonton*. The play suggests much of the work of Thomas Hardy, for it combines in a rustic setting a tragic intensity, a humorous realism, a sympathy with rustic superstitions, and an effusion of sentiment. The drama is intensely national. It comes, however, about halfway to pure tragedy. A humble style, somewhat trivial jesting, and an occasional forced pathos, as in the last act, weaken its seriousness and dignity. In contrast, the conception of diabolism as a pervasive force in human life, effecting both high and low and ranging from the merely grotesque to the deeply criminal, has a kinship with the philosophical or religious inspiration of tragedy in the ancient world. The fiends of Dekker are the furies of Aeschylus translated from the mountains of Greece to the peaceful fields of England.

The authors employed for their story a medley of local events as interpreted by the superstitions of the countryside. From the briefest narration of their plot the moral intention is conspicuous; only a regard for the speeches themselves tells the full story of their sincerity as tragic artists: how tenderly they mirror the sufferings of the characters and with what true imagination they disclose the temptations to crime. The economic genesis of the crimes interests the playwrights less than the last turn of the screw of evil guided by the hand of Satan. Yet they are more tragic poets than homiletic moralists, for they appear more in sadness than in anger.

In the background of the tragic action stands Mother Sawyer, the witch. Through Dekker's indefatigable humanitarianism, scarcely equaled by that of Burns, the portrait of this woman is almost sympathetic. Dekker, like his audience, believed firmly in witchcraft. But he had a profound conviction that this devilish power was merely the curse of hell added to a soul already fallen by free will, much as a pious soul might in addition to its self-wrought virtues receive from heaven a premium of divine grace. As a devil in the play humorously says:

> Let not the world witches or devils condemn;
> They follow us, and then we follow them.

It is the irony of her fate that Mother Sawyer has been a good woman. But her neighbors have corrupted her by their own malice, which she retaliates in kind. Finally when she becomes so venomous as to resort to curses, the minor devils flock in to possess her soul. By her own volition she sells her soul to hell, takes a fiend named Black Dog for her lover, and blasts the neighbors with her spells. Yet Black Dog on his own account does more mischief than ever his paramour directly incites him to. It is he who in a fatal instant tempts Frank to kill Susan. Our sympathy with Mother Sawyer is both oblique and direct. We abhor him but pity her. She protests that bad as she is there are worse devils among men, as perjured judges, corrupted lawyers, dishonest statesmen, and hypocritical priests. Finally, like Frank, she wins our sympathy by her full repentance before her death upon the scaffold. It is she, too, who becomes a mouthpiece of the dramatist in voicing the strongest contempt for the crime of that seducer of honest women, Sir Arthur Clarington. She is unquestionably a genuinely tragic character. If the worst of hell's malice appears in the relations of Black Dog to Frank, the gayer mood of deviltry is shown in his relations to that ridiculous rustic, Cuddy Banks, and an old fiddler named Sawgut. By rubbing against Frank's leg the Dog puts the thought of murder into his mind; in the disguise of Cuddy's sweetheart the Dog leads him into the mire, and at the Morris Dance Sawgut's fiddle is enchanted, so that, much as he tries to play "The Flowers in May," he fails to produce a single sound.

The main action relates the genuinely tragic fortunes of Frank Thorney. He marries Winnifred, a servant in the household of Sir Arthur, where he himself holds a slightly more elevated position. Winnifred, who has previously been corrupted by Sir Arthur, now resolves to lead an hon-

est life. But difficulties lie in their path, chiefly through the
demand of Frank's father that to recoup the family fortune he marry Susan, the daughter of a wealthy farmer.
To retain friendly relations with his father, to secure
Susan's dowry, and to have enough to live on with Winnifred, Frank decides to commit bigamy. Of course, the
atmosphere of tragedy at once thickens. Frank plans to
escape to some distant part of England with his love and
with his ill-acquired funds. Winnifred joins him disguised
as a youthful page. While bidding farewell to the reluctant Susan, a simple girl who loves him dearly and with
whom he has never consummated marriage, he yields to
the Black Dog's sinister suggestion of murder. He kills
Susan, wounds himself as a part of his plot, and pretends
that rejected suitors infuriated by jealousy have committed
the crime. Susan's family at first accept Frank's innocence
and incline to believe his alleged suspicions. But while
Black Dog dances about the room, Susan's sister finds a
bloody knife in Frank's pocket. At the sight of Susan's
corpse he becomes unnerved. Before his execution he makes
a penitent confession.

Frank is thus no less a tragic victim than Mother
Sawyer. He appears a good man tainted by sin rather than
an unmixed scoundrel. The two women who become his
victims are wholly sympathetic figures, admirable in their
pathos in all parts of the play, especially in the highly
ironical scene of their friendly meeting in Act Three. That
scene rivals in tragic irony the plea for assistance that
Desdemona makes to Iago. The reader or audience grieves
at the death of these four tragic figures, impelled by sudden temptation and by desperate ill-fortune. Even some
of the minor parts rise to tragic stature, as those of the two
bereaved fathers and of Ann, a poor girl whom the countryside supposes to be stricken with madness by the devil.

Like *The Duke of Milan* and *Love's Sacrifice*, *The Witch of Edmonton* is not a tragedy of evil or an invective against sin but a tragedy of irony and a sad memorial of human fate.

The pure tragedy, or drama of serious irony, is itself a classic mean between vituperative satire and gentle sentimentality. The satirical drama we have examined in the preceding chapter dealing with playwrights from Kyd to Webster. The sentimental drama as introduced effectively by Beaumont and Fletcher we shall examine shortly. Meanwhile we shall turn to some serious plays more remarkable for their bearing upon the humanist philosophy than for their relation to any phase of the idea of tragedy.

CHAPTER FOUR

THE RENAISSANCE IDEAL

The thirst of reign and sweetness of a crown ...
——MARLOWE

MOST OF THE English dramatists of the Renaissance cultivate the regions about the heart, neglecting the more objective fields of contemporary manners and ideas. We wander with them into vague and uncertain realms, to the seacoast of Bohemia or to the Forest of Arden. The Elizabethans scale pinnacles of fancy, the Jacobean playwrights move through stately woods of aristocratic sentiment. Italy, for example, becomes to them more a romantic fiction than a historical actuality. Thus the serious intellectual controversies of the times are seldom reflected on a stage avowedly devoted to recreational pleasure. Plays from 1590 to 1642 are more often unphilosophical than not. Contemporary politics are as a rule treated obliquely or neglected altogether, and religion is viewed even more evasively. The theatre as constituted in the period was far from an ideal ground for the free expression of public opinion. Even Edmund Spenser, planning a major poem on both the private and the public virtues, actually failed to reach what he conceived to be his greater theme. Definite restraints were imposed upon literature. The words of Ben Jonson that Shakespeare wrote not for an age but for all time have a peculiar validity. Of course the drama expresses the spirit of the age, but it commonly slurs over many of its graver and more specific problems.

In this regard, as in so many cases, Shakespeare proves typical, his difference from his fellow playwrights lying rather in the magnitude of his genius than in the aims of his art. As usual he touches upon many familiar fields of contemporary thought without allowing his work to be ruled by any spirit other than his own. He is fully aware of the favorite conceptions and values of Renaissance culture without becoming in any marked degree a spokesman for commonly received ideas or a mirror of the customs and manners of the times. He generally assumes these to be unchallenged and sufficient in themselves without aid from dramatic propaganda. His plays, almost universal in appeal, cannot be shown to be dominated by either the idealistic or the realistic philosophies of his day, by the conduct books, or by the fashions of the hour. Yet the stamp of his age in thought and manners is so frequently to be noted that a few typical instances may be cited here. We are plunged instantly into the high Renaissance by the opening lines of *Love's Labour's Lost* in praise of fame:

> Let fame, that all hunt after in their lives,
> Live register'd upon our brazen tombs,
> And then grace us in the disgrace of death ...

The entire comedy reflects the stiff, heavily brocaded courtly manners. It comes nearer to exhibiting the taste of a social class than any other of its author's works. Equally in debt to contemporary thought, however, is *The Merchant of Venice*, with its picture of a romantic friendship, a witty and independent woman, and a princely society delighting in carnival gaiety and oratorical exercises. Although the colors of this play have remained fresher than those of *Love's Labour's Lost*, they are scarcely less typical of the times. The idealistic tradition appears in the role of such a gifted prince as Henry V, in the imaginative Romeo, in Brutus, praised by Antony as the ideal man, in Hamlet, the glass of fashion and the mould of form, in the all-accomplished leader, Othello, and in the philosophical Prospero. Courtly taste and morals are well depicted in *Cymbeline* and *The Winter's Tale*. The constituent parts of the ideal king as conceived by the times seem unhappily divided between the poetic Richard II and the coldly scheming Bolingbroke. Doubtless many of Shakespeare's villains, as Iago, evince the acid influence of the realistic school of thought typified in Machiavelli. Yet as a whole the manners and ideas in Shakespeare's plays are not easily dated. And he is more occupied with taste than with philosophy and more concerned with private than with public affairs. Even his portrait of Coriolanus, his most direct excursion into political ideas, shows more regard for the psychology of the individual than for current theories of the state. The most continuous and strenuous assaults of modern scholarship, prying into every conceivable corner left open, have failed to show Shakespeare as primarily a topical writer.

Two dramatists, however, enter with special boldness into the theatre of contemporary thought. Each chants the praises of the Renaissance princely hero or ideal man. What their masterpieces lack in theatrical nicety they make up in spaciousness and splendor of idea. Both were leagued closely together by an unsurpassed devotion to neoclassical humanism. Each was a translator of Greek and Latin poets, one finishing the great poem which the other left incomplete. Chapman is Marlowe's heir, bringing to its logical conclusion his friend's legacy of unfulfilled renown. He is also the complement of Marlowe. In one we see Elizabethan humanism at its radiant dawn; in the other in its zenith and in the smoldering splendor of its decline. Violent death in 1593 left unrealized Marlowe's promise of highly versatile dramatic activity, while Chapman for nearly forty years after essayed a considerable variety of theatrical work, attaining eminence only in four tragedies dealing with contemporary political life. *Tamburlaine*, Marlowe's chief contribution to the theme of Renaissance hero-worship, gives rather more of the soul than of the garment of public life; but in much of Chapman's work a more mature and inquisitive mind carries us into the province of historical realism. In the youthful enthusiasm which produced his *Tamburlaine* Marlowe remains untouched by skepticism, while Chapman reveals the hero not only fallen upon evil days but betrayed by what is false within.

Though Marlowe and Chapman represent different stages in the development of Renaissance thought, the consistent evolution cannot well be ignored. Marlowe's Machiavellian satanism, to be sure, differs considerably from the Senecan virtue preached so continually in Chapman's *Revenge of Bussy D'Ambois*. Yet a fiery pride underlies them both. And in Chapman's other notable tragedies the theme still remains the ultra-aggressive personality, treated flatteringly in *The Tragedy of Bussy D'Ambois* and skeptically in the psychological plays, *The Conspiracy* and *Tragedy of Charles, Duke of Byron*. Behind both playwrights stands a philosophy rising synchronously with the decay of Christian ethics and with the rebirth of the ancient classics. Each depicts the hero as a man intoxicated with the rightness of his own life, acting from the dictation of his own soul and mastered only by the thought of a divine or supernatural force. Their essentially Protestant heroes are aspiring spirits, jealous of their freedom, sensitive of any unwarranted encroachment upon their living, and inclined far more to self-expression than to coöperation with society. Both poets may be viewed as precursors of Carlyle.

In Marlowe there flames up for the first time upon the stage, or for that matter in literature, the soul of the

partially barbarous but peculiarly brilliant English spirit
as awakened by the social and intellectual urges of the sixteenth century. A new paganism and individualism comes
to a sudden blaze of poetical expression. Conventions of
the theatre and of poetry no less than limitations of a
prosaic realism go down before the overwhelming force
of his impassioned thought. Later in his own brief life he
was to question on the stage much of the doctrine so naïvely
and enthusiastically asserted in *Tamburlaine*. The paganism of Faustus was to be called to account by the ideas of
Christianity, and the self-willed and pleasure-loving
Edward II was to be shown in the misery of defeat. But
for Tamburlaine there could be only victory. A philosophical optimism has seldom shown itself so impetuously.
Neither James Thomson, author of *The Seasons*, with his
smug faith in eighteenth-century materialism and England's imperial glory, nor Walt Whitman, with his exuberant belief in America's manifest destiny to mould the
world's future in soul and matter, quite equals the optimism of the first eminent Elizabethan dramatist. Nor is
the childlike innocence of all enthusiastic idealism anywhere more strikingly exhibited. With obvious idolatry
for the figure of his own creation, Marlowe evokes Tamburlaine to be the delight, the admiration, and the envy
of mankind.

An innovator in art, a rebel in ideas, and in every aspect
a creative thinker of unusual force, Marlowe in the earlier
stages of his career becomes peculiarly the radical, and
Tamburlaine a glaring symbol of the anti-Christ. A new
Lucifer, he proves in more senses than one the scourge of
God. Although politically for a while the ally of the
Christians against the Turks, he embodies, ethically speaking, all the ideals decried in Christian teaching. Proud, ambitious, wrathful, irreverent, amorous, luxurious, and

treacherous, with every breath he commits one of the seven deadly sins. He loves war and not peace, cruelty and not mercy, power and not justice. In political morals, though hardly in subtlety, he rivals Machiavelli. The goddess whom he adores is a woman, Zenocrate, whom he has captured on an expedition of mere robbery. He kills the man whom she loves and whom she has been pledged to marry. In war he mercilessly slays men, women, and children, reserving only the chief of his opponents for the last miseries of disgrace and pangs of physical torture. A tyrant enlarging his kingdom and amassing his wealth by slaughter and pillage, he glories solely in his own ruthless power to rule and to destroy. Over his inferiors he assumes a most absolute command, never seeking their counsel but always dictating their actions. His typical mood is boastful defiance. This "fiery thirster after sovereignty" knows none of the scruples, doubts, compromises, and cautions which necessarily appear in any man grown to full maturity in a world of men. At best this impersonation of Satan faithfully reflects that glorified exterior which belongs more naturally to an Asiatic tyrant than to a European ruler, and so, contrary to Marlowe's intention, no doubt, it adheres to the manners of the continent from which the historical Tamburlaine arose. He is, so to speak, Milton's Satan in minority. For the poet's intention so far as he was a philosopher seems to have been rather to express the aggressive materialism of Tudor England than to embody any distinctively Asiatic ideals. The setting in the pagan East simply assisted him in creating his symbols of anti-Christian thought.

Astonishing remains the only epithet to sum up the effect of the plays depicting Marlowe's epic hero. So daring a sunburst of satanic thought and new-minted poetry England had never seen before nor was destined for a long while to experience again. A humble playwright flung impudent defiance in the face of Christian ethics. In the very extravagance of his poetic madness he verged upon the ridiculous; indeed for a generation after his death English playwrights continued to ridicule his lines, scarcely knowing whether it were better to laugh at them or to admire. It is really touching to find the rationalist Ben Jonson sincerely praising the dead poet whose lines he, with all his fellows, so often subjected to laughter. Utterly simple in the integrity of his art, Marlowe remained in a sense baffling. For his play had almost continuously the qualities of both fustian and pure poetry. From one angle a youthful rant, from another it appeared a profound vision. One could neither convict his god of war of a wholly vulgar brutality nor admire him as a purely renovating spirit. For an explanation of so delicate a blending of the extremes of crudity and subtlety, barbarism and civilization, it becomes necessary for us to go to the too-sudden burst of new vitality that was the Elizabethan age itself.

With the audacity of Milton's resplendent serpent, Tamburlaine and his creator, Marlowe, make the brutal god of war also an inspired artist. The hero is endowed with a gift of gorgeous rhetoric. He and his troops are clad in the most splendid armor and garments. A thunder of clamorous but musical sounds accompanies their movements. The entire play proceeds to the rhythm of some august ritual honoring the god of slaughter. Color adds splendor to the scene. Draperies of various symbolical hues are found upon the tents of the general. His helm is carved and plumed after the manner of Arthur's helmet in *The Faerie Queene*. Through all his campaigns he carries a picture of Zenocrate with him to inspire himself and his army. "But what is beauty, saith my sufferings then?" Had he the services of a Cellini, this satanic sovereign would certainly have employed him to make glorious the face of war and conquest. There is something magnificently superficial in this glowing externality.

The fascination of the art of *Tamburlaine* itself and the force of its ideas lie alike in the poet's certitude. A forthright manner distinguishes Marlowe here both as poet and thinker. Never has an English poet written blank verse with greater fluency of movement. The lithe lines leap out at us with animal grace. The rapidity of the movement remains unclogged by parentheses or qualifications, by elaborations or doubts. Lightning-like flashes of thought are accompanied by the thunder of the rhetoric. Though neither the first nor the second play on Tamburlaine has a semblance of plot, each is composed with a definite beginning, progress, and end. A cumulative series of events terminates in Part One with the marriage of Tamburlaine and Zenocrate celebrated by a period of revelry and truce from war; and in Part Two, with the death of the hero and the transference of his rule to his warlike son. A swiftness and sureness of march-like movement grace all Marlowe's characteristic work, including his two cantos of the narrative poem, *Hero and Leander*. When turning from these introductory cantos by Marlowe to the four by Chapman, the reader passes from the exuberant faith of youth to the complexities of an introverted manhood.

The Renaissance hero, stout in his love of personal freedom and inviolable individuality, in his life of action and lust for fame, appears once more in the person of Chapman's Bussy. Less exuberant in his thinking than Marlowe, however, Chapman depicts an ambitious man who fails to fulfill his own promised renown, a gentleman who enjoys a meteoric rise and fall in the court of France. Shifting the scene from a remote Asiatic court to an almost contemporary Paris, Chapman came as near as practicable to theatrical journalism. As it was, his representation of living persons and political events still green forced the state censor to expurgate the whole second act of *The Tragedy of Byron*. By such means Chapman reduces Marlowe's much idealized picture to a far more realistic scene. Yet much of the earlier spirit remains, translated into a more familiar idiom. While the early glamour of confidence has gone, a more thoughtful and solid structure has been built.

In estimating the place of Chapman's tragedies among the more philosophical dramas of the age, it is best, first, to acknowledge their relation to more typical aspects of the dramatic tradition. *The Tragedy of Bussy D'Ambois* has much in common with the customary Elizabethan drama of romantic passion. Its action centers in the love of Bussy for the wife of Montsurry and in the husband's inevitable revenge. Like so many other theatrical heroes, Bussy is a malcontent fond of chastising the vices of a court with his tongue and sword. The motive of revenge so prominent in *The Revenge of Bussy D'Ambois*, the appearance of the ghosts of murdered men, the sententious quotations and nocturnal atmosphere, all belong to the tradition of the neo-Senecan play as developed during the sixteenth century. All of Chapman's four notable tragedies are based upon French chronicles and hence belong in some measure to the type of chronicle-history play cultivated extensively in England. Moreover, since Chapman had a better knowledge of Greek literature than any English poet of his generation, he naturally preserved more of the classical feeling for tragedy than most of his contemporaries. Nevertheless the soul, and the distinction, of all four of his most notable plays is their philosophical idealism. Chapman studies the mind and heart of the typical aristocratic leader gifted with the full power and stature demanded by the idealism of the age. Bussy himself is akin to the impetuous but too rash Achilles; Clermont, his brother, is a Ulysses hardened by stoical doctrine, while Byron represents the decadence of the type fallen before its besetting sins of pride, egoism, and self-infatuation. Each man asserts his own liberty, guarding it jealously; each scorns the vulgar rabble and the corrupted nobles; each pursues the career of arms with a fiery devotion to his own fame. They resemble three generations of a noble family: Bussy, young, arrogant, and supremely adventurous; Clermont, mature, perfect, and admirably self-controlled; Byron, the tragic victim of an excessive aristocratic sensitivity and unlimited pride. Something of Marlowe's youthful and insatiable daring breathes in Bussy; the tragedy of the neurotic cavalier is embodied in Byron; while Clermont is a symbol of the neo-stoical faith as religiously espoused by so many humanists of the age. Chapman's first play excels in the expression of violent emotion, its sequel in an embodiment of a philosophical system, and the tragedy of Byron in its bold portrait of a psychologically fascinating decadence.

Unlike most Elizabethan dramatists whose style makes easy and fluent reading, Chapman likes best a knotty, laborious, and intellectual manner, the sign of his philosophical spirit. Dark, mystical, profound, enveloped in clouds of metaphor and simile, he demands the closest attention. Parentheses are long, grammatical constructions are difficult, the thought is involved. Pedantic even in the use of rare words minted from the ancient languages, the great translator of Homer repels the taste that demands smoothness and clarity.

In his lighter moods, as in his comedies, he could write easily and even with some feeling for dramatic characterization. But in his serious vein he is clearly more the epic than the dramatic poet, as his Homeric similes show. His characters speak as a rule in the same heightened and poetic language, highly artificial and highly uncolloquial. Thus his plays stand among the most splendid monuments of Renaissance rhetoric. His tendency to what he calls "virtuous digression" reaches a climax in *The Revenge,* where the sententious style is at its height and action at a minimum. But all his serious plays abound in long and involved speeches, and all have occasional lapses into a brisker movement. *The Tragedy of Bussy D'Ambois* is the most typically Elizabethan, *The Revenge of Bussy D'Ambois* the most profoundly classical of all plays produced during the period, while the plays on Byron with their inclination to a psychological portraiture of the hero resemble a type of analytical biography popular today.

His philosophical bent and neoclassical technique color even his treatment of minor characters. These frequently have small integrity in themselves, but exist to comment upon ideas suggested by the major characters. Thus before Bussy's death Monsieur and Guise converse on the problems of life and death, goodness and immortality. Shortly before the catastrophe in *The Revenge,* Baligny and Renel, two figures unimportant in themselves, speculate on the consequence of luxurious living and the depravity of the King. Similarly in the last act of *The Tragedy of Byron* scenes between such minor persons as Epernon, Soissons, Janin, Vidame, and D'Escures serve merely as the poet's commentary upon Byron's character. This is virtually the technique of the philosophical chorus as used by Aeschylus transferred to the Elizabethan stage.

Chapman simply inverts the moral outlook of Marlowe's *Tamburlaine.* It was not for the grave, "Senecal" dramatist to make a hero of an avowed villain or to glorify Machiavellian theories of politics. Behind all his heroes is the genuine problem of reconciling the highly prized liberty of the individual with the just claims of society. Bussy is presented as too rash and undisciplined, Byron as too ambitious and self-seeking. Only Clermont successfully fights out the battle within his own soul. But if Chapman is theoretically opposed to the devious ways of Machiavellian diplomacy, he shows no small understanding of political intrigue. The plays of Byron in particular become a really subtle study in the relation of internal dissension and international policy. No Elizabethan playwright comes so close as Chapman to a faithful picture of the political spirit of the day. Allusions to contemporary opinions and events are unusually numerous. English statesmen of the times are referred to or mentioned by name. A story is told of the visit paid by the Earl of Oxford to Duke Casimere. There are covert references to Walsingham and Bacon. Of special moment are the debate regarding the Massacre of Saint Bartholomew's Day which Chapman boldly defends and his championship of Philip II, king of Spain and zealous leader of the Inquisition.

Although many lines in the plays indicate that Chapman himself had some sympathy with the Catholic party in Europe, a romantic individualism places this precursor of Carlyle in line with ultra-Protestant thinking. It is to this party that he belongs. When the priest offers consolation to Byron upon the scaffold, the Duke replies with a Senecal argument familiar to all Chapman's readers, that a just man is a microcosm needing no exterior support. To the Archbishop Byron says:

> Horror of death, let me alone in peace,
> And leave my soul to me, whom it concerns;
> You have no charge of it; I feel her free:
> How she doth rouse, and like a falcon stretch
> Her silver wings; as threatening death with death;
> At whom I joyfully will cast her off.

A similar feeling inspires some of the last words of Bussy:

> Prop me, true sword, as thou hast ever done:
> The equal thought I bear of life and death
> Shall make me faint on no side.

In a genuinely dramatic soliloquy Byron exhibits both sides of the allied problem of destiny and free will. Chapman, of course, holds that true personal freedom is attained by conformity to universal laws. Hence he writes satirically, or at least in a purely dramatic vein, when he pictures the Duke infuriated at the prophecy of the astrologer telling him of his evil fortune as written in the stars. In a fit of passion Byron brags that a cup of wine will for him send the heavens reeling in their courses. He boasts that he will kick at fate, that he will risk his life in a giddy drive like a ship listing in a dangerous wind. Here Chapman still satirizes the ungoverned individualist. In the last words of the speech, however, the poet almost certainly returns to his own positive conviction. It is part of the tragic irony that a madman speaks truth:

> There is no danger to a man that knows
> What life and death is; there's not any law
> Exceeds his knowledge; neither is it lawful
> That he should stoop to any other law.
> He goes before them and commands them all,
> That to himself is a law rational.

Chapman's plays make abundant reference to the social and aesthetic life of the nobility of the age. In the Byron plays, for example, much is said of pictures, tapestries, and statues. The daily life of the captain in command is also well indicated. Like Homer, Chapman, the English Cavalier, loves the sea best of all things and gives his affection next to horses. Superb images drawn from horsemanship ennoble all his tragedies. The fine last act of *The Tragedy of Byron* also affords evidence of the fidelity of his pictures. Byron both in his life and in his death, as Chapman explicitly declares, had been said to resemble the ill-fated Earl of Essex. The dramatist had certainly attended some of the important political executions of the day. The great elaboration and vitality of the scene of Byron upon the scaffold afford strong witness to this. Many a gifted, high-strung, and adventurous nobleman of England during Chapman's lifetime lived and died much as his own hero, playing devious politics with ambassadors from foreign countries and in the end paying the full price. For many years the perilous problem of the heir to the throne of England had been similar to that of the heir to the throne of France as Chapman presented it.

How closely the dramatist reflects both contemporary history and taste is unmistakably to be seen in the fourth act of *The Conspiracy of Byron*. The Frenchman had actually paid to Elizabeth the visit here reported and had discussed with the Queen several of the matters here raised. In avoiding the censor's ban Chapman fails to present the Queen upon the stage, but with extraordinary boldness and a complete disregard for English theatrical practice he has their conference reported at length by two minor characters. In the economy of his play the scene is used as a warning to lead Byron back to loyalty to his king. Chapman imagines Elizabeth urging him to be a faithful subject. Thus the scene has not only a choral value but a place in advancing the action of the drama. Of chief interest, however, is the artful reproduction of the elegant diplomatic speech-making and especially of the courtly flattery as practiced during the Renaissance. Elizabeth's own skill and pride in oratory are well depicted in this scene of neo-Ciceronian eloquence. Here is the language of the humanists as spoken in the affairs of state.

Something of the fiery spirit as well as the external aspect of court life appears in Chapman's work. More than any other playwright he reflects the spacious and strenuous public life led by Elizabeth's boldest servants, Essex, Raleigh, and Drake. Bussy is Tamburlaine brought down to earth; Clermont is the same being doubly fortified with the stoical philosophy, and Byron the same being once more, undermined by his own tragic faults. All evince the powerful romantic element in Renaissance thinking. All are touched by the superstitions of the times. Byron consults an astrologer and believes in witchcraft. Bussy is haunted by ghosts. Even Clermont believes in omens and the Socratic daemon. Clermont, to be sure, subjects his will to some degree of discipline, but Bussy and Byron become the victims of their extravagant zeal. All are audacious spirits, battling a hostile world, cherishing an impossible ideal, and destined to shatter their vessels upon rocks.

With all his grave faults as a dramatist Chapman succeeds, then, in embodying his ideas in four really memorable plays, each of which in turn repays special study. Granting its ornate rhetoric, *The Tragedy of Bussy D'Ambois* remains one of the most stirring of the serious dramas of the period. A little too conventional, perhaps, it is none the less thoroughly alive. Although a thoughtful play, it strikes us first as an emotionally exciting one. Only a waning interest in the poetry of the passions caused it to lose its original splendor in the eyes of Dryden and his followers. Here, although uncommon in Chapman's other plays, the lesser characters have considerable value in their own right. Bussy has by no means a monopoly of the eloquent speeches. The domestic scenes between Montsurry and Tamora, for example, possess unusual power. Written in a fine fury of enthusiasm sustained from first to last, the play will at all times presumably be the most admired of

Chapman's productions. More successfully than any other, it celebrates the ideal of the Cavalier adventurer. In its first scene is a memorable allusion to Sir Francis Drake.

Its sequel, *The Revenge of Bussy D'Ambois*, belongs obviously in a different category. Nowhere is there an Elizabethan drama more richly sown with aphorisms borrowed from the ancients, nowhere a play of the age so barren of vital action. Clermont is content with the most indefinite view of his position as a revenger. Although he has no clear notion as to whether he should or should not kill Montsurry, he suffers none of Hamlet's qualms of doubtful conscience. Being so admirable a Stoic and, it appears, one of the two virtuous men still living in France, he feels no embarrassment in his own position, no tremblings of uncertainty. He resigns himself to fate, reluctant to rush into a violent revenge, but believing that the just Providence ruling the universe will at some time place him in a favorable position to kill his brother's murderer. His character determines the pace of the play. How slight is the action of this static tragedy may easily be discovered by a summary of its story. Strangely enough, from the beginning Clermont is represented as a friend of Guise, his brother's enemy. With Clermont's consent, however, a challenge after much delay is delivered to Montsurry and declined by him. Clermont's enemies now lay a trap for him which he stoically enters fully aware of the danger. He is imprisoned and thereby debarred from prosecuting revenge. Yet presently he is released from confinement. Three women, more eager than he to reap vengeance, are about to bring the act to a consummation when Clermont arrives just in time to perform his fated task. No sooner has he killed Montsurry than he hears of the death of the friendly Guise, and in fidelity to his loved master he falls upon his sword. The action as a whole is reduced to a minimum, all decisive movement reserved for the last act. Moreover, the teaching of the Stoics, especially of Seneca and Epictetus, whom Chapman chiefly admires, would seem poor material for dramatic art, as it is today unalluring food for the literary appetite. Yet in no respect does Chapman more faithfully reproduce the thought of his times than in finding eloquent poetic and even dramatic expression for this doctrine. More explicit than in the vague allegory of *The Faerie Queene* and more moving than in the utterly untheatrical dramas of the speculative Fulke Greville, Chapman's interpretation of this school of thought is the most striking in Elizabethan literature. That he grasped the meaning of the ancient teaching appears in such a passage as the following:

> Good sir, believe that no particular torture
> Can force me from my glad obedience
> To any thing the high and general Cause,
> To match with his whole fabric, has ordain'd:
> And know ye all (though far from all your aims,
> Yet worth them all, and all men's endless studies)
> That in this one thing, all the discipline
> Of manners and of manhood is contain'd;
> A man to join himself with th' Universe
> In his main sway, and make in all things fit
> One with that All, and go on, round as it;
> Not plucking from the whole his wretched part,
> And into straits, or into nought revert,
> Wishing the complete Universe might be
> Subject to such a rag of it as he;
> But to consider great Necessity,
> All things, as well refract as voluntary,
> Reduceth to the prime celestial cause,
> Which he that yields to with a man's applause,
> And cheek by cheek goes, crossing it no breath,
> But, like God's image, follows to the death,

That man is truly wise, and everything,
(Each cause, and every part distinguishing),
In nature, with enough art understands,
And that full glory merits at all hands,
That doth the whole world at all parts adorn,
And appertains to one celestial born.

There remains something still satisfying in this brave fatal-
istic doctrine of brave men.

The Revenge of Bussy D'Ambois contains more long-
drawn-out periods of complicated rhetoric than any other
Elizabethan play. It proves the most individual of all its
author's works, the most carefully written and toughly
labored. A studious reading reveals much more vitality in
it than appears upon its forbidding surface. In its sententious language and studied restraint it comes close to the
drama of the ancients. Most neoclassical drama resembles
the Greek in form but not in spirit; this is like the Greek
in spirit though not in form. It still contains some force as
poetry.

The plays on Byron move almost as slowly in point of
action. Not formless, they are certainly unelastic. They can
hardly have been at any time successful on the stage, for
Byron is too seldom found in truly theatrical situations.
There are no character studies save that of the hero, and
only the most embryonic features of an intrigue. In this
intellectual drama the emotions are seldom portrayed as
powerfully as in *The Tragedy of Bussy D'Ambois,* and of
actual doctrine there is far less than in *The Revenge.*
What remains is an uncommonly pure vein of poetry much
less turgid than in *The Tragedy of Bussy D'Ambois* and
much less frigid than in *The Revenge.* The creative feature of this tragedy is its picture of the neurotic and self-
deluded nobleman, victim of his own passionate pride, the
fall of whom marks the ruin of his ancient family. Al-

though the likeness is more objective and less intimate than the portraiture to which the modern novel has accustomed us, the effect remains none the less vivid. There is nothing in Shakespeare's *Coriolanus,* for example, quite so poignantly real as the spiritual struggle of Byron's last days. The noble idealism of the Renaissance, with its limitless faith in personality, is seen in an hour of trial: the essential meaning of Marlowe's *Tamburlaine* confronted with its own inherent fallacy. In our own age of advancing socialism the limitations of the Renaissance conception stare us in the face. Yet there is not only abiding worth in the ideal but beauty in the tragedy attending its defeat.

Our quest for the cultural philosophy of the upper classes in the Renaissance has led us almost exclusively to two playwrights where in a relatively narrow compass has appeared the spaciousness of their ideal. Some critic might remind us that Hamlet was also an ideal prince, a glass of fashion and a mould of form. The typical revenge plays abound in moral reflections no note of which has been taken here. Nevertheless an impartial view does reveal Marlowe and Chapman as the most powerful and devoted spokesmen of the Renaissance theory. It shows also the breadth of their criticism, an aspect too often neglected by students stressing the doctrines of Machiavelli as a disturbing background and the revenge play as a type. After all, Marlowe and Chapman mention Spenser as often as Machiavelli and borrow from Castiglione and the idealists no less than from Machiavelli and the so-called realists. They are as much occupied with virtue as with sin. As these playwrights never allow us to forget, the ideal gentleman of the Renaissance is a many-sided, Ulyssean character.

CHAPTER FIVE

HISTORICAL OBJECTIVITY

. . . But man, proud man,
Drest in a little brief authority,
Most ignorant of what he's most assured,
His glassy essence, like an angry ape,
Plays such fantastic tricks before high heaven
As make the angels weep . . .

—SHAKESPEARE

WHILE THE Elizabethan censors frowned upon plays on contemporary politics, the audiences delighted in shows on political events well removed in time or place. The moderation and tolerance which have always distinguished the political thought of the Anglo-Saxon people were combined with the aesthetic sagacity of the Elizabethan dramatists to produce some of their happiest work. By no means all their tragedies are grounded on the conception of a world divided between honest men and villains. The dramatists show that sober reflection on political ethics and that willingness to consider fairly the case of every public man which have long been more than merely theoretical ideals in the land of parliaments. As a result the Elizabethan drama contains a considerable number of plays which are meditations upon the political scene without becoming actual propaganda. The English theoretical dislike of the drastic severity so often practiced in other countries characterizes the moral tendency of these dramas. Within the limitations of this feeling the playwrights show a tolerant vision for both the political idealist and the follower of a Machiavellian statecraft. They recognize the fatality of competing political interests in a violent world.

The political censorship of the age which forbade frank treatment of current events on the stage assisted in this sober and philosophical attitude of a politically minded people. A remarkably small number of plays depict recent events or an England at war with foreign powers. Here Shakespeare proves almost an exception, since at least one of his works, *Henry the Fifth*, is on an avowedly patriotic theme. The typical Elizabethan play presenting public affairs deals either with quarrels in foreign lands which the English can, if they will, view more or less objectively or with earlier periods in their own civil strife. In the latter case patriotism itself promotes tolerance. Since all contenders are Englishmen, doubtless some right adheres to the cause of each. A number of plays, usually of no great merit, treat the lives of the English kings who fell from power to misery. Yet such men had ruled England and were not to be scorned. The English kings themselves are generally treated with indulgence. The early playwrights are well aware that the Tudor dynasty was founded in large part upon compromise. Though the Red Rose had passed into the Tudor blood with more potency than the White, this blood is conceived as springing from a union of the two stems. Hence, while Shakespeare shows some partiality to the House of Lancaster, he observes on the whole a moderate attitude. Good and bad men are found in each party, and each cause has some ground to stand upon, the Yorkists having a legal right, the Lancastrians a pragmatic sanction. The tragedy is never that a just faction is crushed by an unjust one, but that English fields are crimsoned with the blood of brothers pursuing revenge and a lust for power from one generation to another. In search for dramatic material the dramatists found rich matter also in the many instances of civil war in England preceding the Wars of the Roses. In their treatment of these struggles a similarly impartial judgment commonly prevails. This holds true not only in the plays but in the verse chronicles of the age, as those by Daniel, Drayton, and Watson composed during the later years of Elizabeth. The poets are quite willing to enlist our pity for a foolish ruler who comes to grief or our admiration for a conspirator who pursues his course with chivalry and valor. Seldom allowing the ethical problems raised by political history to escape them, the playwrights have few theories to champion, axes to grind, deeds wholly to commend or condemn, or melodramatic heroes or villains to celebrate. Occasionally, as in Shakespeare's *Richard the Third,* the melodramatic tradition does, indeed, triumph over the more usual historical outlook. But such being the exception to the rule, a praiseworthy modesty of thought and purity of art are the usual result. The Elizabethans show a commendable inclination to treat their own history in a reportorial spirit.

Early in the sixteenth century the vogue for plays on English history, and indeed for plays similarly based on foreign chronicles, arose and maintained popularity with audiences of all classes throughout the century. The demand became so great that it produced a species of hack writing. In the case of native subject-matter, the popular interest in this type of patriotic instruction tended to vulgarize the productions. Dramatists such as Heywood, Dekker, and a number of anonymous playwrights wrote with more regard for their theme than for their art and with a regard above all for the audience. They resemble mural painters of the past generation in America who decorated the walls of state capitols with patriotic scenes. When the entire story had been told, the fashion was dropped. The main force of the movement accordingly expired with the earlier and less mature period of the drama, or approximately with Shakespeare's *Henry the Fifth* in 1600. The type, indeed, seems less important in itself than in its liberation of the English stage from foreign models. In the writing of historical plays Shakespeare and his comrades received much of their early training. By the middle of Shakespeare's career many dramas had been written on English history before the Norman Conquest; there were plays on every reign thereafter, on a large number of English heroes who had not worn the crown, and on events in the history of ancient Rome, modern Italy, Spain, Portugal, France, Turkey, Persia, the Netherlands, Denmark, Austria, and many another less notable country known to the eager cosmopolitan vision of the English public. The plays have the air of imparting information as well as of giving aesthetic pleasure, of being quite as instructive as entertaining. They resemble our dramatized history on the radio today. In none of their other serious works do the Elizabethans depart so far from literary rules and notably from the formality of classical tragedy. The chronicle histories are as a rule crudely episodic, written by numerous collaborators, treating of disconnected events, and liberally interspersed with purely comic interludes for the delight of the vulgar. If such technique suggested to Shakespeare his superb social and historical pageants of Prince Hal and Falstaff, it also produced a large number of second-rate works by Heywood, Dekker, Peele, Greene, and minor playwrights of loose artistic conscience. In this field even more than commonly, therefore, the work of major interest proves the exception. Nevertheless there are a few fine dramatic poems memorable more, perhaps, for their political speculations than for any other single feature. Such are Marlowe's *Edward the Second*, Ford's *Perkin Warbeck*, and Massinger's *Believe as You List*, all plays with a humane and equable vision. To these might be added Fletcher and Massinger's tragedy on the unfortunate Dutch statesman, Barnavelt.

Despite a certain primitive rigidity (not without its charm), *Edward the Second* proves from the aesthetic viewpoint an outstanding drama. The worst that can be said for it is that a few of its pages sink to the lowest level of the prosaic style found at times in Shakespeare's *Henry the Sixth* plays, works in which Marlowe may also have had a hand. If the scenes are generally brief, like flashes in the motion pictures, their terseness is not without artistic power. If Marlowe's style here is far from the gorgeous rhetoric in *Tamburlaine*, it is not therefore the worse. Often it suggests the bare and unadorned frankness of the dramatic style of Tolstoy. Simple as the rhythmical movement may frequently be, it has enthusiasm and driving force: the march-like sequences of end-stopped lines and balanced speeches, of retorts that echo questions and of formal defiances, admirably accord with the martial subject-matter and the primitive and poetic passions which this most elemental of dramatists selects for his theme. Though not rich, the style is powerful. Though it lacks the splendor of the more sophisticated Renaissance eloquence, it wins the force of a sincere and direct speech, native to England and in essence native to all peoples. Modest in its pretensions, it proves substantial in its effect. Outshone by the more glittering splendor of Shakespeare's *Richard the Second*, which it unquestionably suggested, the tragedy has a right—this literary scholars appear sometimes to have slighted—to stand as a masterpiece upon its own grounds. Neither Marlowe nor any other dramatist has composed a poem fundamentally similar to this most original and vigorous work.

Admirably as Marlowe solves the problems of technique, his imagination is in nothing so notable as in the

implicit morality of his play. He views the whole story
with a fine impartiality. He is tolerant, not skeptical; fair,
not didactic; and sympathetic, not sentimental. Behind his
lines one reads a lively and well-imagined sympathy with
each character. Yet there is only one person, a minor figure, Kent, of whom he seems to approve entirely throughout, and only a brief section of the play, the closing scenes,
where the audience is invited to indulge a warm partiality.
Marlowe's thought can be discerned best by considering his
view of the individual figures. He is disinclined to condemn or approve openly of any action or to retain for any
length of time a friendly or hostile view of a character. It
is not that he discourages judgment or promotes Pyrrho-
nism. Since his mind deals more in feelings than ideas, he
refrains from pressing his issues to ethical conclusions. The
tendency of his thought is not to produce doubt but to
induce caution. There is beauty in his poise, wisdom in his
equity, and reasonableness in his toleration.

Marlowe is no anarchist in morals. His portrait of the
King proves wholly typical. He pictures a ruler at times
capable of courageous action, a humane man loyal and
ardent in friendship and appreciative of a humanistic culture that means nothing to his "leaden nobles." In so far
as the King delights in masques and revels, in allegorical
pageants and foreign arts, in the company of poets and
scholars, he must indeed be a sympathetic figure to the
dramatist. His outbursts against Romanism and superstition
must also be intended by the radical playwright to strike
sympathetic chords in the Elizabethan audience. The heroism with which the King faces his last hours of grief and
torture makes him unmistakably a tragic hero. Yet Marlowe remains uncompromising in his revelation of the
King's weaknesses. Brave as Edward on occasion can be,
he is an effeminate victim of his emotions. When he be-

lieves that he has safely recovered his favorite, Gaveston, he quite unreasonably becomes a friend of all the world. He grows immoderate in joy or grief where his favorites are concerned. There can be no question of his infatuation, though Marlowe prudently slights the familiar charge of homosexuality which his audience certainly understood without the aid of theatrical emphasis. What the poet makes perfectly clear is the criminal inefficiency of Edward's government. His vanity has caused him to lose his only battle. Under his rule England has lost France and important territory on her northern border. While from a Tudor viewpoint Edward was, perhaps, not wholly to be blamed for favoring brilliant upstarts at the expense of an unintellectual feudal aristocracy, he could by no means be defended for unreasonably pursuing this policy to his own ruin and that of his realm. Nor is he viewed favorably by the dramatist in the scandalous transference of his affection and loyalty to Gaveston. A heroic but fallible man, a rash and misguided ruler, he presents a figure ironically compounded of good and ill. With the serenity of the true artist Marlowe watches the tragic unfolding of his life.

The key to our general attitude toward the King is afforded by Kent, the King's brother, who has a small but significant role in all parts of the play. So long as it is not apparent that Edward's follies endanger the realm, Kent remains loyal, opposing the ambitious and meddlesome barons. When it seems clear that in the interest of England force should be used to repress the King, Kent becomes one of the barons' party. Later the increasing arrogance of Mortimer while Lord Protector and above all the cruel treatment of the King cause him, even though he has himself been injured by Edward, to return to his side. This man, whose fortunes resemble those of his namesake in *King Lear*, dies as a loyal servant to his royal master, whom he has vainly attempted to rescue from Mortimer's intrigues. So far as partiality is allowed to enter into the composition of the play, Kent faithfully guides our sympathy.

The younger Mortimer, Edward's chief antagonist, like the King whom he dethrones wins our divided favor. The most striking of all the barons' party, he is drawn on the boldest heroic lines: an English Achilles. His rescue from the Tower by the Earl of Kent reveals him in a sympathetic light. (Drayton made similar use of this part of the story in a heroic poem written shortly after the tragedy.) Obviously drawn in a sympathetic manner so far as his impetuous bravery is concerned, he becomes at last almost a conventional villain. Like Richard III he is effectively hypocritical, vicious toward children, ruthlessly ambitious in love, and savagely cruel in persecution of his sovereign. Yet Marlowe gives him for his last words on the stage a noble speech that must certainly have been heart-warming to the adventurous and anti-Christian temper of the dramatist:

> ... weep not for Mortimer,
> That scorns the world, and, as a traveller,
> Goes to discover countries yet unknown.

The moral complexity of the part is typical of the drama as a whole.

The remaining characters arrayed either for or against the King are developments of the same themes. On the one hand as an Italianate scholar, an adventurer, and an ardent friend, Gaveston must certainly have appealed to the liberal section of the Elizabethan audience which shared the emancipated views of the playwright. On the other hand Gaveston began that undoing of the King and of the kingdom which ended in the darkest tragedy. Much like Gaveston are the subsequent adventurers, the younger

Spenser and the cynical priest, Baldock, who derives all his nobility from Oxford. The older Spenser, a slightly more pleasing figure, acts to support his family and the waning fortunes of his King. The Queen proves well meaning but morally frail. For a considerable time she loyally withstands the advances of Mortimer. That she finally deserts the King, who had for so long deserted her, seems barely criminal even in the light of the Elizabethan view of women; but when she conspires to murder her husband, she definitely passes into the realm of villainy. The character as a whole presents a judicious study in human motives rather than an excursion into moral propaganda.

Finally, the group of nobles is also drawn with marked impartiality. In the episode of Gaveston's capture, there is little to chose between Arundel, who would admit a final interview between Gaveston and the King, trusting the King's plighted word, or Pembroke and Lancaster, who pledge themselves that Gaveston shall die after the meeting, or, lastly, the gray-haired old cynic, Warwick, who, taking matters into his own hands, kills Gaveston by treachery before reunion with his royal friend. With similar impartiality the playwright regards the characters concerned in the King's capture: the self-seeking Lord Mayor of Bristol, the mower who betrays Edward, the Abbot who would gladly save him, and the monks who view the scene with a religious melancholy.

Yet even though our sympathies are generally held in equilibrium, there is an unmistakable shift toward the end of the play. As one after another of Edward's persecutors torment him with added cruelty, our feelings naturally turn toward the now heroic King. Not so much because Mortimer appears as an enterprising usurper as because he acts as a tyrant does this shift of sympathy occur. This point of view shows in many of the English plays of the age. Thus, as we shall presently see, the character of Henry VII in Ford's *Perkin Warbeck* is made the more pleasing because he refrains from torturing Warbeck or persecuting his associates, and Flaminius in Massinger's *Believe as You List* becomes opprobrious not through his political cynicism and moral opportunism but because of his brutality, a vice by no means always condoned by an Elizabethan audience. Brutality in their more romantic plays was one thing, in their chronicle histories quite another.

These two plays have much in common. Each must originally have been built around the conception of the highly theatrical leading role, that of a man who believes himself a king wrongfully deprived of his throne but whom the world at large views as an impostor. This constitutes an ideal tragic figure for the stage. By sheer personal dignity and royalty of speech and bearing the man must stand forth nakedly from his neighbors, a king in stature though clothed in rags. Especially the old audience with its reverence for royalty and for traditional aristocratic behavior must have realized the full dramatic power of the situation. Ford and Massinger particularly appreciated these ideals of the Court. No doubt Perkin and Antiochus were intended to bear themselves with the dignity of a Titian and to speak with the eloquence of a Castiglione. Each was in large part attempting to win his throne by acting the role of royalty up to the hilt. An actor of seasoned powers in gesture and in eloquence could ask no better opportunity to exercise his art. Ford seems rather less at home in the field than Massinger; the former as usual excels in poignancy of expression and imaginative fertility, the latter in the smoothness of his lines and the gravity and rondure of his conception.

The most remarkable feature of Ford's tragedy is the moderation of the ethical judgments implied. Although

many persons are represented in violent conflict, the dramatist enlists our sympathy and regard for almost all of
them in equal degree. While Ford resorts to no soliloquies
or intimate confessions in the part of Perkin, it is certainly
intended that we should believe in Perkin's sincerity, which
leads him unfaltering in royal pride to his death. Had
Perkin renounced his claim to royal birth, Henry would
have pardoned him. But his sense of honor forbade him to
refute a story of which he was wholly convinced. Ford also
makes it clear that he regards Perkin as a man imposed
upon from childhood by persons in authority, some aware
and others unaware of the falsehood of the tale. Consequently Ford respects Perkin for his courage and pities
him for a fault where guilt belongs to others rather than
to himself. By the same tokens the play presents a sympathetic picture of Henry reasonably defending his throne
against a well-meaning pretender and against both his honest and dishonest adherents. The romantic magnanimity
with which James of Scotland champions Perkin wins our
regard at first, though we may disapprove of his sudden
judgment and the rashness of his plan to marry Perkin to
his cousin Katherine. Later, when James deserts Perkin
through motives of policy, we can hardly condemn his conduct. The play preserves a nice balance between reason and
common sense upon the one hand and idealism upon the
other. The caution which James pursues finally and Henry
pursues always stands in contrast to the no less admirable
high-mindedness and devotion of Perkin, Katherine, her
first lover, Dalyell, and her attendant, Jane. Typically
enough, the minor episode of Stanley's conspiracy is treated
with the same moral restraint. Perhaps Stanley actually
believed in the justice of Perkin's claim. But Ford does not
blacken even his hypocritical attitude toward his old friend
the King. Between the traitor Stanley and Clifford, the

betrayer or the traitor, the dramatist makes no choice. His morality plays no fantastic tricks to make the angels weep. Perkin's courtiers comprise the only group of figures harshly treated. These are not condemned for being conspirators, but are ridiculed for being vulgar upstarts and illiterate tradesmen aspiring to the council table of the English realm.

Charity without sentimentality and wisdom without harshness give to this tragedy a moral vision by no means un-Shakespearean. The conception of Henry's government as moderate and reasonable is derived from history and proves Ford's own contribution to the long-gathering tradition of political thought in England. An opportunist in his policy and humane in his affections, Henry represents the pragmatic and humanitarian attitudes which have long been the saving graces of British rule. The Elizabethan audience too, it seems, was not always crudely moral in its judgments and bloody in its spirit. Sometimes it became reserved in its opinion and tolerant in its feeling.

Massinger's tragedy, *Believe as You List*, affords equal interest in the light of its author's artistic detachment and political sagacity. Again we have characters bitterly at odds with each other, realists aligned against idealists, almost all of whom are treated indulgently. By virtue of his peculiar position Antiochus becomes one of the few heroes whose consistently heroic attitude never degenerates into fulsomeness. Massinger intends us to consider Antiochus as the King himself and not as an impostor. The skeptical title of the play refers to ethical, not to historical, doubts. The Romans have cheated Antiochus of his throne and stand morally in debt to him for his kingdom. The powers which offer him aid become accordingly the generous friends of an honest ruler in distress. No blame can attach to Antiochus for asserting his long-deferred rights. But it likewise is obvious that the poet regards the Roman claim as pragmatically justified. He presents the empire as too huge an entity to be judged readily. Probably a benefit rather than a burden to mankind, it remains in its high stage of development a virtually irresistible power. No king can afford to endanger his own fortunes and those of his subjects by resisting manifest destiny. Hence the unscrupulous Roman policy toward Antiochus and the ultimate refusal of Carthage and Bithynia to aid him are largely justified. Massinger presents the two sides of the case fully and impartially. In both Carthage and Bithynia the idealists make eloquent pleas in behalf of the exiled monarch, and the realists in behalf of the continued friendship with Rome. Much as Ford's Perkin is demeaned not by faults of his own but by the folly of his supporters, so Antiochus is served by a meddlesome and ridiculous priest, Berecinthius. This tends to equalize the sympathy with which the conflicting parties are viewed. Certainly Antiochus presents a more commendable figure than Flaminius, the Machiavellian Roman ambassador who is appointed to run him down. But in the affairs of state Flaminius stands intellectually as far above Berecinthius as beneath Antiochus. That the King should be followed by so ridiculous a supporter adds to the tragic irony of his position. Only fools remain faithful to fallen princes.

The political ideas are unfolded with a logicality and orderliness which do credit even to so careful an artist as Massinger. The tragedy proves as consistent as his plays always are, and for him, at least, it is uncommonly spirited. The first scene provides a thoughtful introduction. The Stoic's advice to Antiochus to be prepared for either fortune sets the key to the philosophy underlying the drama as a whole, while the treachery of the servants who rob their master points to the fatality that at all times overtakes him. The cupidity of Flaminius in dealing with the merchants links the first act to the last and prepares the road for the unexpected fall awaiting the ambassador.

The two major episodes which follow, the unsuccessful visits of Antiochus to the courts of Carthage and Bithynia, are of interest in their cumulative power. At Carthage his case is argued on largely intellectual lines; at Bithynia the emotions are heightened. Defending Antiochus is not only the King of Bithynia but the somewhat sentimental Queen; undermining his hopes stands the cynical philosopher, the theoretical statesman who so readily falls a prey to his own ambitions and Flaminius' designs. Here the pretender and his supporter, Berecinthius, instead of making good their escape, are at length taken prisoners. By this succession of parallel incidents the audience infers more than is actually depicted. We seem to see Antiochus pursued over the face of the whole earth, always cordially received, but never actively defended against the ruthless pursuit of Rome. The realists in the end conquer the sentimentalists. Flaminius overcomes Berecinthius.

The execution of the priest can easily be forgiven, but not the torture of the unhappy King. With Act Four the play takes a new turn, our sympathies becoming further engaged for Antiochus and much more alienated from his persecutor. The King meets increasing trials with increasing fortitude. No amount of torture or even the promise of a peaceful retirement with a radiantly beautiful courtesan induces him to deny his personal identity. After subjection to these physical and mental trials he is placed as a slave in the galleys.

The climax proves as powerful as it is uncommonly sober and convincing, and as genuinely dramatic as free from specious theatricality. Our sympathies for the tormented Antiochus reach their height as we witness final proofs of his just claim and moving evidence of his former glory; justice at last overtakes the grasping, cruel, and tyrannical Flaminius; and, needless to add, the power of Rome, mitigated by partial justice, stands supreme.

Flaminius, sailing on the galley in which Antiochus is a rower, reaches the Roman city of Syracuse. Here live the proconsul, Marcellus, once a friend of Antiochus, and his wife Cornelia, once the mistress of Antiochus in accordance with the pure code of chivalry. They ask to see the impostor. When brought before them Antiochus ironically promises to entertain them by juggling tricks. Thus he picks from a score of swords one which he long ago gave as a present to Marcellus and tells Cornelia what inscription lies within a gem which he long ago presented her. An old Moorish servant on recognizing him falls at his feet. These and similar incidents give final confirmation to the King's claim. Nevertheless Marcellus cannot publicly admit the truth, since such admission is denied by the policy of Rome. All that can be done is to alleviate the punishment by sending him to a penal colony at least more merciful than the galleys and to arrest Flaminius through letters from Rome, the merchants having secured their writ on charges of embezzlement and cruelty. The moderation of this conclusion interestingly contrasts with the brutal ending of many a romantic Elizabethan tragedy of blood and thunder. In the entire play no person dies upon the stage, and death is brought to only one character, the absurd priest, Berecinthius.

Written nearly forty years after Marlowe's *Edward the Second*, Massinger's drama affords a significant comparison with its predecessor. One has the poetic energy of the great Elizabethans, the other the suavity of the Cavaliers. Although Massinger's play proves no more intellectual than Marlowe's, it is clearly more sophisticated. Holding a mean position between the generally more effete work of its own author and Marlowe's robust forcefulness, it never grows insipid and rarely becomes elemental. The fourth act, which depicts the torture and temptation of the hero in prison, rises nearest to that youthful vigor belonging to the earlier and more profoundly poetic dramatists. The scene reminds one of Charles Lamb's observation that the old playwrights by dealing boldly in the extremes of fortune avoid the comfortable timidity of a middle-class literature. It is of interest to see both dramatists, the early and the late, friendly to a realistic and pragmatic public policy, but in their conclusion hostile to corrupt public conduct and, above all, hostile to cruelty. The English hatred of brutality or needless bloodshed in political life, expressed so frequently in Elizabethan times through an abhorrence of Spain, marks only one stage of an enduring tendency in British thought. Finally, most important of all is the moderation, the restraint, in moral judgment here commonly shown: a willingness to present and to honor both sides in a public controversy. To such detachment and restraint this group of plays owes at once most of its artistic charm and its intellectual significance.

It is the ripeness of judgment and taste which proves so fundamental to Shakespeare's plays on English and Roman history and, indeed, to all his serious work. Shakespeare marks the apotheosis of all the tendencies reviewed in the present chapter. When it comes to passing final judgment upon the intense human conflicts which his plays present dramatically, the playwright shows, to use his own phrase, the taciturnity of nature. So he views with Olympian impartiality the contentions of the Houses of York and Lancaster, the rivalries of Antony and Brutus, Antony and Octavius, Coriolanus and the Roman people. He, too, hates brutality. His humanitarianism, however, appears more notably in his plays on British than on continental history. One might judge that the death or suffering of an inhabitant of the British Isles meant more to him than similar ills abroad. In any case he feels with special keenness the pangs of civil strife. All these attitudes appear most strikingly, perhaps, in *Richard the Second,* where the playwright so equably balances the causes of the two chief contenders for the throne, Richard II and Bolingbroke. Richard III is a villain largely because of his cruelty; King John and Macbeth are reprehensible on the same grounds. On the other hand Henry VII, the ultimate hero of Shakespeare's long line of chronicle-history plays, retains his place by gracious compromise. Traitors, as Hotspur, are likely to be bellicose; the wiser statesmen are more conciliatory, as Henry IV in the terms which he offers the rebellious factions. Shakespeare is kindly though seldom sentimental. He hates above all other men the cruel dogmatist, who, like Angelo in *Measure for Measure,* plays fantastic tricks before high heaven to make the angels weep. In a broader way this impartiality and this sympathy account for much of the power not only in his historical plays but in his still finer works, for the breadth and purity of his vision in both his comedies and his tragedies. Here is obviously the finest flower of the theatre of the age. Youthful in its enthusiasm, Elizabethan drama shows much maturity of judgment in matters of both public and private morality.

Chapter Six

SENTIMENTAL TRAGEDY

Far other worlds and other seas . . .
—MARVELL

THE ENGLISH DRAMATISTS of the Shakespearean period are
equally remarkable for their gift of insight and their power
to entertain. Thus to Shakespeare the vision of reality and
of art weighs much the same. It is true that from the early
years of the English Renaissance an infatuation with style
and rhetoric distorts much writing, and of this inclination
toward aestheticism John Lyly and his imitators afford
conspicuous examples. But the tendency as a whole is for
the earlier playwrights to interest us primarily in their
substance and for the later dramatists to delight us chiefly
by their form. Even in Shakespeare's work alone the trend
of the times appears. *Romeo and Juliet,* an early play, is
tremendously powerful in its meaning and just a little stiff
and archaic in style, while *The Winter's Tale* and *Cymbeline* excel in artistry but lack the weight and sincerity
of the earlier work. In his last phase Shakespeare becomes
less the enthusiast and more the professional playwright,
less robust in his feelings and ideals but even more uncan-
nily skillful and brilliant in weaving the garment of his
art, in coloring poetic phrases and inventing situations. At
the beginning of his career he collaborated with Marlowe
in plays on English history, and at the end of it he joined
with John Fletcher in work on the same subject. Marlowe
personifies the drama powerful in content and youthful in
artistic form; Fletcher's work is slightly senile in content
and highly mature in artistic virtuosity. The Elizabethans
and their legitimate successors, as Webster and Tourneur,

had more content than their artistic vessels would hold; while the Cavalier playwrights of the courtly school of Beaumont and Fletcher, Massinger, and Shirley mould admirable vessels only half full of poetic wine. Marlowe was an enthusiast who happened to write plays; Fletcher was a professional playwright. Ben Jonson, a stalwart realist, introduced new critical standards; but as medieval earnestness yielded to courtly affectation the course of events was patterned by the culture of the times, irrespective of whatever individual forces might be thrown into the field.

The key to the enjoyment of the Cavalier drama is thus to appreciate the suavity of its form, just as the key to the understanding of the true Elizabethan drama is to enjoy the depths of its feeling and ideas. This does not mean that one school of play-writing monopolizes either tendency. The form of the Elizabethan play is purer for being moulded spiritually from within, while the contours of the Cavalier drama are likewise owing to the feeling hand that wrought it. Only the emphasis is perceptibly or even radically changed.

Neither time nor authorship strictly defines the two schools. To one group belongs the entire reign of Elizabeth and a part of the transitional Jacobean period; to the other, likewise a part of James's reign and the entire period of Charles I. The turning point is roughly marked by the virtual retirement of Shakespeare about 1611 which left Beaumont and Fletcher masters of the field. To the earlier group of tragic poets belong Marlowe, Kyd, Marston, Webster, Tourneur, Chapman, Middleton, and Jonson. For Ford, the Elizabethan inheritance occasionally proves stronger than the Cavalier environment; but far less often than Ford does Massinger incline toward the earlier movement. The moralistic tragedy of revenge for sin, the purer tragedy, the serious plays embodying the Renaissance ideal, and the long tradition of the historical drama belong all to the earlier school. To the later belongs most of the serious work of Massinger and all that of Beaumont and Fletcher. In the time of Charles I James Shirley occasionally labored to revive the Elizabethan temper, only to prove how impossible the task had become. His *Cardinal* and *Traitor* seem admirable plays when viewed beside a score of his own works, but appear shallow when placed beside earlier tragedies which they imitate. Shirley felt most at home when writing dramatic romances of the Fletcherian type and when pursuing the sprightly course of his own comedy of manners. For Elizabethan tragedy in the high poetic vein he had no gifts whatever. Beaumont and Fletcher ruled the Cavalier stage with Massinger and Shirley as competent understudies.

Most of Beaumont and Fletcher's plays may be called dramatic romances. The authors of no plays so properly in the tragic tradition as those of a dozen of their contemporaries or predecessors, and of relatively few unadulterated comedies, they composed a large number of works on what one historian of dramatic literature has well termed a sliding scale from the more to the less serious. Their chief contribution was undoubtedly the genre of tragicomedy. But to view this contribution in too narrow a sense would be a mistake. The important thing is not that Beaumont and Fletcher wrote many serious plays of the trials of princes which end happily, but that in three-fourths of their works they confuse the tragic and the comic spirit. In their Cavalier exuberance they fly boldly in the face of all that Horace forbids, creating with Renaissance extravagance mermaids, centaurs, and chimeras. To tragedy they bring the complexity and artificiality proper to comedy, and often to comedy the semblance, at least, of those serious emotions proper to tragedy. Where the Greeks had theoretically held that love had little or no place in tragedy and that little or nothing else had a place in comedy, Beaumont and Fletcher deal with little else in either genre. Hence their relative impoverishment of ideas and circumscription of vision; for they not only monotonously repeat the romantic love theme, but fail to feel so deeply as their older rivals. Although sometimes uncommonly frank, they are also pedantic. They cultivate standards of morality belonging less to fact than to fiction, pursuing quixotic ideals of chastity when chastity is least of all in their minds. With a gift for elaborate theatrical storytelling, a fondness for multiplicity of characters and situations presented in superficial relations and without deep imaginative synthesis, they never develop a single passion or idea with thoroughness, as Shakespeare did in *Romeo* or in *Othello*. Most of their plays have their sources in the late romances, especially the Spanish; and the dramatists were destined to pass on still more of their art to the English romantic novelists in prose, notably to Sir Walter Scott. Their plays are thus admirable as pastime and entertainment but of no equal service for the enrichment of the human spirit.

That Shakespeare himself came under the spell of the Jacobean innovations has been well recognized by critics, at least since A. H. Thorndike in 1901 published his essay, *The Influence of Beaumont and Fletcher on Shakespeare*. The precise dating of some of Beaumont's early masterpieces and of Shakespeare's latest plays has not been established; but on the whole Shakespeare seems rather to have followed than to have led in the direction of Cavalier sentimentality. The important thing is obviously not the influence of one individual upon another but the rising shadow falling with greater or less intensity upon all the dramatists during the second decade of the seventeenth century.

Shakespeare was no man to remain insensitive to the world he lived in. Unquestionably he escaped further influences from the Cavalier spirit only by the drastic step of virtual retirement from theatrical life in London to provincial life in Stratford. *The Winter's Tale*, still in many respects Elizabethan (using the word in its broadest sense), also reflects most clearly the spirit of the age which moulded the art of Beaumont and Massinger. While *Cymbeline* resembles such a baroque Fletcherian extravaganza as *Bonduca, The Winter's Tale* has much of the suavity, idealism, artificiality, tenderness, impersonality, and courtliness to be found in such plays as *A King and No King*, where the hand of Beaumont is dominant, and Massinger's *Maid of Honour*. But *The Winter's Tale*, after all, merely approximates the younger school, which became thoroughly established only after Shakespeare's retirement.

A noteworthy distinction appears between the more serious art of Beaumont, or in any case of Beaumont and Fletcher, and the work of Fletcher done independently of his friend. In making this distinction it is unnecessary to employ a subtle and intuitive divining rod to divide scenes of single plays between the two dramatists. This delicate task, which has naturally fascinated persons of taste such as E. H. C. Oliphant, half as scholars and half as connoisseurs, has led to only partial agreement and success. The plays were commonly written and published deliberately to obscure the authorship of individual scenes or passages. But enough plays were produced after the death of Beaumont in 1616 and under Fletcher's sole name to evince a striking change in style. Professor Oliphant warns against too rash judgment in the case of the earlier plays, owing to the deferred development of Fletcher's marked idiosyncrasies. The plays are anything but crude collaborations of inartistically fused workmanship. When the two dramatists worked together, they showed their peculiarities least; and especially Fletcher, who had the more eccentric genius, kept his excrescences pruned, or perhaps Beaumont pruned them for him. Thus the masterpieces which the two wrote together, as *The Maid's Tragedy*, *Philaster*, and *A King and No King*, fall into one category, while the tragedies solely by Fletcher, as *Valentinian* and *Bonduca*, or those produced by Fletcher with the aid of Massinger, as *Thierry and Theodoret* and *The Double Marriage*, fall into quite another. Beaumont seems to have had the dominant hand in the earlier plays, that is, in those which he wrote with Fletcher. This may partially account for the desire of Fletcher—who appears to have had a generous character, whatever may be the moral delinquencies of his Muse—to have his own work forever associated with that of his more deeply inspired friend. Beaumont's genius led to definition and control, Fletcher's to exuberance and fertility. One excelled in form, the other in fancy, one in depth, the other in expansiveness. Beside most other dramatists Beaumont seems extravagant, but beside Fletcher he appears conservative. Beaumont is known to have been much under the restraining influence of Jonson. He presumably needed Fletcher's warm fancy to fructify his critical nature, while Fletcher, in serious work at least, profited immensely by Beaumont's guidance and relative sincerity. In comedy or in sheer romancing Fletcher might be trusted to go his way alone. When writing tragedies unaided he attained at times some brilliant results, but only with an inimitable vein of extravagance that divorces his tragedies still further than his earlier work from the tragic norm. Beaumont and Fletcher together, the former leading the way, produced work something like the relatively chaste and comely *Winter's Tale*. By himself Fletcher wrote plays reminis-

cent of the epical *Cymbeline*. Before Beaumont died
Fletcher was actually in his own right nearer to Beaumont
than thereafter. Later he continued to tell good stories on
the stage and composed even more dashing lines than
ever; but, unaided by his great partner, he never wrote
plays so admirable in point of construction and form as
their three serious masterpieces already mentioned. Massinger possessed something of Beaumont's architectural
sense, but what was positive genius in Beaumont becomes
in Massinger mere facility. Beaumont has obviously a
poetical power not only superior to Fletcher's but vastly
superior to Massinger's.

The limitations of the Cavalier school as a whole may
be seen by comparing their treatment of the emotions, of
character, and of comedy with the practice of their predecessors. Although the lesser Elizabethans deal in much
cool-blooded fustian, the better poets of that more robust
age possess a surer grasp of the emotions than the Cavalier
playwrights. The peculiar type of inflation found on the
Cavalier stage can best be examined later in connection
with the amazing extravaganzas of Fletcher; but the most
revealing contrasts in the best plays of the later period
concern the marked rise in sentimentality. With the Cavalier playwright sentiment commonly does the work of
more genuine feeling. Beside the exaggerated and almost
incredibly masculine Evadne stands the melting and sentimental Aspatia, beside the gruff Melantius the pathetic
Amintor. The tragic is increasingly replaced by the pathetic. Through the false idealism of the Cavalier morality,
through the fondness for fantastic renunciation and melancholy introspection thereon, the scene becomes peopled
with wet-eyed women, the Aspatias, Euphrasias, and Spa-
conias of the tragic stage. So far did John Ford regard
himself as spokesman for this fashion that he composed an

entire play, his masterpiece, well entitled *The Broken Heart*, in celebration of this passive and self-pitying fortitude. What had been merely a significant vein in Beaumont and Fletcher becomes for him, this one time at least, the sum and substance of his art. The fiber of life is weakening when such a fashion prevails. The Cavalier plays express the spirit of the Court as opposed to the life of the nation. They have the pallor as well as the charm of a too-cosmopolitan life, of translation rather than spontaneous work.

The readiness with which characters of all sorts in Beaumont and Fletcher admit of typification points to the relaxing of the artistic imagination. Beaumont has clearly more sense for character than Fletcher, as appears in his work upon such figures as Arbaces and Amintor. Yet in the plays as a whole the repetition of characters becomes even more notable than the duplication of incidents. We are far removed in such art from the true genius of Shakespeare or of Jonson. One looks in vain in the Cavalier plays for characters so marked as Marlowe's Edward II, Chapman's Byron, Webster's Flamineo, or Dekker's Friscobaldo. The dashing and impecunious gallant, the romantic heroine, the lustful court lady, the irate old man, the rough and honest soldier, the pure patriot, and the tyrant king are reduplicated time after time in mechanical fashion. The failure of these playwrights to conceive original or even eccentric characters restricts definitely the scope and freshness of their comedy. There is no more fertile and facetious author of comedy in the world than John Fletcher, but there are many whose comedy is more exhilarating. Especially a poverty of social ideas renders the Cavalier playwrights deficient in the salt of comedy, which is satire. Beaumont inherited enough salt from Jonson to season one admirable burlesque; but he neglected to carry his gift much further and bequeathed little or nothing of it to his peculiarly irresponsible partner.

The general failure of the Cavalier dramatists to compose brilliant reflections of reality appears both in their tragedy and their comedy. Compared with James Shirley, Beaumont and Fletcher have no doubt considerable power for grasping emotional reality, but compared with Shakespeare and the Elizabethans their power seems limited indeed. Lightly amused with gay trifles, in their comedies as a rule they view manners superficially. In their tragedies it becomes significant that they do best when discarding any serious historical allusion. It is not for them to write plays upon English history, or to study the history of another land, as Chapman studied France or Jonson Rome. Their best serious plays have scenes in a romantic nowhere, again emulating not Shakespeare's tragedies but his comedies laid in Arden, Illyria, or Bohemia. The three masterpieces of Beaumont and Fletcher are laid in a romantic Rhodes (a cloudland compared with Shakespeare's Cyprus), in an imaginary Messina and a fantastic Iberia. Following this course Ford writes a semipastoral tragedy, with oracles as in *The Winter's Tale* and *Cymbeline,* laying the scene in a most unwarlike Sparta, a land of languishing women. Each play becomes a web of dazzling improbability.

The plot of Beaumont and Fletcher's *King and No King* is the simplest and so proved the most pleasing to the neoclassical taste of the age of Dryden. Nevertheless it remains a fantastic story, treated with ingenuity and a rare sense for form. We are moving essentially in the world of Sidney's *Arcadia*. The type of artifice employed by the poets was precisely that most admired by their own age and least tolerated in ours. We are too likely to demand a feeling of actuality which the highly artificial

Jacobean poets have not to give. Thus to start off their story they depict a duel fought between two kings to decide the fate of their armies and kingdoms. Fantastically generous, the victor offers his sister to be the bride of the vanquished. The woman whom the vanquished Tigranes loved follows him in disguise to become the servant of the Princess and to hinder their alliance. When Arbaces, the victorious monarch, arrives at his house, he falls in love with his sister whom he has not seen since infancy. The incestuous passion is natural enough, but the tragicomic denouement of the play owes vastly more to romance than to probability. The King is discovered to be no relation to the Princess. The latter is true heir to the throne, the former an impostor foisted in infancy upon the people at a time when the former King desired a male heir and despaired of having offspring of his own. Arbaces marries the Princess, and Tigranes his faithful Spaconia. In the center of the comic relief stands Bessus, an extravagantly exaggerated poltroon. From first to last the ingenious plot and its developments are excellently handled. But to accept such a tale with pleasure it is essential to have at all times a considerable fondness for sheer romantic fancy. With these allowances the play has the beauty of a truly classical form. A smoother or more rounded dramatic story becomes almost unthinkable. The playwrights show a command of leisurely and graceful beginning and ending that often escaped even Shakespeare. But the situations and the highly artificial rhetoric make an illusion of reality quite impossible. Beaumont and Fletcher, like the scenario and popular-fiction writers today seeking first of all for entertainment and preferring the pleasures of ingenuity of those of profundity, make no claim to the higher species of artistic reality. In the aesthetic problem which their art raises the wisest course lies midway between the

Cavalier worship of artifice and our own bourgeois contempt for it. *A King and No King* then appears as a masterpiece of the second order of excellence.

The Beaumont and Fletcher plays such as this compromise, in fact, between artifice and realism by presenting a largely fantastic plot with incidental imagery and a spirit quite in keeping with the manners of Cavalier life. The events depicted prove incredible, while the trappings remain true to court usages. Court ceremonies, masques, assemblies, small talk, gossip, and intrigues are painted to the life and much of the dialogue is graceful and easy, whereas the enveloping design belongs to the most artificial realms of literature and the theatre. A harmony is achieved because the court life of the Renaissance proved itself so artificial and highly decorated with affectation. Naïve stories and sophisticated manners paradoxically join to reflect the world whose taste Inigo Jones moulded into gorgeous court spectacles and baroque palaces.

Philaster, or Love Lies a-Bleeding, exhibits the qualities of *A King and No King* in a more complex and advanced form. The artifice and convention formerly assumed by comedy is here introduced into serious drama. Echoes from *Hamlet* and *Othello* come to us deliciously softened through airs of Arcadia. Euphrasia, a girl disguised as a page and named Bellario, carries love messages between Philaster, the man she adores, and Arethusa, the woman who is scandalously declared to be her lover. In short, we find ourselves halfway between Othello's Cyprus and Viola's Illyria. An affected court steeped in amorous intrigues owes in itself, perhaps, an equal debt to essential reality and to romantic fiction. But the incidents of this play belong, of course, to the latter. By a theatrical convention highly convenient to the playwrights of the age, anyone immediately believes what he is told or what the plot requires. The testimony of a minor courtier and a notorious woman weighs more with the King and Prince than the avowals of innocence by the incorruptible Princess and her female page. The word of an evil woman is never doubted, that of a virtuous lady never believed. Characters exhibit incredible devotion and magnanimity and are as adept in forgiveness as in repentance. When love actually lies a-bleeding in Act Four, the romance is at its height. The credulous Philaster, otherwise a worthy knight, wounds the Princess and her devoted page with his own sword in a fit of jealousy. Because a bad conscience has miraculously weakened his powers as a fighter, he is himself wounded by a countryman. It would be more accurate, however, to observe that in the genre of tragicomedy no one dies. Since the injured women show fantastic devotion in the time of his own greatest danger, Philaster recovers his faith in their honesty. Thus after the pageant of absurdities which occurs in the forest, the situation becomes precisely reversed. Philaster now believes his friends honest, but is himself in danger of death or severe punishment. Arethusa, the Princess, willfully joins him in his confinement after she confesses her love. The highly quixotic trio is rescued through a convenient uprising of the populace in Philaster's behalf. The King being humiliated, the marriage of Philaster and Arethusa is secured and the party of the Prince no longer holds their threat of revolution over the realm. Bellario, in reality Euphrasia, is made a perpetual attendant upon Philaster whom she still platonically loves, while Arethusa trusts fully in their honesty. The last act proves as artificial as an Italian opera. Extremities of impossible virtue are reached by Philaster, Arethusa, and Euphrasia, and no less incredible wickedness or despicableness in the King, Pharamond, and Megra. The audience is invited to take sides as in a crude melodrama; and if the melancholy and impressionable Philaster falls at times from grace, there is never a moment's doubt of his inherent magnanimity.

The play remains a success, first, because it is always consistent with itself, though seldom with probability, and, second, because of the able writing, rising at times to inspiration. Seldom if ever weakened by diffuseness, the style attains such real excellence that *Philaster* belongs with the few Elizabethan dramas not far below the level of Shakespeare. It is a *Cymbeline* robbed of ethereal poetry but graced by a more definitely aristocratic and courtly temper. Less rounded than *A King and No King* and far less powerful than *The Maid's Tragedy*, it stands beside them as a dramatic poem. Both Beaumont and Fletcher achieve in it the highest mastery of style of which they are respectively capable.

The Maid's Tragedy, finest of the three plays, although nominally a tragedy, is in spirit and execution also a tragicomedy. Too serious to be ideal tragicomedy and too artificial to be pure tragedy, it hovers in that aesthetic limbo where the suave Beaumont and the mercurial Fletcher breathe most naturally.

A tendency to advanced artifice appears in the opening speeches. The dramatists comment modestly upon their art:

LYSIPPUS: Strato, thou hast some skill in poetry;
             What think'st thou of the masque? will it be well?
STRATO: As well as masques can be.
LYSIPPUS: As masques can be!
STRATO: Yes; they must commend the king, and speak in praise
             Of the assembly, bless the bride and bridegroom
             In person of some god; they're tied to rules
             Of flattery.

Much of the first act is comprised of a masque, as the fore-going promises, highly artificial and yet within its given limitations admirable as poetry. Especially the conventional but exquisite bridal songs in the masque merit a place beside the choicest lyrics of Robert Herrick.

The plot becomes only less farfetched here than in *A King and No King* or *Philaster*. Evadne, mistress of the King, is induced by her irrepressible brother to kill the King, who has spoiled her honor, although by arranging her marriage with Amintor he would seem according to familiar court standards to have been exceptionally considerate. Indeed the whole play is permeated with the most exaggerated Cavalier notions of honor. In place of passion the major plot substitutes fury, the minor plot sentimental melancholy. In the Aspatia story the dramatists employ just such ingeniously artificial devices as once were widely admired and now are commonly disapproved by the more sober literary opinion. Seeking only death at the hand of her lover, Aspatia disguises herself as her own brother, taunts Amintor, kicks him, forces him into a duel, runs upon his sword, and dies with words of gratitude upon her lips.

Beaumont and Fletcher, who always excel in elaborate stage pictures, bring their conscious command of theatrical effects to notable heights in the climax and the catastrophe of this tragedy. The most stirring scene is the quarrel between Melantius and Amintor, a passage worked out with elaborate balance. First Melantius draws his sword to kill Amintor, on the ground that his sister has been traduced; Amintor is about to fight when both think better of it; next Amintor draws his sword to kill Melantius, on the ground that the latter may kill the King; Melantius is about to fight, when again they change their minds. Amintor goes off the stage leaning upon his friend's shoulder.

The finale of the play proves considerably more complicated. A stage tableau is provided. As in *Philaster*, the hero-lover is placed between the two women who love him, a situation especially agreeable to these amorous playwrights. In one play Philaster stands between Arethusa and Euphrasia. In the other Amintor kneels between the dead bodies of Aspatia and Evadne, each of whom has committed suicide for his sake. He himself generously responds by committing suicide for theirs. Behind the three prostrate figures are grouped three mourners. Melantius, the faithful friend, stands behind Amintor; Calianax, the grieving father, behind Aspatia; and Diphilus, the mourning brother, behind Evadne. Diphilus, indeed, seems to have been created chiefly for this tableau, since he takes only a trifling part in other scenes.

An episode of a lighter character further illustrates the fusion of conscious design and delicate fantasy meeting in the art of Beaumont and Fletcher. Melantius wishes to win control of the citadel and therefore is compelled to draw Calianax, the foolish old counselor, into his plot. This he does by taunting the old man with treason so many successive times before the King that in sheer exasperation Calianax yields completely. The most open course gives Melantius the most assured secrecy, as though he were hiding in an excess of light. The cleverness rather than the literal probability of such an intrigue strikes our attention. A political truth is much exaggerated in the interests of art.

The elevation of true tragedy is lost to the play by its picture of an essentially incredible court, wherein the sole business is love-making. Dignity is lost still further by the importance of the sentimental element, personified in Aspatia. True, scarcely an English tragedy presents such a relentless series of high-pitched scenes as those of the last four acts of *The Maid's Tragedy*. The fiery interviews between Amintor and Evadne, Amintor and the King, Amintor and Melantius, Melantius and Evadne, Amintor and Evadne once more, and Evadne and the dying King, are not easily duplicated in their boldness. But too many types of artificiality are at work to allow the play to breathe in the atmosphere of tragedy attained by other Elizabethan dramatists. As works of refined artistry no Elizabethan plays except Shakespeare's surpass the three principal works of Beaumont aided by Fletcher; but as specimens of serious tragic writing these will not bear comparison with plays by Marlowe, Chapman, Jonson, Middleton, or Webster.

The versatile and imitative Ford writes now in the tradition of the tragedy of sin and revenge, now in the purest vein of tragic feeling, now with historical objectivity, and finally in a romantic manner that proves a masterful elaboration of the sentimental or pathetic theme so clearly sounded by Beaumont. *The Broken Heart,* one of the most perfect works of the period, carries to logical conclusions the sentimental tendencies in the Beaumont and Fletcher plays. To begin with, Ford's Sparta is essentially the world of the Greek so-called pastoral romances, and no historical kingdom whatsoever. Once more man's business consists in love and his chief wisdom in cryptic oracles. The passivity and melancholy expressed in the secondary roles of Aspatia, Euphrasia, and Spaconia here become the dominating notes of the play. Calantha and Penthea die of grief, the latter, to be sure, refusing all nourishment. Ithocles pines away with melancholy reflection upon a youthful error in judgment. The King sadly ebbs out of existence, one hardly knows why. Bassanes lives to regret his mad jealousy and to smile in pensive retrospection, while Nearchus willingly renounces the hand of Calantha. All is renunciation and sadness. Only the undying anger of Orgilus, long concealed, finally breaks into violent action. He himself, typically enough, chooses a lingering mode of death, cutting his own vein and bleeding his life away. The morbid strain in the earlier Cavalier drama becomes in this piece wholly dominant. Yet the change is really one of evolution rather than of mere accretion. The consistently objective type of writing practiced by Beaumont and Fletcher is subtly but drastically discarded by Ford in favor of a subjective and introspective one. The effect of Ford's play, as Havelock Ellis well discerned, is the negation of action. It is a masque of melancholy, not a tragedy of deeds. We witness a tableau of grief, the figures frozen in tears. Ford gives little or no dramatic suspense and no real plot. Instead, he composes a series of scenes each in much the same spirit. From time to time joy flickers with a sickly light, merely to give outline and definition to the pervasive sorrow. Volition is dead. Bassanes, for example, suffers from an attack of jealousy as a man might have an attack of the mumps and recovers from it simply in the course of nature. Mankind as a whole is depicted as sick with a diseased heart for which all remedy is fruitless. We witness a hopelessly ailing world, the long decadence of the introspective aspect of the Cavalier tradition. While Burton wrote the medical analysis of melancholy, Ford composed its artistic synthesis. His melancholy is not philosophical, as Hamlet's, but sentimental, as Poe's. Within its own limits, *The Broken Heart* becomes an almost perfect work of art, the dramatist weaving every imaginable variation upon his given theme. From the discussion of bookish learning with which the play opens to the funeral pageant of its conclusion, he shows a complete awareness of his task. Each scene is harmoniously composed. In the more important episodes Ford rises unmistakably to the height of his argument. Such, for example, are the bitter interviews between the two chief characters, Orgilus and his wronged

sister Penthea, Penthea's renunciation of Ithocles, her ironical legacy to Calantha, her madness begotten of despair,
the deaths of Ithocles and Orgilus, the tragic nuptial dance
of Calantha, and the closing ritual, where Calantha at once
weds her kingdom, her lover, and her grave.

In style as well as in content Ford follows the footsteps
of his masters. At times he shows an ability to reproduce
the essential features of Fletcher's manner, as in the love
scene between Katherine and Dalyell in *Perkin Warbeck*.
But Fletcher's style was as a rule too expansive for Ford's
more precious nature. More often he found himself at
home in the less mannered style inaugurated by Beaumont.
Although his language is less inevitable, less dramatic, and
less musical than Beaumont's, he has his predecessor's gift
for comely, dignified, and calculated expression, weighted
with some genuine feeling and rounded into courtly grace.
Each poet is an architect in words, sometimes, no doubt,
too self-conscious but seldom lacking in the lofty realization of his art. With Beaumont the sentimental tragedy
of the Cavaliers was first unfolded; with Ford it fell full
blown to the ground.

CHAPTER SEVEN

TRAGIC EXTRAVAGANZA

... Here's a large mouth indeed,
That spits forth death and mountains, rocks and seas,
Talks as familiarly of roaring lions
As maids of thirteen do of puppy dogs! ...
He gives the bastinado with his tongue;
Our ears are cudgell'd; not a word of his
But buffets better than a fist of France:
Zounds! I was never so bethump'd with words
Since I first call'd my brother's father dad.
— SHAKESPEARE

BY NO MEANS a monotonous terrain, the three-score plays loosely ascribed to Beaumont and Fletcher show many divergent extremes in style and taste. Among the more serious works some preserve at least a relative sobriety in language and situation, while others run to a type of dramatic extravaganza called tragedy only by courtesy. Allowing for the possibility of many errors in the ascription of this or that scene to one of several authors, sobriety is the mark of Beaumont, while the love for all kinds of extravagance in tragedy belongs chiefly to Fletcher and the most exuberant of the tragedies are largely, if not wholly, from his hand. Most of these plays seem to have been written after Beaumont's death. A further question is raised by the probability of Massinger's collaboration in a large number of plays, especially those of a late date. Collaboration among Elizabethan dramatists, as previously observed, often produced work in which the eccentricities of the authors are pruned and something approaching a mean between the extremes of their most marked style is attained. So successful are the friends in working together that few obvious discrepancies show. In their earlier days of play-writing Beaumont seems to have influenced the style of Fletcher more than Fletcher that of Beaumont, while Massinger appears to have been buoyed up by the stronger and more volatile genius of Fletcher. Very definitely Massinger did his best when working side by side with his most gifted friend. Such is the commonly accepted and plausible theory of the partnership of the three men in serious plays. But whatever may be the truth about authorship, the fact remains that some notable tragedies of an almost fantastic nature exist, as well as some a little declined from this supreme exuberance. We may regard as the sole work of Fletcher those high-flying works, *Valentinian* and *Bonduca,* and as typical tragedies inspired by Fletcher and partially executed by Massinger those lively and colorful dramatic stories, *Thierry and Theodoret* and *The Double Marriage.*

All four plays are indubitably tragedies in the narrow, technical sense of the word. They present actions of high state where the most sympathetic characters, indeed the majority of the figures, pass through much sorrow to ultimate misfortune. The stage is swathed in tragic black. Yet these dramas miss the highest seriousness as well as the highest poetry because of inveterate exaggeration. Once among the most admired of their authors' works, they now stand in a precarious position because of this very exuberance. Their plots and language we find unnatural and overstrained. One wonders whether to regard an episode as genuinely fantastic or merely grotesque and a speech as truly eloquent or merely fustian. Like the word fantastic itself, Fletcher's audacity will bear either a good or a bad connotation. Overdone in their romantic morality, their hyperbolic rhetoric, and their incredible incidents, these plays have often been damned; yet the enthusiasm with which their most baroque art was at first received may

in part be recovered. In any case the critic must wonder at
what is almost a miracle of theatrical ambiguity: work that
comes within a hairbreadth of burlesque upon the one hand
and true tragedy upon the other. Although English poetical drama from Marlowe to Shirley—indeed, one might
say from the medieval Passion plays exploiting the character of Herod to the present day—abounds in examples
of similarly commingled rant and poetry, in no playwright
is the paradox so marked as in Fletcher. These ultra-Eliza-
bethan, ultra-Renaissance dramas mark the final development of the heroical fustian before the closing of the
theatres in Cromwell's time. It was a tradition to be renewed
with much alteration by Dryden, Otway, and Lee—Fletcher's rhetoric pruned to accord with Augustan taste. But
while others rival Fletcher in heightened oratory, none
quite equals him in the fantastic exaggeration of heroic
idealism and in the conscious and artful defiance of probability. Tendencies of dramatic degeneration and sophistication apparent in Beaumont's work attain their culmination
in his friend's. The most paradoxical relation of sincerity and absurdity reaches its height in these avowedly
serious plays. The less high-flying of the tragicomedies,
the dramatic romances, and the pure comedies have, of
course, little to offer in this particular vein of tragic extravaganza. Beaumont, apparently unaided by Fletcher,
wrote a most logical and consistent burlesque of Elizabethan spurious heroics in *The Knight of the Burning
Pestle*. He was there ridiculing the absurdities of the plebeian stage. But Fletcher popularized for courtly and
Cavalier audiences a type of theatrical inflation really
more extreme than anything produced not only by the
plebeian Heywood but by the genius of Marlowe, Chapman, Webster, or his most romantic predecessors in the
tragic field. Fletcher's tragedies cannot be taken wholly

seriously, nor can they be read attentively without admiration. By no means the finest, they are among the most representative, as once among the most popular, of Jacobean plays and are to the modern eye the most extraordinary. On viewing these gorgeously and deliberately inflated works we see the daring convolutions of baroque architecture lifted against vast, sun-drenched thunderclouds.

Although the plot of *Valentinian* has relatively few flights of fancy, by the extravagance of its idealism and its prodigious rhetoric this masterpiece well represents Fletcher's boldest manner. None the less improbable are a number of its incidents. The historical setting of the play by no means curbs the author's melodramatic proclivities. Lucina, wife of Maximus, on being ravished by the Emperor Valentinian follows the path of Lucrece to suicide. On plotting revenge against the Emperor, Maximus thinks it necessary to contrive the death of his best friend, Aecius, a general whom he believes so loyal to the Emperor as to avenge even such a righteous blow raised against their master. But if there is no great reason why Aecius should die, there is still less in the immediate circumstances of his death. The Emperor's guards prove too cowardly to kill him. Even when he commands them loyally to execute the murder, when he pledges them to stand motionless and gives them his sword, they fly from his presence. This fantastically faithful and courageous servant is thus forced to kill himself for the sake of his treacherous master. It is worth remembering that Aecius became one of the most popular roles in all Fletcher's plays. The death of the Emperor proves equally sensational. Two brave soldiers take poison themselves, knowing that their plot affords no escape, and then poison Valentinian. While the murderers die heroically, Valentinian dies as a coward. The playwright omits nothing in the picture of his physical torment.

The tragic extravaganza is indeed merely the old tragedy
of horrors sentimentalized. The play ends with another
highly theatrical poisoning. In the height of wine and triumph Maximus tells the former Empress, whom he is
about to marry, that he has killed her nefarious husband.
Resenting this, the Empress sprinkles poison on the laurel
crown which symbolizes the elevation of Maximus to the
throne. Critics have expressed disappointment regarding
the scenes of the play after Valentinian's death without
perhaps studying Fletcher's intentions carefully. On the
one hand the closing scenes are undeniably rapid and sparing in literary development; a new group of characters is
abruptly introduced; and the catastrophe falls with great
suddenness. On the other hand this inconsistency is more in
seeming than in fact when we remember the Elizabethan
demand that retribution shall overtake the guilty, that
Maximus in accepting the crown has allowed ambition to
replace justice, and that nothing can entirely exonerate him
from the murder of his friend Aecius or, indeed, from that
of Valentinian. Although the lightning falls abruptly, it
falls upon a head already dedicated to death in a morally
conceived universe.

The chief peculiarity of *Valentinian* lies, however, as
we have said, not in its fantastic situations but in its extravagant idealism and rhetoric. Lucina's chastity and Aecius'
loyalty are as hard to believe on the one hand as the vices
of Valentinian and his sycophants are upon the other.
Clearly the play inherits much from the moral tradition
of melodrama, wherein are opposed the incredibly good
and the monstrously bad. Yet as a work of art it belongs in
another and better category, for it abounds most of all in
a gorgeous prodigality of speech, a magnificent effusion of
eloquence. It contains the finest harangues, the most over-
powering language, which Fletcher ever wrote. Flashes

of a purer poetry at times shine behind the great clouds of rhetoric in *Bonduca,* but here the writing proves remarkably of a piece. One page much resembles another. An expansive manner Fletcher might, to be sure, have learned from Jonson. But there is a fine liquid fluency in Fletcher's eloquence that the latter never quite attains. Although Jonson, the better poet, is more intellectual and architectural, more substantial and less inflated, his periods are more clearly built and not born, while Fletcher, with less real power of eloquence, has the greater spontaneity.

The presence of this masterful and grandiloquent style calls for exemplification, which several score of passages might equally well afford. The dying rant of Valentinian gives as fair an instance as any:

> More drink!
> A thousand April showers fall in my bosom!
> How dare ye let me be tormented thus?
> Away with that prodigious body!—Gods,
> Gods, let me ask ye what I am, ye lay
> All your inflictions on me? hear me, hear me!
> I do confess I am a ravisher,
> A murderer, a hated Caesar: oh,
> Are there not vows enough, and flaming altars,
> The fat of all the world for sacrifice,
> And, where that fails, the blood of thousand captives,
> To purge those sins, but I must make the incense?
> I do despise ye all! ye have no mercy,
> And wanting that, ye are no gods! your parole
> Is only preached abroad to make fools fearful,
> And women, made of awe, believe your Heaven!—
> Oh, torments, torments, torments! pains above pains!—
> If ye be any thing but dreams and ghosts,
> And truly hold the guidance of things mortal;
> Have in yourselves times past, to come, and present,
> Fashion the souls of men, and make flesh for 'em,

> Weighing our fates and fortunes beyond reason;
> Be more than all, ye gods, great in forgiveness!
> Break not the goodly frame ye build in anger,
> For you are things, men teach us, without passions:
> Give me an hour to know ye in; oh, save me!
> But so much perfect time ye make a soul in,
> Take this destruction from me!—No; ye cannot;
> The more I would believe, the more I suffer.
> My brains are ashes! now my heart, my eyes!—fiends,
> I go, I go! more air, more air!—I am mortal!

Here are exhibited the familiar features of an expansive eloquence, wherein emphasis is achieved by repetition, prolonged periods, rhetorical questions, exclamations, and similar language patterns. All produce an impression of grandeur and magnificence, a clamorous and metallic splendor, like a baroque temple or a blare of trumpets.

In *Bonduca* the spirit of unrestraint is carried still further, aided by the nature of the theme. The play combines Fletcher's classical and patriotic enthusiasm. An epic drama, it deals with wars of the Romans and Britons, the former speaking a neo-Ciceronian eloquence, the latter for the most part a barbaric rant. Much is made of Bonduca and her daughters, who inveigh against their enemies in a manner that even their fellow countrymen find raucous, unbridled and vain. Burlesque is frankly introduced into a large number of the scenes. Sport is made of the gaunt and hungry Roman soldiers, even more greedy for food than for battle, and of captains who grow lovelorn when commanded to charge the foe. Bonduca rants; her ravished daughters make but doubtful heroines; and by humorous irony the fates of the Roman captains, Petillius and Junius, are wholly transposed: first the former ridicules the latter for loving Bonduca's younger daughter living, then the latter mocks the former for doting on Bonduca's elder daughter dead. These courtships are conceived in the vein of raillery of which Fletcher is master. The spectacle of Roman soldiers in love with the ungentle British viragoes who have just been ravished is fantastic enough, but still more preposterous is Petillius enamored with a girl because of the bravery of her suicide. Even the name Judas, the famished corporal, points to the burlesque nature of this role. The wonder is that with so much deliberate fooling there should be so much heroic poetry. Yet the two elements in Fletcher's play grow even more harmonized than contrasted. Besides Judas, who is always absurd, are Petillius, Junius, and Bonduca, who are sometimes absurd, and Caratach, Suetonius, and Poenius, who are always heroic. It is the ridiculous Junius, the laughing soldier, who lays the trap for the one charming and pathetic figure in the play, the child Hengo, nephew to Caratach. The play, in short, has ludicrous episodes in the spirit of Fletcher's comedy, *The Humorous Lieutenant,* and flashes of poetry worthy to place beside the best and most serious verse of Beaumont. Unique as a work of art, it faithfully represents the boldest contradictions in the Cavalier soul.

The proud individualism and lack of discipline, which undermined the cause of Charles I, show best in the episode of Poenius. When this brave captain is ordered by Suetonius, the general, to lead his company against the Britons, he refuses on the ground that he has never been accustomed to hearing the words "must" and "command." The generosity of Caratach, real tragic hero of the drama, proves as astonishing as the insubordination of the unsoldierly Poenius. When Caratach captures Judas and his starving company, instead of making them prisoners of war the general gives them a banquet and releases them to participate in the engagement. More than once the Romans permit Caratach to escape out of admiration for his cour-

age and pity for his young nephew. He attends the
obsequies of his enemy, Poenius, apparently during a
magnanimous truce in the reality of which it becomes difficult to believe. The death of Poenius affords another instance of farfetched high-mindedness. Although Suetonius
would forgive him, the captain prefers death to shame.
But by far the most astonishing scene in this most astonishing of plays is that of the British women on the battle-
ments of their town. In the hopeless state to which
Bonduca's feminine rashness has brought them they are
besieged by the Roman victors. On the left side of the
Queen stands her timorous daughter, on her right her
brave one. Beneath the taunts of her family the weak girl
grows courageous and, rather than fall again into the hands
of ravishers, takes poison. This is passed about in a huge
bowl, the braver girl dying second and Bonduca last, with
many lofty and defiant speeches. Meanwhile Petillius, who
has jested at the love of Junius for the younger daughter,
falls in love with the elder, his infatuation growing after
her death. But in the end, as British treachery and hard
blows converted Junius, hard fighting cures Petillius. The
death ceremony of the British women provides an unex-
ampled flight of impassioned hyperbole. Throughout the
play, however, the extravagance of pseudo-epic poetry is
pushed to the uttermost. The bragging of Bonduca's first
rant sets the key for the whole. Less thrilling and real than
Marlowe's *Tamburlaine*, but no less eloquent and animated, it proves the wildest flight of Fletcher's fancy as
a tragic poet. Still popular as heroic rant on the Restoration stage, its burly extravagance was no doubt pruned and
its burlesque as far as possible omitted. The eternal commonplaces of the martial ideals have never been presented
more colorfully or seasoned with more dramatic action.

For another instance of Fletcher's tragic muse on a

somewhat drunken spree, exemplifying the wilder flights of Jacobean fancy, one turns to *Thierry and Theodoret.* This play may have been written in part at an early date, Beaumont may have had a hand in its first draft, and probably Massinger had a larger part in its present form; but if the work is not chiefly by Fletcher himself, at least it represents the strange form of tragic extravaganza that he popularized. Several passages of really notable poetry are sprinkled among mountains of hyperbole and improbability, resulting in a play far from displeasing as a whole and even inspired with tragic feeling in its conclusion. Something of the elemental spirit of the earlier Elizabethan playwrights breathes in its scenes of blood and horror.

The action merits brief review in the light of its extreme melodramatic extravagance. The evil characters are grouped about Brunhalt, mother of two virtuous kings, Thierry and Theodoret. When Theodoret rebukes her for her wickedness, she flees to Thierry. Always ready to credit eloquence in any cause, Thierry at first believes his brother a villain, but on hearing his defense holds him innocent. A shallow reconciliation is effected between the sons and mother. She kills Theodoret by the use of a trap door beneath his throne and then excuses her action on the ground that he was foisted upon the royal family and is not her true son. Thierry accepts the apology. She now proceeds to avenge herself on Thierry's new queen, Ordella, toward whom she feels a desperate jealousy. To achieve her end she gives the King a drug rendering him for the time being sexually impotent. When he finds his wife still content however, he becomes happier than ever at being married to such a miracle of chastity. Defeated in her plan, Brunhalt now cheats the King with a false oracle. He is told that he can have an heir only if he kills the first woman leaving the temple after morning prayers. His wife appears, veiled. When he confronts her with the prospect of being a sacrifice, she willingly promises him his wishes. But when she unveils, he becomes so horrified that he goes off leaving his design unfulfilled. The honest counselor, Martell, reports that the Queen has killed herself in deference to the oracle. Martell's account of this death is wholly fictitious and nevertheless the most ambitious flight of rhetoric in the play. The Cavalier playwrights must indeed have taken seriously Touchstone's precept that the best poetry is the greatest lying. When the King, to fulfill Ordella's desire for him to have children, proposes to marry his niece, Theodoret's daughter, his mother declares, in order to check the match, that she lied in denying Theodoret to be her son. The fear of incest, she hopes, will prevent the union. But for once Thierry will not believe a palpable deception. Driven to her last extremes, Brunhalt gives him a poisoned handkerchief to aid him in weeping for Ordella, his supposedly lost bride. This poison prevents him from ever closing his eyes in sleep. From this torment he dies accompanied by Ordella, who expires in sympathy. The mother, off stage to be sure, chokes herself to death on witnessing the torments of her paramour, the cowardly soldier, Protaldy. The minor characters harmoniously add to this fantastic major plot several scenes of broad and grim comedy. De Vitry, a humorous and impoverished soldier with a disillusioned outlook but a sense of honor, plays picaresque tricks on Protaldy and others.

Some scenes, as the death of Theodoret, are in the rapid and unliterary language of the crude and early melodramas; others, as the death of Thierry, are in Fletcher's most poetic style, and still others, as those centering in that priggish moralist, Martell, appear in Massinger's reflective and comparatively wooden manner. But from first to last the play is an extravaganza. The miracle is that so much tragic feeling and poetry can come out of such fantastic flights of speech and plot and that true beauty can coexist with such lurid violence of deed and word. The plot of *Thierry and Theodoret* was imitated in a more reasonable but less successful work, probably by Fletcher, Massinger, and Chapman, *The Bloody Brother*. There is less of Fletcher's peculiar vein in the latter play, however. Without his extravagance, Fletcher is likely to become tame.

Probably with the aid of Massinger he composed a tragedy less exuberant in act and language than the three plays so far considered in detail but still typical of his unrestrained manner of thinking and writing. *The Double Marriage* represents the lofty Massingerian style more prominently than in *Thierry and Theodoret* though still subordinated to Fletcher's mercurial vein. A drama with some tragic gravity but much lively action and robust fooling, it is too weighty to be a mere dramatic romance and too extravagant to place beside the more serious Elizabethan masterpieces of tragedy.

The chief passage in the first scene is a typical strong speech wherein Juliana, wife of Virolet, convinces her husband of her more than masculine valor and patriotism by renouncing his embraces to aid him in his honorable conspiracy. In a less rhetorical but more violent scene that follows she refuses to betray her husband although Ferrand, the tyrant of Naples, tortures her on the rack.

The second act is highly representative of the dashing Fletcher and more romantic than tragic in feeling. It depicts a fight at sea, with much thunder of cannon and clash of arms, between the party of Virolet and the implacable Duke of Sesse, aided by his Amazonian daughter, Martia. The bravery of Virolet as a prisoner in defying Sesse makes Martia madly—though inconveniently—in love. To free her lover she leaves her father's ship in a longboat, pursued by shots from her father's guns.

As the play advances its spirit grows less violent but more tense. Virolet has promised Martia marriage in order to preserve himself and a susceptible youth, Ascania, for their heroic task, the destruction of the Neapolitan tyrant, Ferrand. The scenes that follow make the usual dramatic capital of the theme of love and honor. When Juliana hears of the valor and sacrifices of Martia, she willingly releases Virolet from marriage. Since he has already offered Martia marriage, he effects a divorce from his wife on the ignoble ground that the torture suffered in his behalf has made her sterile. Nevertheless out of loyalty to Juliana he refuses to lie with Martia. The martial virago at once repudiates him and endeavors to conspire with Juliana for his death. Despite all her wrongs Juliana remains faithful, only insisting that so long as she and Virolet are legally divorced they shall neither kiss nor embrace. Juliana becomes the familiar type of highly quixotic honor and chastity in woman. Planning to fight in her husband's cause, she even takes sword in hand. Meanwhile the wicked King of Naples has been driven to his last redoubt by a rebellion led by the Duke of Sesse and his sailors disguised as Switzers. To win the honor of killing the tyrant, Virolet disguises himself as one of the sycophants who has access to the court. Juliana kills him, thinking him to be the rascal whose appearance he has assumed. The evil Martia, repudiated by Virolet, has now become the tyrant's mistress. After a lively battle Sesse enters bearing Ferrand's head. During the last moments of the play Sesse launches a terrific invective against the daughter who has robbed him of his prisoners and become the mistress of his worst enemy. A sailor kills Martia, saving her father the crime of the actual murder. Sesse goes back to the piracy that he loves, and the young Ascanio reigns in Naples.

The profusion of oratorical speeches and violent actions combined in one play makes *The Double Marriage* typical of the distinctively Fletcherian school. Likewise representative is a fantastic underplot afforded by the fool Castruccio, who fancies himself to be a king. Once while dressed in royal robes he is mistaken by Sesse for the King and attacked. The free use of disguises and unnatural situations also betrays the type of highly artificial tragedy. The incredible wickedness of Martia and Ferrand, the no less unbelievable virtues of Juliana, the violence and valor of Sesse and his followers, and the pervasive gusto betoken this dramatic tradition. The general style of the play is Fletcher's unrestrained by Beaumont. Like the other plays discussed in this chapter, it lacks even such dignity and sobriety as are attained in the better-known masterpieces of the Beaumont and Fletcher collaboration.

In conclusion we may recall that the extraordinary plays just examined are by no means alien to the Shakespearean spirit. Shakespeare shared to some degree Beaumont's fondness for decorous sentimentality and Fletcher's love for grandiose heroics. Just as the former tendency is mirrored the most clearly in *The Winter's Tale*, the latter appears best in *Cymbeline*. The most natural comparison is between *Cymbeline* and Fletcher's *Bonduca*. In each case the dramatist deals with ancient Britain and its wars with the Romans, shaping his scenes in vast, epic proportions, using a swollen and tumid rhetoric and a highly complicated plot. There is a profusion of bombast and idealism. Shakespeare's martial harangues describing the battle with the Romans much resemble those depicting the wars of Bonduca. The visionary pageant in the last act of *Cymbeline* suggests Fletcher's most extravagant manner. Moreover, Shakespeare's play is written to please the courtly audience that especially enjoyed Fletcher's productions. The elaborate comparisons made by Morgan and his supposed sons between court and rustic life show a conscious address to this restricted audience. Such parallels with familiar Shakespearean work should help us to appreciate Fletcher's neglected masterpieces more sympathetically and to understand how, as it seems, Shakespeare came actually to collaborate with Fletcher in *Henry the Eighth* and *The Two Noble Kinsmen*.

CHAPTER EIGHT

DRAMATIC ROMANCES

No weighty matter, nor yet light . . .
—FLETCHER

THERE IS a type of dramatic romance, reaching neither the seriousness of tragedy nor the hilarity of true comedy, in which the poetic dramatists, especially those of the Fletcherian period, excel. Such plays cannot well be described as tragicomedies, since it is customary and reasonable to reserve that term for works of a really grave and stately cast, containing some feeling of tragedy but resolved in the last act to a happy ending. The plays discussed in the last two chapters are tragedies or tragicomedies; those to be discussed now are properly neither. Again there is a great difference, easily recognized, between the play with comic major plot and one with a sentimental or more or less serious major plot aided by secondary comic relief. Some plays here designated dramatic romances were by the Elizabethans termed tragicomedies; a greater number were called merely comedies. But in the age of their birth men were not pedantic in using such terms. To distinguish a variety of plays of varying degrees of seriousness, but all clearly midway between the gravest and the lightest, has its real usefulness. It helps to reveal a group of dramas with stories derived from or imitating, continental prose romances and located midway upon a sliding scale: on one side the tragedies or heroic tragicomedies, on the other the gay or the satirical comedies of manners.

The group is further defined by the social class of its major characters. The most ambitious types of Elizabethan drama deal with the fortunes of princes, while the pure comedies present chiefly the humble classes. A prince may, to be sure, be the *deus ex machina* in a farce, as in *The Comedy of Errors*, or a clown may appear in a tragedy, as in *Hamlet*. But a tendency to observe the decorum of rank is the rule. In the dramatic romance the major characters are noblemen or highbred gentlemen, neither so illustrious as the kings of tragedy and tragicomedy nor so vulgar as the commoners of comedy.

One reason why so many of the most successful plays of the school of Fletcher are dramatic romances of this description doubtless is that they were addressed on the stage to the social class which they represent. The earlier play had as a rule reached a more popular audience; but as the puritanical city of London drew away from stage plays and the other vanities of Merry England, the drama became increasingly the property of gentlemen and courtiers. The first Stuart kings, spending vast sums on masques, showed a less discriminating patronage of the legitimate stage than their Tudor predecessors. Plays were largely, then, for the upper class rather than for either prince or people. The drama always reflects its social setting.

Fletcher, lacking the high seriousness requisite for pure tragedy and the capacity for social criticism found not only in the comedies of Jonson but in those of his pupil, Beaumont, was quite as qualified in dramatic romances as in tragedy or pure comedy. He accepted a loose view of dramatic forms exhibited in Dekker and others older than himself and immensely influenced the less gifted dramatists who surrounded him. Thus there are notable plays that may properly be called dramatic romances by Dekker and the true Elizabethans, as well as a considerable number of such works by Beaumont and Fletcher, Massinger,

Middleton, and Shirley. The effect of the dramatic romance is to make us neither grave nor merry but to afford mild entertainment. It is a pleasing theatrical pastime, taking itself none too seriously, unimportant in philosophy or satire, rich in narrative and adventure. Usually with the aid of a remote and unrealistic scene, it preserves a considerable distance between itself and the more intimate emotions of the audience or reader. It resembles dinner music played at a fashionable restaurant.

In his less inspired productions even Shakespeare stooped to satisfy the demand for this ever-popular type of play. But his only close approximation to the mood about to take such firm possession of the Cavalier stage is *All's Well That Ends Well*. The somewhat peculiar position of this comedy among Shakespeare's works shows how seldom he subjugated his more discerning and poetic genius to a secondary type of inspiration. The play has often been described as the ugly duckling among its author's flock of swans. It is one of the "she comedies" so popular in the times or, in other words, a play dominated by a woman. Bertram, the man, is cold and passive, Helena, the woman, enterprising and ardent. The story, following a formula of continental literature most brilliantly represented by Boccaccio, deals with Helena's ruse to win her beloved. Exactly as in Shakespeare's *Sonnets*, there is something wry and unconventional in the poet's development of his theme; yet at bottom the art and temper of the piece are as familiar as the plot. It is a simple love story, not greatly enriched by poetry, philosophy, or realistic characterization. It altogether lacks the satirical energy of *Troilus and Cressida* or *Measure for Measure*, the sprightliness of *Much Ado about Nothing* or *The Merchant of Venice*, or the tender fancy of *Twelfth Night* or *A Midsummer-Night's Dream*.

Helena seems almost drab beside Rosalind. The farcical elements of the play appear tame beside those of *The Taming of the Shrew* and *The Merry Wives*. And it wholly lacks the grave and elevated idealism of *The Tempest* and *The Winter's Tale*. Yet it is only because Shakespeare has so much more alluring work in most of his comedies that *All's Well That Ends Well* has frequently been neglected. It is neither more nor less impressive than a score of competent dramatic romances by the Fletcherian school; and like these plays as a group it has received, perhaps, rather less than justice.

Although prose fiction has always cultivated these romantic moods at considerable length, they have enjoyed less general vogue in the theatre. The moods of comedy and tragedy have successfully retained their traditional preëminence. Hence anthologists and critics of English drama have relatively neglected this type of play as it flourished lavishly in Fletcherian fields. And so it becomes of interest to reëxamine the possibilities of the type by reviewing a considerable number of plays diverse in spirit and ranging from the more to the less ambitious. They extend from exotic melodrama to the comedy of sentiment and from the exuberant to the polite. With rapid glances we may view four or five pieces chiefly by Fletcher and as many others by his fellow dramatists.

Who and how many of the leading dramatists wrote such plays, and in what proportion do they stand to other types of theatrical entertainment? The following table gives at least a fair picture of the situation, showing the types of plays written by the four most prolific playwrights. It must, of course, be read without any misapprehension as to complete accuracy. The authorship of the plays is not always assured; and even some differences in classification might legitimately be allowed.

	Tragedy	Tragi-comedy	Dramatic Romance	Pure Comedy
Beaumont and Fletcher	8	11	13	20
Massinger	6		11	
Middleton	2	1	7	11
Shirley	7		13	10

From this table certain conclusions are readily discerned. Especially notable is the claim of Beaumont and Fletcher to almost all the loftier tragicomedies. Equally conspicuous is the absence of pure comedy in the works of Massinger. Two of his plays, to be sure, approach this type, but cannot be said to attain it. *A New Way to Pay Old Debts* and *The City Madam* are partly satirical and realistic, though they are hardly ever risible and usually serious, sentimental, and romantic in tone. They may best be described as dramatic romances slightly off-color. The first has proved a memorable, though I believe a somewhat misunderstood and overpraised, work. Romantic critics delighted in its picture of Sir Giles Overreach in madness. The British of the commercial age have noted with favor its bourgeois morality. But its straightforward dramatic storytelling, which must have chiefly afforded its original charm, seems to have been overlooked. A number of better plays in its author's unmistakably aristocratic idiom were meanwhile slighted. *The City Madam* would have been a pure comedy in the hands of any other playwright than the ever-serious Massinger, so singularly in want of a robust sense of humor. Notable in a less degree is the numerical strength of Middleton's comedies. This playwright had very infrequent success with his dramatic romances and even fell short with his one tragicomedy. A poet of extremes, he wrote two fine tragedies and nearly a dozen comedies so light as to border upon farce. Shirley's work tends to the lighter side of the scale. With questionable success he attempted to write a few tragedies, wrote no real tragicomedy in the grand manner, but did compose many dramatic romances of a rather airy variety and a large number of sparkling comedies.

To indicate more precisely, by differentiation, the territory occupied by dramatic romance itself, one may cite a representative tragicomedy. Such a play is *The Knight of Malta*. Fletcher's hand can unquestionably be traced in many of its scenes, especially in those depicting "Norandine, a valiant merry Dane, commander in chief of the gallies of Malta." The play was evidently much revised a considerable time after its first appearance, for the opening scenes, and possibly other sections, are in the style of pre-Fletcherian melodrama. The lines are bristling and abrupt as spearheads, expressions are sententious, moralizing is too glaring, and the artificial soliloquies are reminiscent of a technique which flourished more in the time of Shakespeare's *Richard the Third* than in that of Beaumont and Fletcher's *Philaster*. Yet so little did the essence of melodrama change even while the trappings altered that the discrepancies in *The Knight of Malta*, though inimical to complete harmony, prove by no means fatal. The work of two and probably more authors, it remains still very much of a piece. Once popular and still enjoyable, it was acted by one of the most distinguished casts of the period including Burbage, Field, Underwood, Sharp, Condell, Benfield, Lowin, and Holcome.

The setting is in the grand manner. The isle of Malta is defended against the Turks by the Knights of the Order vowed to war on the infidel and to observe strict chastity. With the Order itself are several allies. Two knights are candidates for initiation, the lighthearted Dane, Norandine, and the idealistic and admired Miranda, an Italian gentleman. Montferrat, a Frenchman and a villain, contrary to his vows of celibacy seeks to seduce Oriana, sister of Valetta, Grand Master of Malta. Both Miranda and the noble Spaniard, Gomera, honorably seek her hand. Montferrat, failing to seduce Oriana, accuses her of lust and of treason toward the Turkish general, producing forged evidence of her alleged crime. A trial by combat is arranged, with Montferrat as accuser and Gomera as defendant. Before the battle Miranda arranges with Montferrat to fight disguised in his armor. To defend the lady Miranda then deliberately loses the tournament to Gomera. True to the letter of her oath, the lady marries Gomera.

The action passes into many highly romantic complications. When Gomera is led to suspect the honor of his wife, she sinks into a trance which appears to be death. A negro servant in love with Montferrat gives her a drug with powers similar to that taken by Juliet. Montferrat comes by night to ravish the tomb, and Gomera to pay his obsequies. They meet, a pistol is fired, Gomera is wounded, and the villain seems victorious, when Norandine appears and conquers. Later, Oriana, long supposed dead, is restored to Gomera, whom she forgives. Miranda has rescued her while fulfilling his vigils in the church. He renounces love in joining the celibate Knights of Malta, while for lust and treachery Montferrat is unfrocked. In the course of the play Miranda tempts two women to try their virtue, first, a Turkish captive named Luscinda, who is later united with her husband and converted to Christianity, and, second, Oriana herself. Norandine is shown principally as a laughing cavalier in contrast to the more serious-minded Miranda. The former will have nothing to do with the vows of the Knights of Malta: he remains loyal but unregenerate to the last.

The play entirely answers to the familiar phrase "a rattling good melodrama." Its opening sentence perfectly sets the key: says the villain, "Dares she despise me thus?" Too fantastic in both action and ideals to be taken altogether seriously, it is far too mature and skillful a work of art to be described as vulgar. Not only are every scene and character highly actable and well set off by its context. The style is always vigorous, even occasionally trespassing upon a higher vein of poetry. This tragicomedy belongs not unworthily to the neo-epic tradition that culminated in the *Jerusalem Delivered*. Its brilliant theatrical potentialities can hardly be exaggerated.

The Knight of Malta is a little less poetic and more artificial than the best of Beaumont and Fletcher's tragicomedies, but more serious than their typical dramatic romances. This vein is exhibited by plays such as the dashing but outwardly rather serious *Custom of the Country*, the facile *Love's Pilgrimage*, and *The Coxcomb*, a play despite its humorous scenes too rich in sentiment properly to be set down as a comedy. All these plays, to be sure, are comedies in the sense that they have a happy ending, but they show more sentiment than laughter and much more romance than satire.

The Custom of the Country offers a perfect fusion of Fletcherian gusto and Massingerian eloquence, both colored more deeply by sex than is attractive to most English audiences today. Much as in *The Knight of Malta* and *Love's Pilgrimage*, there is an idealistic young hero who may be partially the creation of Massinger and a humorous and free-living young cavalier who is certainly the creation of Fletcher. The tone of the play is lightened by the humorous Rutilio and by the implausible and even magical events of the plot. We have strange and exotic customs, improbable disguises, fights at sea, sudden turns of fortune, and a sorceress who practices sympathetic magic—all somewhat in the manner of the Greek pastoral romances which inspired much of Renaissance prose and verse and indirectly produced such plays as Shakespeare's *Winter's Tale.* The atmosphere seems highly un-English: its warm airs are of the Mediterranean or even of the neighboring shores of the Near East. In the *Arabian Nights* one reads similar tales of adventure.

A nameless principality of Italy has a custom that the prince is privileged to lie with the bride before the bridegroom. Clodio, the governor, in the case of the fair Zenocia even makes a promise of marriage. But she scorns his advances. Disguised as masquers she, her lover Arnoldo, and his brother Rutilio escape by sea, only to be pursued by the angry Clodio and the girl's sorrowing father.

The lovers are attacked by a Portuguese ship off Lisbon. While Zenocia is being captured, her protectors escape bondage by leaping into the sea. The Portuguese captain, long a lover of the renowned beauty, Hippolita, gives his fair captive to her as a maid, requesting Zenocia to sing his praises. But Hippolita's eyes fall upon the young Arnoldo in the street. She has him brought to her house, offers him gifts, and woos him ardently. Loyal to Zenocia, he refuses the lady. For a moment the two young lovers are jealous of each other, Zenocia suspecting Arnoldo of loving Hippolita and Arnoldo suspecting her of corruption in lax society. Though the enraged Hippolita at first has Arnoldo condemned, when her former passion returns she procures his pardon. Learning of his love for the servant, she has Zenocia put under a deadly spell by a sorceress. At the sight of the two lovers about to die, one from the charm, the other out of pure sympathy, she relents and marries her long-faithful captain.

Rutilio's fortunes are largely independent of his

brother's. Having no wealthy admirer, he is threatened by
poverty. Chance leads him to a brawl in which he wounds
and supposes that he has killed Duarte, an arrogant young
nobleman of the town. Fleeing for safety, he asks sanctu-
ary in the home of Guiomar, who unknown to him is
Duarte's mother. She vows to protect him, remembering
that her quarrelsome son may need similar aid. Even when
she learns that her guest is the murderer of her son, she
refuses to violate her sacred oath. Wandering again in the
streets by night, Rutilio falls into a cellar where the am-
munition of the city is stored. He is accordingly threatened
with the galleys, when to his vast relief the mistress of a
male bawdyhouse pays his ransom. He finds this house of
prostitution harder labor than slavery with the oar. From
its trials he is rescued by Duarte, who, remarkable to say,
has not only recovered from his wounds, but experienced
a conversion and a burning desire to reward the man
whose sword has effected the cure. Believing that Guiomar
really loves him, Rutilio sends Duarte on a love message
to his own mother. She lures Rutilio to her house now in-
tending to kill him for his audacity, but, impressed with
his behavior and finding her son alive, she marries him
instead. Such is the busy action of the play. A livelier series
of scenes would be difficult to discover; and though naturally such a play never rises to lofty heights of thought,
feeling, or expression, it remains truly remarkable how
well it is conceived and written throughout. If it were not
for the vile custom of the country and Rutilio's bawdyhouse it would certainly have retained a greater degree of
favor among English readers. But artistically considered it
is all good work, whether in its morally pure or impure
passages.

A more pleasing play, even closer to the norm of dramatic romances, *Love's Pilgrimage* has been somewhat

neglected amidst the wealth of similar material in the
Beaumont and Fletcher plays. Less extravagant and im-
posing than *The Custom of the Country*, it proves gayer
and still more artificial. One of the most delightful and
implausible of all dramatic plots, sentimental in tone and
agreeable in effect, is interwoven with a number of excellent scenes of light comedy. Stated in its simplest form
the plot tells the conversion of the madcap Marc Antony
from irresponsibility to fidelity. The stock humorous characters include two jovial innkeepers, a fantastically minded
bailiff, and a pair of irritable old fathers, one of whom,
though so lame as to be confined to his chair, still wishes
to fight duels on the least provocation. Marc Antony himself is a gay young blade only with difficulty tamed to take
life seriously. It is his eccentric practice to offer fair ladies
marriage and then desert them practically at the church
door, leaving them with hearts broken but virginity intact.
For the recovery of love and honor two of these ladies disguise themselves as young men and, unknown to each
other, pursue their love over the length of Spain. The
events which ensue are distinctly amusing. To insure her
safety Theodosia hires both beds in a wayside inn graced
with but one room to let, only to find in the course of the
night that the avaricious innkeeper has been bribed to
admit a man. After some vague talk in her sleep, she confesses to the stranger the nature of her quest. Daylight
reveals him to be her own brother. Presently they meet
Leocadia, the second girl, in the mountains. Theodosia sees
through the masculine disguise of her rival, but Leocadia,
blind to that of Theodosia, makes many savage remarks
regarding her. Marc Antony's cure is now arduously effected. With great impudence he accosts in the streets the
wife of the governor of Barcelona and attempts to seduce
her. At her instigation physicians frighten him into believ-

ing that wounds which he has received in a scuffle must prove mortal. He repents his sins, meets his former sweethearts, regrets that he cannot marry them both, and follows the law in choosing the first. After long and dutiful service, Theodosia's brother persuades Leocadia to resign affection for Marc Antony and to accept him. The angry fathers being pacified, a happy ending is achieved.

So much tender and lovely poetry is lavished upon this plot that the result is a gay romance rather than a true comedy. As the prologue nicely declares, the play is "no weighty matter, nor yet light." A more charming and accomplished work of the kind is nowhere to be found. *Love's Pilgrimage* has more body and substance than either the generally solemn romances of Massinger or the artful fantasies of Shirley.

Often the playwrights of the age conceived plays with homelier and less exotic plots than the foregoing, with scenes outwardly much like those of the pure comedy of manners but with sentiment still in advance of humor. Such is the domestic type of dramatic romance, well illustrated by a very pleasing work of Beaumont, Fletcher, and Massinger, *The Coxcomb*. This piece, beloved by Charles Lamb, is comprised of a major and a minor plot only slightly integrated. The minor plot, of distinctly secondary interest, is strictly comic. A foolish merchant fancies that it will be to his greater glory to have his wife in the arms of his friend. Although the friend is at first reluctant to betray his host, and the woman no ardent lover, the absurd plots of the husband to effect his own undoing prove in the end successful. While he purposely announces his own death, the two have their desired meeting. This fanciful story, however, pales beside the really moving scenes of the major action. A young man has arranged to meet a girl by night in the street, with plans to elope and marry. Tempted by riotous companions, the lover becomes drunk, and not recognizing the girl, insults her. Leaving her home, she wanders through city and country, here robbed by rascals and there befriended by kindly men and women. She secures a position in a dairy farm under circumstances not unlike those of Tess of the D'Urbervilles. Her repentant lover, quite distracted by grief, follows her. They are finally united, the girl being far too humble and devoted to protest her injury. Throughout the scenes fluent verse and prose are artfully blended, the former, of course, carrying the more eloquent and emotional passages, the latter the more comic or realistic. Fletcher's fine ease and freedom of dialogue appear at their best. The play is so modest and unpretending that its true merits can easily be overlooked.

After Fletcher, Massinger; and after Massinger, Shirley. The cycle is complete when we recall Shirley's pious editing of Fletcher's plays in 1647. In the later authors as well the dramatic romance ranges between eloquent tragicomedy and true comedy, passing through many levels of gravity and style. Thus among Massinger's plays *The Bondman*, *The Maid of Honour*, and *The Bashful Lover* belong to the more high-flying and ambitious type of romance. *The Renegado* is of about the average seriousness, while *The Guardian* inclines to the lighter side. Since it is Massinger's tendency to be sober without being profound, the two last-mentioned and less pretentious works stand among his more rewarding plays. They show various aspects of the romancing tradition.

Ever a lover of colorful rhetoric, Massinger finds himself especially at home with an Eastern scene, as evident in *The Emperor of the East*, *Believe as You List*, and *The Renegado*. The setting of the last is painted with an almost Venetian warmth and, incidentally, with a Venetian hatred

of the Turk and zeal for Christianity. The religious spirit
of the piece may not be profound. Even in *The Virgin
Martyr* Massinger's faith has appeared, at least in Protestant eyes, to be lacking in depth and richness. But he is
certainly no hypocrite. The story of *The Renegado*, as is
usual with Massinger, is far simpler than the type beloved
by Fletcher. A daredevil named Francisco has desecrated
the Cathedral of Saint Mark, stolen a Venetian lady, and
taken up piracy in behalf of the Turk. Vitelli, the lady's
brother, is in vengeful pursuit. At Tunis Donusa, the niece
of the great Amurath, wins his love. Here, too, he en-
counters the renegade, Francisco. But his Jesuit confessor
persuades him to renounce both love and vengeance. His
affair with Donusa being discovered by Amurath, the pair are
condemned to die unless she converts him to Mohammed-
anism. Instead he, of course, converts her to Christianity.
Meanwhile Vitelli's sister, who has long resisted the advances of a noble Turk, smuggles into the jail a pie concealing a long rope in the center. The two prisoners escape
through a window. Francisco repents his crimes, and all
four Christians merrily sail away. The Turks are left to
languish even more over their lost women than their lost
gold.

Massinger has two styles, one eloquent and poetical,
distantly reminiscent of the language of Sidney's *Arcadia*,
the other fluent and easy, resembling the style of Fletcher
denuded both of its eccentricities and its resonance. *The
Renegado* represents the former style, *The Guardian* the
latter. This quick-moving and romantic play, Italian in its
lightness and gaiety, owes a part of its plot to Boccaccio,
not unworthily translating into drama the charming narrative of its great original. By far the most striking scene
depicts the device by which Iolante rewins the confidence
of her husband Serverino. After a long exile he returns

disguised to his home, only to find ample evidence that on this very night she has prepared to entertain Laval, her lover. He blindfolds and binds her. While he is absent for a moment and the room is darkened, she changes places with a faithful servant. On his return he brutally wounds the maid. Affairs call him once more temporarily out of the room, and the women resume their former places. When he returns he finds his wife uninjured. This he accepts as a miracle to persuade him of her real innocence. A scene contrived of such fortuitous events falls far short of tragic reality, but admirably accords with dramatic romancing.

The remainder of the play shows some graceful plotting and effective though not profound contrasts in character drawing. Durazzo is the ribald and humorous old guardian of his prim and idealistic nephew, Caldoro. The libertine Adorio first wins and then loses the good graces of the enterprising Calista. Mirtilla, the maid, unblushingly pursues Adorio, while the hypocritical Iolante hesitates over her lovers. By an ingenious plot Adorio is won to elope with Calista: she sends him a jewel on which is carved the rape of Proserpine. By a wittily conceived train of circumstances Caldoro supplants Adorio, and Serverino Laval. The numerous lovers are usually depicted as sincere; but one judges by many a turn that the author himself embraces a sophisticated philosophy. "Jest, but love not," as Shirley advised. Durazzo, the guardian, further casts a disillusioned light upon the whole action, much as Pandarus, guardian of Criseyde, does upon Chaucer's poem. While the play is not thereby made in the strictest sense of the word a comedy, it inclines to the lighter and airier type of dramatic story.

Nearly half of Shirley's works, all written between 1625 and 1642, falls under this general head of dramatic romances. Many are very pleasing productions, as *The Wed-ding, The Grateful Servant, The Example, The Royal Master*, and especially *The Doubtful Heir*. All are grace-ful dramatic narratives with some feeling and some flights of poetry but with little genuine tragedy or humor. They exhibit the drama as an idle and aristocratic pastime, ex-celling in a limpidity of manner rather than in a profun-dity of matter. In view of the history of the heroic drama on the English stage, perhaps the most interesting of all is *The Young Admiral*. This work contains some moving and well-written passages, but is comprised chiefly of brief and sketchily composed episodes wherein the meaning lies largely in the plot. Shirley brings to serious drama a fond-ness for intrigue even greater than Fletcher's and com-monly found only in comedy. This play deals almost exclusively with scenes of love and war, wherein there is much more of the former than of the latter. A Sicilian Princess aspires to the hand of the philandering Neapolitan Prince. Her father brings the armies of Sicily before her lover's gates. Meanwhile Naples has exiled her best war-rior, Vittori, the Young Admiral. With him he has taken Cassandra, his mistress in platonic courtship. Both fall into the hands of the Sicilians. Vittori finds himself caught in a perfect dilemma. If he refuses to fight for the Sicilians, they threaten to kill his sweetheart; if he declines to fight for his Neapolitan countrymen, they now declare that they will kill his father. But further complications soon change the face of events. Vittori's mistress, Cassandra, becoming a friend of the Princess, promises to lure the Neapolitan Prince from his city with a love letter, so that the Princess may meet her beloved. The Prince comes, but the meeting itself is thwarted when he is betrayed and taken prisoner. To prevent his maltreatment the Princess, after entering the gates of Naples in disguise, offers herself as a hostage for her lover. This act of self-sacrifice at last thaws his heart, and the peace between the countries is accompanied by a double marriage. These situations are contrived to afford a maximum of theatrical effectiveness. If Shirley in this case only partially availed himself of the opportunity for poetic declamation, he did perhaps a wiser and happier thing: he let the situations all but speak for themselves.

Such is the general course of dramatic romancing among the chief Cavalier playwrights. By gradual transformation they achieved a type of their own, which has neither the penetration of tragedy nor the humor of comedy—a play composed not by alternating scenes grave or gay but by uniform scenes blending into a passive contentment throughout. The more robust and outspoken Elizabethans did such things differently. Dekker's two great plays, the first and the second part of *The Honest Whore* (written with the assistance of Middleton), likewise fall evenly between tragedy and comedy, but are intrinsically finer poetry and drama than anything in Beaumont and Fletcher or their school. His work by comparison betrays the limitations of his successors. For Dekker penetrated more deeply than they into the realities of the private heart and of the social structure. In the story of Infelice and Hippolito we have a romance comparable to that of Romeo and Juliet. Even if a bourgeois and sentimental morality occasionally mars the realism, the inner fidelity of the picture of the converted prostitute admits no doubt. The bizarre poetry of the madhouse scenes in Part One and the general construction of both parts warrant admiration. The humane humor of the scenes depicting Candido, the patient man, has a fragrance of Dekker's own. In certain episodes of Part Two the dramatist rises to his height. The oblique conversion of Hippolito, the moralist, to evil is well conceived; the cruel spendthrift Matheo is still better; and

best of all is, of course, the eccentric father, Orlando
Friscobaldo, who loves and serves his fallen daughter,
though he is long unwilling openly to admit her as his
own. The major action and indeed the entire conception of
these companion plays shows them to be the type of the
dramatic romance. But precisely because of Dekker's grasp
of actuality they prove to be romances nearer to *Measure
for Measure* and the art of Shakespeare than to *Love's Pilgrimage* and the pleasant but definitely inferior art of
John Fletcher and his associates. Unfortunately there are
few romances in the Elizabethan period remotely equal in
power to *The Honest Whore*.

CHAPTER NINE

THE CAVALIER PSYCHE

. . . the sage
And serious doctrine of virginity.
—MILTON

LIGHTHEARTED as are the majority of dramatic romances by the Cavalier dramatists, these plays cannot in either intention or achievement be divorced from serious meaning worthy of at least a passing consideration. Since their subject matter is preëminently love, one of their chief attractions lies in their development of this theme; and since the plays deal largely with the ideals and manners of an aristocracy, they afford an attractive and faithful mirror of the thought and taste of the highest social class. When the dramatists look inward they perceive the workings of their hearts; when looking outward they see the pattern of the gentleman. In the one case they reveal the Cavalier psyche, or soul disturbed by passion, in the other the Cavalier life in its more social appearances.

A large number of important scenes in the plays are built about clear and uncompromising standards of honor readily expressed in action. Since all non-marital sexual relations of women are presented as unethical and all such relations of men with women of their own rank are frowned upon, though somewhat less severely, the possibilities of ringing changes upon the moral theme become innumerable. Men seduce women, women pursue men, the honor of wives and virgins is threatened; and upon such materials the drama flourishes. Virtually all the plays of Beaumont and Fletcher, Ford, Massinger, and Shirley turn upon these themes. Evadne kills the King for corrupting her; Maximus kills Valentinian for corrupting Lucina; brothers avenge injured sisters, sons avenge injured mothers. Especially in Massinger is honor championed above desire, and with the most quixotic nicety. Thus in Fletcher and Massinger's *Double Marriage* a man has divorced his wife through a pressure of circumstances. Although they are in love with each other and the second woman has repudiated him, she denies him her embraces. In Fletcher's *Wife for a Month* the husband is forced by the King to deny himself to his wife and to conceal the cause of his conduct. Loyalty conquers desire under the most trying conditions. Three types of women are represented: the immoral and luxurious; the honest wives who frankly acknowledge their sensual pleasures; and women who, whatever their conduct, have at all times the appearance of being untouched with desire. The chief dramatists present all three types. The very significant third type we have seen eloquently represented in Ordella in *Thierry and Theodoret*.

The outstanding paradox of the plays is this perverse wooing of Eros, now drawing him nearer and now turning him away. No poets express the allurement of sex more warmly or repeatedly than the Cavalier dramatists, and yet few dwell so commonly on the sinfulness of all sexual pleasure. Love, at least as a spiritual disturbance, is frequently represented as a disease, deserving the whip no less than the madman. Love without sexual fulfillment is extolled as noble; the frank acceptance of sex as a pleasure worthy of refinement and gratitude is commonly denied. Such is the vein of platonic courtship extending widely through the thought of the Renaissance, subject of praise in Castiglione and of occasional doubt in John Donne.

Shakespeare's relation to the idealistic theories and fantasies of his times naturally supplies a useful commentary both on them and on him. He is more concerned with passion as an emotional excitement than as a force for good or evil, which passes through certain transformations to become exalted purity and idealism or debased by certain carnal instincts into infamy and lust. Although the great dramatist was certainly aware in a broad way of the doctrines expressed in *The Faerie Queene*, he seems to have been little allured by them. He is too genial to accept on its face value Ovid's view that passion is a disease and too worldly to hold the Neoplatonic doctrine that it becomes angelic or even to anticipate the indefinite romantic notion of it as half angel and half bird. Love he presents in his tragedies as a fatal force, in his comedies as a remediable or a friendly force. Many of his characters are inspired by love, but they are scarcely purified or debased by it. Once or twice in his *Sonnets* he speaks metaphorically of making a religion of love, but these very poems as a whole reveal a mind far removed from conventional Neoplatonism. Thus many of the sonnets addressed to the beloved man severely criticize him and represent the poet's devotion as infatuation, while all the poems regarding the Dark Lady present both her and her lover in the most unfavorable light. In his comedies Shakespeare shows too active a sense of humor to view love religiously. In short, he has more in common with Boccaccio and Ariosto than with Dante and Petrarch. The passions of Romeo, Othello, and Antony are pitied, not praised or condemned. Like most poets, he frequently depicts lovers, but he neither accepts an old theory nor formulates a new. Although his scenes are passionate, they are always in the best sense of the word realistic. He has no real interest in an academic psychology that elevates purified love to heaven and is little concerned with love as spur to chivalrous conduct. While his preoccupation with romantic passion is itself evidence of his fundamental

debt to medieval thought and poetry, he makes distinct
departures from the medieval tendency to view romantic
love in relation to a code of ethics or a system of psychology. He seldom depicts the forced and virtually incredible actions common in the heroic and ultraromantic
play from Massinger and Shirley to Dryden and Lee, and
he shows small regard for the fashionable Neoplatonism
which appealed to many of the courtly dramatists and even
to such worldly men as Jonson and Fletcher. The English
Renaissance produced many Neoplatonic plays. But it is
highly interesting that no play by Shakespeare is among
them.

Although the chivalrous code of honor plays a larger
role in the dramas than the Neoplatonic theories of the
fleshly life, the pastoral dramas in particular, always modeled in large part upon Italian sources, reflect this cult of
chastity. It appears in all the pastoral plays of the age, as
in works by Peele, Daniel, Shirley, Randolph, Jonson, and
Milton. Indeed without the cult of virginity the pastoral
drama becomes almost unthinkable.

John Fletcher, ever dedicated to the service of love,
whether in a Lais or a Diana, was the logical author to
develop the theme most fully. No other Englishman had
the lightness of fancy necessary to appreciate and translate
the gaiety of the Italian pastoral. Something in Fletcher's
nature, too, responded to the catholic attitude inherent in
the Neoplatonic spirit. He knew Eros with a fervor that
necessarily made him acquainted with Anteros. To the
lament for the vanity of the flesh, heard in Theocritus,
Virgil, Horace, and Catullus, he lent a sympathetic ear.
More than any of his contemporaries save Shakespeare, he
was qualified to sing the threnody of the falling rose. With
the soul of a libertine and the heart of a Robert Herrick,

he was able to epitomize at least one phase of Renaissance thought in a play of undying beauty.

The Faithful Shepherdess has received less critical study than it would seem to warrant, for it states with the greatest clarity an ideal difficult for the modern mind, and especially the Anglo-Saxon mind, to grasp save under the most favorable conditions. Much closer to the spirit of the Italian pastoral than any other English play and even in its title an echo of Guarini's *Pastor fido*, it occupies a norm, or central position, amidst the many somewhat surprising variations which Englishmen wrought upon the theme. The frigid and decorative pastoral of Peele, the grave and comely plays by Daniel, the pastoral turned folklore in Ben Jonson and turned puritanical in Milton—all evince the flexibility of the genre without real fidelity to the Italian pastoral, the parent stem from which it sprang. Among the longest of pastoral plays, *The Faithful Shepherdess* proves by far the most comprehensive in its utilization of legitimate pastoral material. Its scope may be instanced in its use of themes from the subspecies of the piscatory or eclogue of fishermen. No actual fishermen, to be sure, appear among its characters, but the conclusion of the third act, with the elaborate scene of the River God, brings much watery imagery into the play: it has distinctly a more fishy smell than the last scene of *Comus*. Milton's play, after all, is called a masque, while Fletcher's is a legitimate drama or, as he himself termed it, a tragicomedy. In Milton there are five fairly well-marked scenes, woven together by the choral figure of the Spirit. In Fletcher there are five acts with eighteen scenes according to the English manner of computation and nearly fifty according to the continental manner, which records a new scene with the entrance of each new character. Fletcher has more than

twice as many characters as Milton. Moreover, in developing the amorous theme Milton has only one lover, the
lustful Comus, whereas Fletcher has nine lovers in thirteen
different relationships. One author attempts a comprehensive picture of the microcosm of the pastoral world, the
other to build out of that world a lofty temple which
"never yet was heard in tale or song."

Behind all Fletcher's imaginative fecundity and poetical
fluency lies a purist's conception of what is proper to true
pastoralism. By the beginning of the sixteenth century the
pastoral element in poetry had gone through a considerable
range of transmutation. Following the hints of Virgil, pastoral writing had been boldly used to present political,
religious, and philosophical subjects. Far from being a
secluded glade for the innocent sports of the amoretti, it
had become a garden which the gravest sages made their
philosophic walk. Any subject, even the Crucifixion, might
be given a pastoral dress. Thus the scope of the pastoral
was much enlarged by Spenser, Sidney, Raleigh, Giles
Fletcher, and many other notable poets in England. Yet
always in the background was the awareness that the pastoral was essentially a light form of verse, the pastoral
realm a region of little loves, and love itself in its hum-
blest dress its rightful theme. An Anacreontic paradise was
still the homeland of the pastoral; whatever territory it
might further acquire was granted by courtesy rather than
by right.

As Fletcher's preface would alone be sufficient to show,
he composed his work with much conscious art. In order to
reach the gist of his thought, it is well to begin by a review
of the pieces with which his pastoral chess game is played.
Each character has a central import, much as in a strictly
allegorical poem. Clorin, the Faithful Shepherdess, stands
for a love wholly purged from the flesh. Since her lover, to

whose memory she remains faithful, is dead, her industry is solely employed in plucking out the thorns of desire from the flesh of less fortunate beings than herself. Amoret is true love less pure and religious. Perigot, her lover, having no sexual desires is essentially sound, yet in some respects is frail with jealousy, passion, and mistrust. He twice attempts to kill Amoret when, as he believes, she even mentions a sexual wish. Amarillis is likewise a lover capable of nobility, but less constant and true than Perigot. She stoops to deceit and even to intended infidelity to win the physical consummation of her desire. Thenot represents infatuation without desire: he loves Clorin because she remains true to the memory of her own lover. Clorin cures him of his error by the amusing device of pretending to be in love with him. Daphnis is a singularly interesting study of bashfulness. Alexis represents looseness in men, Cloe looseness in women, and the Sullen Shepherd the depth of unredeemable lust. Each character speaks and acts throughout in accordance with the formula on which he is conceived. The play may be considered as following very literally the theory behind Jonson's comedy of humors. And, as in more than one of Jonson's plays, the comic irony lies in the dishumoring of the characters at the conclusion.

The title of the play might well have been "Love's Cure." As already observed, the nine characters are in love in thirteen distinct situations, not including the love of Clorin, a veritable north star of constancy, for her dead sweetheart. In all cases but one the conclusion of the play brings about a change of heart. Amoret, though obviously representing a lower order of perfection than the all-accomplished Clorin, has entertained a pure affection for Perigot throughout and to the last continues so to do. But Perigot overcomes his jealousy of her, while Thenot,

Daphnis, Alexis, Amarillis, and Cloe are entirely freed from the pangs of love or desire by the art of Clorin. The Sullen Shepherd, a pathological type and last and lowest of those who are smitten, is judged by her to be beyond cure and banished from the pastoral realm. The lesson of the play is precisely that of Ben Jonson's famous epode on the same subject. Not to love at all is best; but if one must love, then so to love that purity dispels desire. This is the gist of Fletcher's Christian Neoplatonism.

A strong current of Christian or religious imagery proves, indeed, one of the most attractive poetic features of the play. As in Herrick's amorous land of faërie, the inhabitants of the pastoral realm practice a ritualistic religion obviously a brother of Catholicism. In this realm of devotion Clorin represents the grace of the Holy Spirit; the River God and the Good Satyr, the pure forces of nature; the Priest, the Church; and Pan, God. Clorin and the Priest engage in an elaborate service and sacerdotal system. They practice aspersions, benedictions, prayers, and numerous formal devotions. Clorin lays much the same charge upon the Priest as Milton in *Lycidas* lays upon all good shepherds of the flock. The clergy in pastoral-land are to preach and to blame sinners fearlessly, to correct errors gently but firmly, and to keep as close a guard over the shepherds and shepherdesses as these should keep over their flocks. The beauty and seriousness of the inner meaning of Fletcher's poem come to us much enhanced through this delicate allegory.

Only a supersensitive taste wholly hostile to Renaissance modes of verse will find his language banal or insipid. Closely as he follows his predecessors, he makes his material altogether his own, so that, with the freshness that accompanies all Elizabethan works of genius, his poem nowhere reads like a translation or paraphrase, though in fact it may be so. Behind his success lies the thoroughness with which he has thought his materials through. Although there are numerous characters and episodes, there is no duplication. The entire play is focused upon Clorin, the Faithful Shepherdess, and the idea of chastity which she embodies. The imagery remains scrupulously within the confines of the strictest conception of the Theocritean pastoral. Fletcher neither neglects any essential aspect of his subject nor introduces larger and irrelevant themes. With graceful tact at the end he settles the fate of all his characters. An interesting evidence of his artistic design lies in his observance of the dramatic unities, in which he merely carries out more strictly a scheme implicit in Shakespeare's semipastoral, *A Midsummer-Night's Dream.* There the first act seems laid in the afternoon of a summer's day, and the three ensuing acts that night in the forest. Dawn breaks at the close of the fourth act. A brief interval follows, and while we are actually a few days advanced, the closing scene appears almost as a continuation of the enchanted night in the woods. A breath of the morning in the last lines scatters upon the wind the last gossamer threads of the comedy. In *The Faithful Shepherdess* the first act also is a prologue at evening. All the remaining acts recount the events of the night, which occur in the forest. In the first act the Priest of Pan gives the shepherds the benediction of vespers, and in the last act the blessing of matins.

In estimating the value of Fletcher's poetry in this eminently poetic drama there are two errors equally difficult to avoid: that of describing the style as commonplace because it is low-pitched or that of calling it admirable in the highest degree because it proves altogether adequate to its subject. To judge it best a nice experiment is to place by its side a merely average work, such as Peele's *Arraignment of Paris,* and a supreme pastoral poem, such as

Comus. Something too admirable for the average hand appears on every page of Fletcher's work, yet he never soars to the heights reserved for less artificial and more imaginative authors. His aim is not to astonish but to charm. Yet even Milton in his great masque may give an impression of striving a little too hard. So does Jonson in his admirable but unhappily unfinished pastoral, *The Sad Shepherd.* Fletcher attains the maximum accomplishment consonant with no expense of superlative effort. His style is often in direct imitation of the relatively humble verse in which is written most of that sylvan, if not actually pastoral, drama, *A Midsummer-Night's Dream.* In his solid accomplishment without trace of strain Fletcher stands rather with Shakespeare than with his two other chief competitors for renown, Ben Jonson and Milton.

While no lyric flights or enchanted lines occur equal to those in pastorals by Milton and Herrick, Fletcher maintains his remarkably high average of excellence through a poem much longer and more complicated than theirs. He echoes Shakespeare without demeaning himself and foreshadows Herrick and Milton without being overshadowed by them. Puck himself is scarcely superior to Fletcher's delightful Satyr. Moreover, Fletcher's Satyr not only resembles Puck. He looks forward to both Ariel and the Spirit in *Comus.* Fletcher also led the way for Herrick in some of the latter's most attractive devices, as the practice in light verse of placing the rhyme on slight words, such as "it," "yet," and "of." With this refinement the rhymes skim the more rapidly across the moonlight. Like both Shakespeare and Herrick, Fletcher makes delicate reference to moths, flies, birds, squirrels, and the smaller creatures of the forest that fly or leap with the movement of an allegro. Like those masters, too, he introduces a considerable number of rustic images with humorous effect.

Frequent turns of phrase and especially of rhythm look forward to Milton. Thus octosyllabic verse with a subtle blending of trochaic and iambic measures appears equally in *The Faithful Shepherdess* and *Comus*. In the very first speech of the play occurs a repetition of phrase distinctly prelusive of *Lycidas*. In the manner later to be so elaborately developed in Jonson's pastoral, *The Sad Shepherd*, Fletcher with much fancy introduces many beliefs from folklore. Lovely and playful in its simple pastoralism, enriched with popular superstitions, hardened with a definite doctrine of sex, and polished with the hand of a learned and accomplished artist, Fletcher's play is one of the ripe fruits of the Renaissance theatre. Although philosophically less brilliant than Milton's *Comus*, it is in some respects happier and wiser, much as the central tradition of Italy is more graceful and cosmopolitan than the more idealistic and fantastic tradition of Puritan England. Fletcher has here the sagacity of a man who takes himself and his art neither frivolously nor too seriously. This is why his poem charms us, as we are charmed by Chaucer, but never inspires us, as we are exalted by Milton. While *Comus* is like a mountain to which we occasionally lift eyes and heart, *The Faithful Shepherdess* resembles a pastoral valley where it remains a delight to dwell.

The charm of the light and conventional pastoral with its romantic fairyland of little folk had small allurement for Milton's sterner genius. Using pastoral forms because of a pleasant and prevailing fashion, he wrote a loftier vein of poetry than these had as yet embraced in England. Piety and Puritan politics intrude upon the Sicilian calm in *Lycidas*, while towering flights of imagination no less in imagery than in abstraction dignify the verse of *Comus*, as thunderclouds rise upon a sunny pastoral landscape. Like Plato in his later years, Milton will not allow himself to be enslaved to a merely effeminate doctrine of the beautiful. He writes a poem literally considered in praise of virtue and physical chastity. But such continence becomes in reality a symbol for the idealistic mind that spurns delights and lives laborious days. Like Shakespeare's *Tempest*, *Comus* is a marriage masque, and in each case we have an idealization of chastity. This patently means not only that lovers shall obey the moral law which demands first virginity and then married continence, but that sex as such shall be relegated to a mean and subservient place in the human mind. The poet not only preaches the negative virtue that forbids both illicit relationships and overindulgence; he proclaims the duty to rise above the flesh to higher things. A heavenly paradise of virtue lies beyond the earthly paradise of sensual love, and is the lovelier far. One does not even lead to the other; one is, indeed, almost the contrary of the other. It is the convention of all such poetry that the virtuous man or woman is above sensual desire, treading it down as George trod down the dragon. Milton declares in substance: behold how beautiful appears this earthly paradise of the flesh and of material things; but the true paradise is so much fairer that it makes us see the earthly one for what it really is, a sty for Comus. The physical world, declares the poet of *Comus*, is indeed fair and to be enjoyed. Woman's beauty is of this fair the fairest and so is to be appreciated. But desire is base. And there is a fair beside which all the beauty of earth and woman becomes as dust: the heroism of the valiant mind. In Plato's doctrine Milton finds a moral duality rather than a moral unity.

Behind Milton's gorgeous veil of images sparkle these turrets never wholly scaled by humankind. *Comus* is haunted by the presence of Milton's youthful and eternal idealism, by the thirst for goodness, by the high art, in

Spenser's words, "to fashion a gentleman or noble person."
It is these overtones of high-mindedness that make the
poem truly and sublimely Miltonic. The author concerns
himself far more with the virtue to be won than with the
vice to be disowned. To Milton the simple truth that man
is to rise in dignity superior to the slavery of sex represents
merely the beginning of an eternal quest. This quest is the
theme, and the poet's function is the portrayal of virtue in
figurative terms befitting poetry. Milton accepts Fletcher's
ascetic conclusion, but begins where Fletcher ends. Where
the earlier dramatist makes no effort to develop the more
positive side of the idealistic attitude, to the more vigorous
mind of his successor this task appears preëminent. As a
consequence Milton's poem gains vastly in richness and
elevation, but also acquires a didactic tone and lack of simplicity. Because Fletcher's humble drama is perfectly self-
contained, it bears mention beside the great poem in many
ways modeled upon it.

CHAPTER TEN

POLITE MANNERS

Eye nature's walks, shoot folly as it flies,
And catch the manners living as they rise.
        —POPE

PLAYWRIGHTS of the age of Shakespeare have as a rule
more success in the poetic than in the realistic drama. The
spirit of the times was more given to romance than to the
faithful portraiture of manners, more to a poetry of emotion than to the picture of the externalities of life. The
drama, as a whole, stands closer to the idealistic painting
of Italy than to the genre painting of the Netherlands. Yet
if only a minority of plays excel in scenes from daily life,
this does not mean that such works are of small value. A
considerable number of excellent plays are to be found
depicting the objective and external side of experience.
Both phases of art meet in the richly blended work of
Shakespeare. As a great satirist and egoist Ben Jonson
misses the purest realism, though he certainly triumphs in
the drama of manners. Some of the earlier plays on court
life, as *Cynthia's Revels* and *Love's Labour's Lost,* depict
the stiff, exotic, and not wholly interesting surface of aristocratic life under the Tudors. Most of the scenes of middle-class or low life occur in middling or inferior comedies
by Heywood, Middleton, Webster, Dekker, Marston,
Rowley, and Brome, plays generally representing the less
conscientious labors of their authors and addressed to the
taste of the average London audience. Highly artificial
comic situations as a rule vitiate not only the fidelity of
the picture but the integrity of the art. Thus no real comic
masterpieces emerge from Middleton's numerous and

lively plays on city manners. One explanation of this wide-spread defect doubtless lies in the transitional and inchoate condition of middle-class life in Elizabethan and Jacobean London. But as the Stuart period advanced, as wealth grew, as influences from France were increasingly felt by Court and aristocracy, a genteel tradition came into being. A society was born capable of producing and enjoying polite comedy, which mirrored the life from which it arose. While the tremendous poetical-satirical-burlesque comedies of Jonson surpass all Cavalier drama in imaginative power, they are in turn outdone in direct portraiture of manners by several plays produced in the period of Charles I. The weakening of the strong poetic vein inherited from the true Elizabethans proved a positive aid in producing this more charming, if less exciting, type of theatrical diversion.

How such gusto debars dramatic pictures from literal fidelity appears most strikingly in Shakespeare. The most powerful comic scenes which he ever wrote are presumably the Falstaff scenes. But Falstaff himself talks not only as Falstaff inspired but as Shakespeare inspired. He is one of the most essentially poetic of all the dramatist's characters. His chief speeches are virtually lyrical; the scene with his ragged army is written antiphonally, with the force and balance of a great ode. The farcical scenes of the Athenian tradesmen in *A Midsummer-Night's Dream* are scarcely closer to a photographic art than the romantic adventures of the princely lovers in the forest or the antics of Puck and the fairies. Every one of Shakespeare's comedies is full of allusions, if only in metaphor, to Elizabethan manners. All are true to a fundamental and emotional reality. But none is in the strictest sense a comedy of manners. *Love's Labour's Lost,* with its picture of the stiff affectations of Tudor courtiers, perhaps approximates the genre.

The nearest approach, however, is *The Merry Wives of Windsor,* where Falstaff's poetic genius is relatively in abeyance and the poet, though still in a high degree artificial, gives at least something of the flavor of English provincial life, with its aroma of pippins and cheese.

John Fletcher, also, possessed too much poetic genius, gusto, and fancy to be a master of high comedy. His plays express the Cavalier psyche rather than Cavalier habits. He stands much closer to Shakespeare than to Molière. It remained, then, for his successors under Charles I to bring this type of play to a perfection which dramatic historians too often postpone in their narratives to the period of Charles II. Although more poetic and idealized, less cynical and bawdy, than Restoration comedy itself, a type of play had arisen long before the Restoration which pointed the way toward the later stage. Massinger depicted the more idealized phase of Cavalier manners, and Shirley the rising of London's leisure class.

Charles Lamb knew a masterpiece when he saw it. Among his favorite plays was Massinger's most graceful dramatic romance, *The Great Duke of Florence.* No work is more eloquent in expressing the fineness of Cavalier taste in realms of social behavior. In the field of drama the play occupies the place held among the so-called conduct books by Henry Peacham's *Complete Gentleman.* Life is presented essentially from the point of view of etiquette, and etiquette itself from the point of view of the beautiful. An aesthetic taste or sense of style is represented as the flower and perfume of civilization.

The story of this tragicomedy serves as a convenient frame on which to hang an embroidered garment representing the pattern and decorum of courtly life. Prince Giovanni, nephew of Cozimo, Duke of Florence, has been placed with a tutor, Carolo Charomonte, in whose villa he has met and adored his tutor's daughter, Lidia. His character and his relations with both tutor and girl are depicted idyllically. Giovanni is a young prince perfect in every grace of thought and action, skilled in manners, discourse, studies, horsemanship, and soldiering. Shortly after he returns to his uncle's court at Florence, the Duke hears of Lidia's beauty. Should the Duke, who is a widower, marry and have heirs, Giovanni would lose claim to the throne. Attracted by reports regarding Lidia, the Duke sends Sanazarro, his favorite, to give an account of the girl's appearance and character. The favorite himself falls in love. To discourage the Duke he reports that Lidia is plain and stupid. Moreover, by playing upon Giovanni's self-interest he persuades the Prince to confirm his story. The Duke, however, has indirectly heard the contrary from Giovanni and determines to investigate for himself. Lidia and the conspirators join in a vain plot to deceive Cozimo. They present to him as Lidia a hard-drinking housemaid, Petronella, whose rudeness proves so far overdone that Cozimo immediately detects the deceit. In great anger he arranges a trial whereby the two men are judged by the women whom they have wronged, namely, by Lidia whom they have belied and by Fiorinda, Duchess of Urbino, a princess whom Sanazarro has rudely rebuffed. The women forgive the men; the Duke, remembering his dead Duchess, determines to renounce his present suit, and Giovanni marries the humble Lidia, Sanazarro the noble Duchess.

An artificial but graceful vein of polite compliment runs through the greater part of the dialogue. The Duke is a model of dignity, Giovanni of charm, Lidia of sweetness, Charomonte of hospitality. The Horatian sincerity and purity of manners in Charomonte's family are contrasted with the more elegant manners of the court. Absurd affec-

tations of elegance by persons not to the manner born are
ridiculed in minor characters. Calandrino, for example, is a
merry country fellow who on going to court as servant to
Giovanni cleverly assumes the extravagance of court etiquette, making his way briskly in the world. He frowns
upon the mere thought of his rude and rustic upbringing.
But where the error of the Court is affectation, that of the
country is boorishness. Consequently Massinger depicts in
the household of Charomonte a group of rustic but good-
natured country people, such as the butler, the master of
accounts, and the gentleman of the chamber. Above all
stands the hussy Petronella, in strong contrast with the
gracious Lidia whom she preposterously attempts to imitate. In the manner of the most courtly scenes in the polite
romances of the period are the interviews between the loving Fiorinda and the discourteously cool Sanazarro. The
last act has all the ceremony of the feudal courts of love, a
theme which in several other plays proved attractive to this
moralizing dramatist.

Much of the courtesy is mere compliment, some of it
genuine delicacy of feeling; but all of it is charming and
none of it profound. One atmosphere, one brilliance of
tone and grace of line, characterizes every scene. The play
resembles a painted Florentine chest, the youthful figures
like gleaming puppets, ever light of foot and limb, with
curled hair and softly smiling faces. A charm pervades the
whole, irresistible to any reader who does not take his two
hours with the book overseriously. So perfectly is the mood
sustained that one passage serves almost as well as another
for purposes of illustration; and so elusive is the genius
of the old courtesy that only by example (or in other
words by itself) can the spirit be conveyed. In Shakespeare's *Winter's Tale* and other of his most courtly and

mature plays appears some such feeling for polite manners; but precisely because Massinger is so defective in the
sterner qualities of the poet's mind his lesser graces shine
more conspicuously. Discussion of Massinger's play may
be elucidated merely by quotation of the four opening
speeches:

CHAROMONTE: You bring your welcome with you.
CONTARINO: Sir, I find it
    In every circumstance.
CHAROMONTE: Again most welcome.
    Yet, give me leave to wish (and pray you,
        excuse me,
    For I must use the freedom I was born
        with)
    The Great Duke's pleasure had com-
        manded you
    In my poor house upon some other service,
    Not this you are designed to: but his will
    Must be obeyed, howe'er it ravish from me
    The happy conversation of one
    As dear to me as the old Romans held
    Their household Lars, whom they believed
        had power
    To bless and guard their families.
CONTARINO: 'Tis received so
    On my part, signior; nor can the duke
    But promise to himself as much as may
    Be hoped for from a nephew. And 'twere
        weakness
    In any man to doubt that Giovanni,
    Trained up by your experience and care
    In all those arts peculiar and proper
    To future actions, being grown a man,
    Make good the princely education
    Which he derived from you.

This type of writing betrays at once the most ingratiating
phase of Cavalier taste and the weakening of the fiber of
English life under the continental influences felt in the
courts of James and Charles. On the one hand is a gracious
and humanistic culture, on the other an effeminate want of
broad, realistic, and intellectual vision. This relaxing of the
nerves of the drama helps to explain how the Cavalier culture was found decadent under the attacks of a Puritan
Commonwealth.

Where the grave Massinger is courtly, the sprightly
Shirley becomes urbane. One affords the blues of a sentimental distance, the other the brightness of a superficial
foreground. Although Shirley wrote a few plays almost as
idealized as Massinger's—witness such a work as *The
Arcadia*—the poetic vein ran even thinner than in his
predecessor, and thus his most rewarding works have a
realistic flavor. Standing in an interesting position between
the poetic dramatists of the Elizabethan age and the prosaic playwrights of the Restoration, he writes in a verse
that has all but tumbled into prose and must be read virtually as prose to be fluent and attractive. His own contemporaries admirably estimated his genius, as is well shown
in the numerous prefatory verses to his tragicomedy, *The
Grateful Servant*. There he is praised for introducing
smoothness and sweetness into an English style hitherto
distinguished by ruggedness and grandeur. One realizes
that Jonson was companion of the tempestuous Donne,
Shirley of the serene and lucid Waller. Swinburne did
Shirley's comedies an injury when he lamented the decline
of the drama from Marlowe's *Tamburlaine* to Shirley's
Hyde Park, while Sir Edmund Gosse perhaps overrated
Shirley's tragedies by comparing them with those of his
predecessors. Just as Shirley's most successful style curiously compromises between genuinely poetic verse and

honest prose, so his best plays preserve all the Elizabethan love for fantastic intrigue side by side with Stuart fondness for polite conversation and witty banter.

The drama of the age faithfully mirrors the social and economic evolution. Jonson's comedies reveal a court life frozen by etiquette, a city life rude in its turbulence, and a country life bestial in its crudity. Although strivings are visible towards an upper-class society in London, as witnessed by the gallants and the "collegiate ladies" of *Epicoene*, no picture of a really urbane and gracious social order emanates from this burly and profound dramatist. But a London society only indirectly tied to the Court was being formed by a fairly numerous group of wealthy aristocrats mingling with the plutocrats of the city and establishing town houses, a social season, and a regime of idleness. The ideal of the soldier-courtier as expressed in the tragedies of Chapman thus gave way to that of the polite gentleman as depicted by Shirley. A civil society gradually gathered force, governed by fashions imported from France and embellished with considerable opulence. For its members Shirley wrote, and with such persons his happiest plays deal.

Lacking Fletcher's manlier grasp of emotion, Shirley possesses his fondness for witty intrigue in a really superlative degree. Shirley's dexterity in this field we have seen happily exhibited in his dramatic romance, *The Young Admiral*. That his Pegasus is after all no prosaic nag, as Swinburne insinuates, may be seen from the highly artificial intrigues in *Hyde Park*. The fantastic plots in this play are all the more amusing because it is so surprising and refreshing to discover them among speeches in a familiar style and scenes faithfully reproducing much of the spirit of London life.

The situations are typical and witty enough to bear recounting. Three plots are nicely interwoven. One deals with the loves of Fairford and the sprightly Mistress Carol. The episode is an early version of a theme popular in the age of Dryden: two lovers, witty, independent, and unwilling to acknowledge an attachment which they are unable to avoid, lead each other through a rapid dance of pursuit and escape. To draw Carol toward him Fairford uses the trick of pushing her away. He asks her to do whatever he demands, allowing her to make any preliminary reservations. She declares that she will not love him, marry him, lie with him, grant him her parrot or anything else that is hers. With these and similar provisions understood, let him make his request. He promptly tells her never to see him or make love to him again. Piqued by this denial, she is shortly, of course, once more upon his trail. She sends messages to him and on their meeting denies that she has done so. Affixing his name to an unsigned letter announcing the intention of a rejected suitor to commit suicide, she tells him that she will marry him out of pity. There are more turns and wiles to this plot than necessary to recount here, but its lively character is readily inferred.

Plot number two incongruously though happily borrows conventions from classical comedy. A more indulgent Ulysses has gone to sea granting his wife the privilege of a second marriage if he is absent for seven years. The play of course begins with the seventh anniversary of his departure. The wife is celebrating a morning party with Lacy, projected as her second husband. As an unbidden guest to the party comes the first husband disguised. His rival ungenerously urges him into performing an uncouth sailor's dance. At noon the party goes to the races at Hyde Park. The two men quarrel over bets till the true husband challenges his would-be successor to a duel. Making a just retribution for the earlier insult, the husband employs a bagpiper to play, so that their swords may keep pace to his notes and they may contrive each other's deaths to music. The merry scene is broken off by the entrance of a lord. In the last act the husband, still incognito, returns to participate in the festivities of his wife's wedding. The company is in fantastic dress, engaged in revelry and dancing. In his arms he bears branches of symbolic willow, which he distributes to a number of persons unlucky in love, last of all to his rival. The comedy ends when he reveals his identity.

Plot number three is typical of Cavalier and Restoration comedy in its artificiality and immoral implications. Trier, suitor to Julietta, strangely decides to try his mistress's fidelity by exposing her to the company of the free-living Lord Bonvile. The Lord attempts to seduce her, notably during the afternoon at Hyde Park. But she preaches him so eloquent a sermon in praise of chastity and honor that he makes an offer of marriage, which she, more sensitive to her fortunes than to her own honor, promptly accepts. Poor, foolish Trier remains incredulously in the cold.

Behind these giddy plots, remarkable to relate, is a flow of easy, natural, and graceful dialogue reproducing without material improvement the conversation of polite society. This society, moreover, is the real world of London, not the paradise of aristocratic courtesy envisaged by the grave Massinger. The chief scenes present the races and other amusements of Hyde Park. Runners all but naked compete under the admiring eyes of the ladies. The men find the horses more exciting. Venture, suitor to Mistress Carol, rides his own horse against one mounted by a professional jockey. The gentleman is thrown in the ditch. The chief riding masters are French, the chief runners Irish. Venture sings an excellent ballad in honor of the horses. When he apologizes for the simplicity of the song, his friends protest that only professional singers perform the more difficult music—the simpler tunes best suit a gentleman and an amateur. Near the racetrack in the Park are woods and thickets where the lovers wander. According to old superstitions those hearing the nightingale are destined to good fortune, those hearing the cuckoo to bad. The play of course confirms the auguries of the birds. But the mundane atmosphere is never damaged by the extravagant plots or by theatrical conventions. Behind it all we discover real life, if not real people, and a vivid image of a pleasure-loving, idle, amorous, carefree aristocracy. No one would suspect from this picture that a civil war was brewing in England—these shadows of reality are wholly absent. Whatever realism befits a fanciful and witty play appears, however, making this at once one of the gayest and most memorable of English comedies of manners. It contrasts happily with heavier productions in similar fields, as Jonson's *Every Man Out of His Humour*, Massinger's *New Way to Pay Old Debts*, or Brome's *Northern Lass*. For Shirley realized that it is quite as important for art to entertain as to enlighten.

He himself, and presumably anyone acquainted with his plays, takes more seriously *The Lady of Pleasure*. Fundamentally much the same type of comedy, it none the less differs from its predecessors in many ways. The intrigues are here few, unimpressive, and relegated to the later part of the play. The language, instead of being light and airy, grows relatively eloquent and accumulative, reminding the reader at least distantly of Ben Jonson. In place of amusing situations we find witty speeches, in place of clever plots wittily conceived characters. The best part of the play remains static: an impressive canvas of upper-class London life seasoned with just a touch of the artist's satirical wit. But *The Lady of Pleasure* is rather an apology than a

satire. While it ridicules certain types and follies, on the
whole it presents a flattering picture of the life of the
privileged classes. The key to its unemotional tone lies in
the advice which Celestina, the all-accomplished widow of
sixteen, gives to her friends. She advises them to live a life
of amiable flirtation: "jest, but love not." The truth is that
Shirley is a master of jesting and no master at all of the
passions.

Since little of consequence happens, only the barest elements of the story need be kept in mind. Lady Bornwell
has persuaded her shrewd but less highborn husband to
come from the country to live amid the gaiety of the new
London. Here Shirley borrows and alters a plot from
Beaumont and Fletcher's *Noble Gentleman*. To recall her
from her extravagance and looseness the husband pretends
to be even more reckless than she, giving luxurious ban-
quets and courting the witty widow, Celestina. Shortly
Lady Bornwell becomes so much alarmed at her husband's
expense and freedom that she discontinues her own wild
courses. Meanwhile she has an adventure in the dark with
a foolish gallant named Kickshaw. In his company are
other foils to the witty, such as Scentlove and Littlewit. A
perfumed barber, named Haircut, masquerading as a gentleman and suitor, adds considerably to the amusing picture. Most diverting and significant of the minor characters
is a callow scholar from Oxford, Master Frederick, who
offends his aunt, Lady Bornwell, by his dullness and
pedantry. She sets him to school to the foolish gallants who
haunt her house, with the result that he gets drunk and
explores the world. This character has been pleasantly
foreshadowed in the Tim of Middleton's slight farce, *A
Chaste Maid in Cheapside*. Celestina, Lady Bornwell's
rival in fashion, conversation, and extravagance, is surrounded by a throng of suitors. A lord vainly attempts

her seduction. The dramatist hints in profound secrecy that Celestina may not be wholly chaste, but an elaborate exchange of compliments with her suitors is her greatest indulgence witnessed by the audience.

Shirley's first three acts giving the tableau of polite life much excel the following acts, which are vitiated by not-too-lively intrigue and some deliberately pedantic rhetoric. But the foolish gentlemen are always well contrasted and lifelike, Master Frederick is always amusing, the jealousy of Lady Bornwell and Celestina, who exchange compliments in French, is lively, and the quarrel between Lady Bornwell and her husband is vigorous. Cavalier society is here depicted not as yet disillusioned with itself but already somewhat fatuous and ineffectual. Shirley gives a vivid picture of the manifold trappings of luxury in seventeenth-century London, the dress, furniture, plate, paintings, coaches, Venetian glass, and knickknacks of the times. An admirable reproduction of the spirit of the age lives on in his play, no dull museum piece but an animate creature of the poetic imagination. There is scarcely a better comedy of high life in English or a more faithful image of its glittering dress and shallow mind and heart.

CHAPTER ELEVEN

SATIRICAL COMEDY

He rather prays, you will be pleased to see
One such to-day, as other plays should be;
Where neither chorus wafts you o'er the seas;
Nor creaking throne comes down, the boys to please . . .
But deeds, and language, such as men do use:
And persons, such as comedy would choose,
When she would show an image of the times,
And sport with human follies, not with crimes . . .
I mean such errors, as you'll all confess,
By laughing at them, they deserve no less:
Which when you heartily do, there's hope left then,
You, that have so graced monsters, may like men.
                                        —JONSON

IN ALL MODES of expression the Elizabethans were an
eclectic people, medieval and modern, Christian and pagan,
national and cosmopolitan, naïve and supersubtle. It is next
to impossible to make rules for them. Here they are highly
pedantic, and there no less licentious. The difficulty of
classifying Shakespeare or any of his works is but one phase
of the problem confronting any student of the Elizabethan
mind. Opulent, spacious, inconsistent—so are they in all
fields of thought. Their art is a gallimaufry of styles from
the Egyptian to the Gothic; their music runs the gamut
between popular ballad and Italian madrigal; their theatre
ranges from the neoclassical to the puppet stage. Seneca
cannot be too heavy for them, nor Plautus too light. Comical, historical, pastoral, tragical mingle in one scene. Even
their most attractive works are likely to be alternately delightful and unpleasing, and for this reason pedantry
chiefly accounts for those rare occasions when an Elizabethan play appears on the modern stage without expurga-

tions and alterations to fit the taste of the producer and
audience. We find ourselves amidst a jungle of incongru-
ous riches; things good, bad, and indifferent; an entangled
wilderness.

Readers have long been familiar with the motley garb
of Elizabethan tragedy, the stately pall of black dashed
with splotches of comedy. Farce, nonsense, and burlesque
are introduced both for diversion itself and with overtones
of irony. This motley appears in some of Marlowe's tragedies as they have come down to us and in the chief plays
of Shakespeare, Ford, Middleton, Fletcher, Dekker, and
many others. Although a minority of the tragic dramatists,
as Jonson, Webster, and Chapman leaned away from the
most excessive eclecticism, the typical and popular tragedies of the period have an abundance of "comic relief."
The natural converse of this situation occurs in comedy,
pure comedy being as rare as pure tragedy. Satire or sentimental romancing, moral or emotional earnestness usually
play an important part in the most humorous plays. The
elements of Elizabethan comedy prove indeed so much
more complex even than those of tragedy that the heterogeneous character of the former has been commonly overlooked by critics, blinded as it were by an excess of light,
while the case of the latter has given rise to a critical commonplace. Even Jonson, the most scholarly English clas-
sicist, did more than any other man to produce hybrid
forms of comedy and to demonstrate that such forms may
be attended by notable success.

The most obvious and least interesting aspects of Ben
Jonson are those wherein he differs from Shakespeare, his
most interesting features those which he shares with his
friend. That Shakespeare's plays are first of all emotional,
and Jonson's intellectual, that Shakespeare is intuitive and
androgynous, if not feminine, while Jonson is logical and

masculine, are differences too obvious to bear emphasis. That one poet is often light, the other almost always heavy need only a passing comment. During the romantic period a foil to Shakespeare, Jonson has in recent generations proved a stumbling block to critics. Throughout the neo-classical period the equal of Shakespeare in fame, he has now become a classical author obviously more generally revered than understood. Some frank critics, finding him hard to read, speak ill of him without adequately explaining their position; others speak favorably with even less explanation. Scholarship proves Jonson beyond dispute to have been himself a wide scholar and a remarkable personality, at once like and unlike Doctor Johnson; but it remains to be shown how he was also a great artist. While no critical problem in English literature should be approached with more caution, none invites a richer reward; and in the spirit of trial rather than of dogmatism the task is here attempted. The crux lies in Jonson's truly Elizabethan eclecticism: his reputation must stand upon some seven or eight comedies which are in fact comical, historical, tragical, satirical, farcical, burlesque. The magnitude of their author is to be measured by his prodigious powers of vital assimilation which enable him to create plays baffling in their richness. It is as hard to read such heavily laden works easily as to paddle through dancing rapids a canoe loaded to the rim.

Whatever excellence such a writer attains must obviously result not from a mere virtuosity in heaping together a mad mass of subject matter but from harmonizing all parts with artistic effect. Yet Jonson is clearly at his best in his most complex work. Ever an aristocrat in literature no less than an autocrat, he achieves his final goal only where he exerts the greatest audacity in amassing his sharply contrasted materials. By universal consent his tragedies are inferior to his comedies. Nobly written as his tragedies are, they possess a monotony of tone utterly unlike Shakespeare's and one from which his masterpieces in comedy remain wholly free. One doubts if there is another writer who can boast plays so variegated in attitudes as each of Jonson's major works. In these cases his imagination swings between equally successful scenes of high seriousness, Juvenalian savagery, lofty idealism, delicate satire, uproarious comedy, farce, burlesque, bawdiness, philosophy, realism, and fantasy. It is possible to produce these plays, to be sure, in only one key. Stefan Zweig, for example, after radically altering Jonson's text in his German version of *Volpone*, created a sheer farce. Some amateur performances of this play in English have rendered it as serious as a sermon. But Jonson's intention is truly represented only in a richly diversified presentation. To realize his meaning becomes no slight task, since we are accustomed to far easier and less complicated patterns. Even Shakespeare is actually less elusive in dramatic mood. Far more aware than Jonson of the varieties of human passion and human character, he follows a simpler course in the conception of his scenes. A Shakespearean play is likely to be much more consistently tragic or comic, heavy or light, serious or gay than is a Jonsonian play. The so-called comic relief in Shakespeare's tragedies savors strongly of tragic irony, and the sentimental scenes in his comedies, as in *As You Like It*, have as a rule more latent mirth than real seriousness. The historical plays presenting Falstaff contain, it is true, two sets of radically contrasted scenes, but the very purity and simplicity with which each group is conceived, the one soberly, the other hilariously, produce a pattern that is utterly unlike Jonson's effects. The scholar-poet would not for a moment have countenanced such technique. One poet enjoyed contrasting radically opposed elements, the other

enjoyed blending them. With a more rational and controlled attitude than the romantic Shakespeare, Jonson
aspired to see life all of a piece. Or, looking at the matter
from another point of view, being far more of an egoist
than Shakespeare, he presented life in his comedies as a
reflection of his own complex and self-disciplined mind
even more than as an impersonal pageant of diverse men.
And since Jonson's mind consisted in much more highly
compacted and limited impressions and expressions than
Shakespeare's vision of humanity, in each play of Jonson's
we find the varied strata of his own personality. His comedies are much alike because they are written to the formula of the author's own literary character.

Shakespeare's comedies are either too gay or romantic
to resemble closely the moral and satirical comedy as written by Jonson and a few of his associates. Robustious farces
or tender fantasies belong to categories far different from
the serious-minded and yet highly complex comic creations
of Jonson. Only three of Shakespeare's so-called comedies
have generally been recognized as deviating from the more
familiar paths of light dramatic entertainment. *All's Well
That Ends Well* is simply a conventional dramatic romance
robbed of its customary moral idealism and poetic bloom.
Its humorous elements are of secondary importance. *Measure for Measure* and *Troilus and Cressida* are made of
sterner stuff. Each is romantic and satirical, but neither is
truly comic. Amusing characters, to be sure, appear in both
plays, as Lucio and Pompey in the former and Pandarus
in the latter. Such figures, like Polonius, create humorous
scenes. Yet *Measure for Measure* is morally one of the
most serious plays that Shakespeare ever wrote. The implausibility and complexity of its plots chiefly debar it
from the sober tone of tragedy itself. The Jacobeans themselves would probably have termed it a tragicomedy. On

the other hand *Troilus and Cressida* is an unconventional tragedy terminating with misfortune instead of death and adorned with much buffoonery but still fundamentally grave and ironically tragic. In general temper these two works are like Marston's *Malcontent*. They evince the deep vein of dramatic satire which appeared in the drama of the last years of Elizabeth and the first of James. Without this tradition Jonson's comedy would hardly have flourished, but satirical comedy is a very special form of dramatic satire.

The best and simplest way of envisaging the typical work of Jonson is to regard it as a synthesis of all familiar types of drama save pure tragedy and romance. Each play, as has been said, is didactic, playful, satirical, farcical, realistic, and fantastic. It is written to instruct and to delight, to make men think and to make them laugh, to make them sneer and to make them smile, to produce equal vehemence in moral earnestness and boisterous mirth, but never to make us weep or fear or pity. Sentiment and compassion are utterly banished, as befitting either tragedy or romance. Whatever remotely touches true comedy, whether in the tradition of Aristophanes, Plautus, Terence, or any other classical dramatist, intimately concerns this comic Jove of Elizabethan London.

The seriousness of his intentions both moral and intellectual admits no question. To be sure, in the earliest part of his career, when he wrote romantic tragedies now known only by title and comedies which he never cared to preserve as literature, he took his task as a comic poet relatively lightly. *The Case Is Altered* and *The Tale of a Tub*, the latter a play early in conception though late in execution, evince this lightness of heart. Nothing can be more untypical of the great Jonson than his discarded and Italianate play, *The Case Is Altered*, with its languishing lovers and recollections of chivalry. The case was altered indeed. Strange that as Jonson pruned the excrescences and flourishes of his style, he flourished apace in his own more fundamental eclecticism. Mixed metaphors and purple passages vanish from the second version of *Every Man in His Humour;* but this play is straightforward compared with its immediate sequel and its successors. Moral earnestness is clearly less felt than in *Every Man Out of His Humour,* and the whole proceeds from a lightness of heart. Bobadil still retains some of the pleasantry of Falstaff; the town and the city "gull," Master Stephen and Master Matthew, are sketched with a hand only a little less indulgent than that which drew Shallow and Slender. Long episodes of pure farce occur, as the antics of Tib, the water-bearer, and the errors of Kitely, the jealous husband —parallels to the scenes of Grumio and Master Ford in Shakespeare's jovial farces. The edge of moral justice in the play is much tempered by mercy, as the mere name of Justice Clement suggests. This comedy has little of the asperity or the fresh play of ideas apparent in all Jonson's subsequent comedies. While a moral intention is apparent, satire always remains definitely subordinate to comic fun. To perceive the strata which compose Jonson's more mature masterpieces it is convenient to keep in mind the foundation laid by this important play. To his love for humor which persists till the last he adds an increased devotion to good conduct and to ideas. In the case of his major works it is especially important never to lose track of this level of true comedy underlying even scenes of considerable serious import.

Although Jonson seems most at home when flushing the gutters of Jacobean London with his torrential satire, he occasionally approaches the spirit of high comedy. More in this field he certainly would have accomplished had he lived in a less dynamic society. Much of Renaissance continental culture was as new to England in Jonson's lifetime as eighteenth-century culture to Russia in the age of Catherine the Great. Court life was still colored by robust crudities, and the aristocratic society of the Augustan period lay still three generations removed. Although well ahead of his own times, Jonson could not anticipate so remote a future, and even fifty years later England was unprepared to produce or to entertain a Molière. But something of high comedy already appears in the scenes depicting court etiquette in *Cynthia's Revels,* in the episode of the music lovers in the second act of *The Poetaster,* in the scenes of the "collegiate ladies" in *Epicoene,* and in those parts of *Volpone* which give a flattering picture of Venetian culture. An artificiality and dignity of manners without pedantry or stiffness constitute an ideal at least within the scope of Jonson's art.

But urbanity is not the chief distinction of this Gargantuan soul. His polish is more often that of the intellect than of taste. In *Every Man Out of His Humour,* Jonson's first play in his own humor, he does not chuckle over human follies; from a superior eminence he smiles coldly upon them. With the detachment of a physicist and the interests of a psychologist, he scrutinizes the whims of men. Bidding us smile or even laugh at their absurd attitudes, he censures them as unworthy of the promise or hope of mankind. Carlo Buffon is a perverted poet, Fallace a foolish and sentimental woman, Deliro a doting husband, Sordido a farmer distorted by avarice, Sogliardo a wealthy boor or, as his coat-of-arms has it, a boar ramping to gentility, Fungoso a silly student whose mind is more on his dress than on his studies, Puntarvolo a gentleman of quaint affectations, and Macilente a victim of the envy begotten of his intellectual pride. These are the chief persons in the play. They do little. A summary of such a plotless work is impossible. All that need be said is that each character at last gets into such difficulties with his neighbors that he is, to use the playwright's words, cast out of his humor. *Every Man Out of His Humour* is thus a dry, some would even say an arid, country, where men grow into fantastic plants like cacti.

One must not, however, identify the poet's mood with that of Macilente, the character whom he unquestionably most favors. The fact is that in this play he really approves of no one and yet is never entirely bitter toward anyone. Throughout he observes a grim humor, enjoying the distortions of his characters as a child might be fascinated by the writhings of an insect. There is no dark metaphysical tragedy in the case of Ben Jonson. Successfully tenacious of his own ideals, though these he finds more abused than realized by the world at large, he never withdraws into the clouds of melancholy and romantic cynicism. He never grows pessimistic as do Chapman and Marston. This preserves his "comical satire," *Every Man Out of His Humour*, as a comedy, even though the acids of satire etch all parts of the play. True, life is shown by this most impartial of satirists to be widely corrupt. The country is depraved, composed of barren and earthy clowns; the city is a scene of bourgeois sentimentality, and the court is guilty of ridiculous affectations. The three orders of Tudor society are thus infected. Carlo, with his new-fangled metaphors, is as perverse as Puntarvolo with his old-fashioned euphuistic speech, his dog on a leash, and his cat in a bag. The errors of London are not, thinks Jonson, to be amended by a trip to Constantinople. Yet however base all his characters are, they are all ridiculous. When their errors are viewed collectively one sees the tragedy of society. But when one sees each of these fanatics dwelling in his little world hopeless of coöperation with his neighbor or of personal achievement, his life appears futile and amusing. Jonson is neither concerned nor hopeful for the state of society. Merely for dramatic effect he pictures each folly as exhausting itself after running its own unchecked course. He has no conception of political, educational, or economic reform, of the hope of progress or the fear of social calamity. To him the world is a stage for a collection of follies from which a few men escape by their individual intelligence. Humanity at large can never be redeemed. Thus Jonson, the intellectual aristocrat, realized many of the displeasing aspects of Puritanism, but never sensed its full menace to the peace of England. Hence he never writes out-and-out propaganda, though almost always preserving a hypercritical tone. With a general notion of the reasonable life and with no specific institutions calling upon him for support, he remains free to smile, so that even in the most bitter of his works the comic mood is sustained. How naturally he introduces his comedy into serious situations appears in his picture of the attempted suicide of the farmer Sordido. This knave is so contemptible that no sympathy could be felt for him even in his death. After the fool has vainly attempted to hang himself, he bitterly regrets that his rescuers have cut the rope, "and in the midst too." It is Jonson's satirical comedy at its most corrosive best.

In appreciating the comic or farcical element in his plays it is helpful to keep their theatrical presentation well in mind. The theatre definitely provides for laughter which can be reflected in the library only by some special exercise of the imagination. This appears conspicuously in *Volpone*. The entire story is accompanied by an undercurrent of beast fable. There is but one exception, Celia, who because of her virtue earns the right to a name better than that of her beastly neighbors. The cast of characters includes the greedy fox, the vile flea, the voracious crow, raven, and vulture, and a male and a female parrot. In costume and pantomime these parts exhibit their allegorical meanings. Even the minor episodes in the play frequently strike the eye more strongly than the ear. Thus the parts of the dwarf, eunuch, and hermaphrodite, Volpone's contemptible household, contribute relatively little to the literary value of the work, but provide considerable amusement on the stage. Volpone's pantomime throughout, as well as his disguise first as a mountebank and finally as an officer of the police, helps to enliven the theatricality of the play with small addition to its poetical merits. But the sensitive reader will make the necessary effort to reconstruct the comic elements by no means obvious upon a hasty perusal.

A rich blending indeed is this celebrated comedy. Written in verse, and often in powerful verse, it has much of the poetic force and sincerity of the Juvenalian satires which it frequently paraphrases. Volpone's wooing of Celia rises to a lyrical enthusiasm. Almost all the characters give way to vehement passions. The moral violence of the conclusion, an ending unconventional to say the least in pure comedy, Jonson himself felt obliged to defend. A single villain may be expected to be banished or dismissed at the end of a comedy, but what shall the pedants say of a professed comedy which sends all the chief characters to disgrace in its last scene? Jonson, following Terence, declares that comedy should sport with human follies, not with crimes; and yet few deeds can be more criminal than those of the characters of this work. Volpone pretending to be mad or on his deathbed suggests many a tragic scene. One hardly knows whether to regard the play as a macabre tragedy or a sinister comedy. In either case, for his more serious scenes the poet does provide a comic relief of a kind in the episodes of Sir Politick Wouldbe, his wife, and

his companion Peregrine. Even the farce here has bitterness. There is a touch of misanthropy in the caricature of
the hateful and loudmouthed woman; and keen satire
against those commoners who presume to a knowledge of
politics sharpens the portrait of the unfortunate traveler.

Equally remarkable for blending comic and serious
themes is the greatest of Jonson's masterpieces of architecture in comedy, his *Alchemist*. It is as though the author
had in a single play foreshadowed the sobriety of *Le Mi-
santhrope* and the mirth of *Le Médecin malgré lui*. Written, like *Volpone*, in verse, it depicts some of the most
passionate cravings of mankind. The love of wealth and
the fear of poverty lead a host of men and women upon
the most desperate adventures. Blinded by avarice and
superstition, they penetrate into the strange religion of
alchemy. Ananias and Tribulation Wholesome seek to
establish the only true Church of Christ through their
profits in dealing with the alchemist, Subtle. Kastril has
sold all his lands in order to learn from Subtle and Face,
the butler disguised as a captain, how to live as a roistering
gallant. He also believes that he is to make his sister's
fortunes for life by marrying her to a noble Spaniard.
Surly, one of the most severely treated of the characters,
attempts to uncover the nest of rascals in the sacred name
of truth. Poor Drugger and Dapper are citizens who have
staked at least all the goods they possess on the hope of
becoming rich by magic. Sir Epicure Mammon aspires to
reap the finer riches of the world and even to control the
earth and the heavens by Subtle's art. Finally, the three
knaves, Subtle, Face, and Dol, risk everything they cherish
in their desperate imposture. All are for a time hopeful,
and every one but the supreme knave, Face, is at last
cheated out of his fortune and his "humour." Sir Epicure
Mammon is, to be sure, the only heroic figure comparable

to Volpone, but a certain tragic seriousness is evoked by the spectacle of miserable mortals staking their all upon a dream. Every one of the cheated is a fanatic in the cause, laying his most dearly beloved treasure at Subtle's feet. Jonson draws the alchemist as a priest of evil who evokes reverence and awe from his ignorant worshippers. He, Face, and Dol are playing with the most sacred things of life, buying and selling men's hearts, souls, and honor.

On the other hand the play is a better comedy than *Volpone*. The author delights in the tricks of the cheaters whereby they take in their spoils and indefinitely postpone the day of payment. Especially he shows comic gusto for the war between the two chief rogues themselves and a joyful satisfaction that the greater rogue and meaner man is in the end overcome by the more reputable cheat. For sacrilegious alchemist and vile prostitute Jonson can have, of course, far less sympathy than for the witty servant who from the time of Menander has been the ideal hero of comedy. The play combines the mirth of *Every Man in His Humour* with the satirical energy of Jonson's tragedies. Laughter becomes much freer and less harsh than in *Every Man Out of His Humour* and *Volpone*. Although Dapper and Drugger are more intellectually conceived than Matthew and Stephen, they are considerably more amusing. They are, indeed, almost ideal simpletons and are admirably contrasted, the mean tradesman with the no less mean but vastly more ambitious lawyer's clerk. Ananias and Tribulation Wholesome prove perfect sketches in the vein of light and witty satire. Even the quarreling boy and his fatuous sister contribute something to the general mirth. The situations prove especially diverting. One of the most amusing is the explosion which ends so tragically all Sir Epicure's hopes of affluence. Another is the entrance of Ananias to the household already in a storm over the disclosures of Surly. To an aroused tempest the man of God with magnificent irrelevance declares:

> Peace to this household;
> Casting of dollars is concluded lawful.

Not only is there no peace. The situation has nothing whatsoever to do with the casting of dollars; and there can never have been a doubt that the pliable Puritan conscience would find a way to sanctify its own interests at the expense of the state. With the faith of the ungodly shattered, an open warfare established between Subtle and Face, and the witty servant in control of the situation, the last act becomes at once less poetical and more obvious comedy than the preceding. The dupes pass in and out of the house on great waves of fear and disillusionment. As usual Jonson takes his jibe at public opinion. The people will believe anything they are told. What good, implies Jonson, is to be expected from the typical citizen who sits up all night mending his wife's stockings?

Just as in the case of *Volpone*, the comic nature of *The Alchemist* may easily be underestimated if the play is read too narrowly as literature. It undoubtedly affords a serious and eloquent indictment of the wishful thinking of superstitious, emotional, and unintellectual people, but it also may seem heavy in its reiterations and overemphasis if the theatrical situation is not taken into account. Subtle uses long and even preposterous rants to pound his victims into submission and belief. Dol engages in a similar debased eloquence when she assumes madness at the mention of Broughton's works. As literature such passages, if read unimaginatively, are insipid. But the intention is evidently that Subtle shall talk so fast and furiously that his longest speeches will take only a few moments to deliver. His vehemence, not his sense, draws the simple flies into his web.

Evidence of Jonson's eminently theatrical conception appears in the quarto, which prints certain speeches of Dol's mad scene in parallel columns. The speakers are to talk simultaneously. Most modern editions overlook this refinement, thus doing a great injustice to the playwright's art, concealing its theatrical effectiveness and its real vivacity. Indeed, one must always hear Jonson's speeches with the mental ear. Much of the humor lies in the tone or tempo in which they are delivered. Scenes between Truewit and Morose, Otter and his wife, and Otter and Cutbeard in *Epicoene* are litanies in form and triumphs of comic gusto in spirit. In *Volpone* Jonson creates highly original comedy from the hard-of-hearing Corbaccio. The playwright's prose has the quality of stanzaic verse, strophes and antistrophes gushing out at us in the robust idiom of the London streets. With a fine musical ear he even pitches his dramatic speeches as though writing one of his masques. The last scene in *Bartholomew Fair*, for example, contains music in three parts: the bass of the roaring Busy is effectually answered by the treble of the squeaking puppet, while Leatherhead's mean represents the normal human voice. Such are the inspired inventions of the most successful contrapuntal writer for the English stage.

Less emotional than *The Alchemist* and written wholly in prose, *Epicoene* becomes serious first of all because of a strong undercurrent of intellectuality. A gigantic farce it has well been called, but it is also a critical study. Each character and each scene is the product of a coolly analytical mind. The ingenuity with which the complex situations are manipulated indicates this; the learning displayed so freely points to it still further. Jonson has a set of theories which he commits to the laboratory of the stage. Thus there are two types of fools, those who can be moulded to any shape which a designer wishes and those ridiculous through their very stubbornness. Monsieur La Foole, John Daw, and the "collegiate ladies" belong to the former class, the more dignified, heroic, and truly British Morose to the latter. Because Jonson selects for this play a group of characters largely from high life, he introduces more mental acumen than in his plays with more vulgar scenes. Thus throughout Clerimont has an argument with True-wit on the Horatian problem of whether art or nature better adorns a woman. Only in the conclusion of the play is Clerimont convinced of the superiority of art. La Foole is a subtle study in the affectations of well-to-do society, John Daw in those of false scholarship. The learned and hilarious dispute in Latin between Cutbeard and Otter on the twelve grounds for divorce adds weight to the play. A certain dignity and courage pertains to Morose despite his ridiculous weaknesses. All these considerations, however, are outweighed by the farcical plot centering in Epicoene himself, and the play, though a serious study of manners, becomes in still higher degree a roaring bonfire of mirth.

Similar in its intellectuality is Jonson's great comical pageant, *Bartholomew Fair*. On the one hand this is a serious study of the lower orders of London, on the other a humorous burlesque of city life. In striking degree it is designed to instruct and to entertain. The sheer intellectual feat of following the complicated pattern of the play tends, especially in the reader, to induce sobriety. Act One, really a prologue, is laid not in the fair but at Littlewit's house. A group of figures ever mounting in number and importance gradually fills the stage, the arrival of Zeal of the Land Busy supplying an appropriate climax. The formula for the remaining acts is a simple but not too obvious one. The central scene is always occupied with Bartholomew Cokes, the type of simple-minded creature without whom

the fair could not exist. The carnival is for his pleasure and
for the profit of those who live off his purse. But his fair
has two enemies attempting to outflank him on two sides,
the conscientious Anglican judge Overdo and the fanatical
Puritan preacher Busy, and one or the other or both are
present in the first and the last episodes of each act. To be
specific, in Act Two Cokes loses his change purse, in Act
Three his major purse, in Act Four his coat, hat, and par-
cels, and in Act Five he is seen upon his true level playing
as a child with the puppets. Opening Act Two, Overdo lays
plans to spy upon the fair and in its conclusion is beaten by
Waspe. Act Three begins with Busy's triumphal entry into
the fair and ends with the arrests of both Busy and Overdo.
In the commencement of the next act the two are placed
in the stocks, and in its conclusion they are miraculously
released. In the opening of the last act Overdo offers his
misguided charity to Troubleall, the madman; at the fin-
ish of the play he is disgraced by his wife, and Busy is
"put down" in argument with the puppets. So deliberate
a plan is typical of the serious mind of its author, equally
zealous in his study of technique and his criticism of public
morals.

Although a burlesque in its exaggeration of the folly
and stupidity of the citizens, his play deals with once important matter and cannot be regarded as mere trifling.
The bitter tang of reality clings to it. Overdo is a telling
satire on the overzealous reformer, in this instance vainly
upheld by classical learning and the authority of the Anglican Church. Busy supplies a terrific satire on vulgar
puritanism, its brutality, ignorance, pride, and hypocrisy.
Dame Purecraft, the Puritan widow, is an expansive foot-
note to the same effect. In drawing the fair itself, with the
pigwoman Ursula, the horsecourser, pickpocket, ballad
singer, puppeteer, wrestler, boxer, and the rest of the un-

ruly clan, Jonson makes the city appear not only ludicrous but vile. A Juvenalian animosity enters into all parts of the picture. The only reputable characters, Grace, Winwife, and Quarlous, are never warmly drawn, are briefly sketched, and scarcely afford an exception to the foregoing remarks. It is typical that Jonson gives Overdo a silly wife who is last seen drunk in the company of Whit, the pimp, and Alice, the prostitute. Just as he satirized pedantic learning in John Daw, so here he mocks the pedantic temperament in Waspe, the irritable guardian and tutor. Jonson views such fools as Cokes, Master Littlewit, and his wife with even more scorn than amusement. The play is comical and no doubt is more risible on the stage, when well produced, than when read in the library. But at most it represents once more the curious Jonsonian compound of censoriousness and burlesque, the sharpest satire and the broadest mirth.

On these major comedies, all much the same in spirit, Jonson's fame chiefly rests, and little need be added regarding his minor pieces. Much the best of the plays unmentioned so far is *The Poetaster*, another instance of Aristophanic humor blended with Juvenalian seriousness. It shows Jonson's views of poets, playwrights, and their art through scenes in Augustan Rome, he himself masking in the disguise of Horace. It was motivated by an ephemeral literary quarrel between Jonson, champion of the new realism and classicism, and Dekker and Marston, the romanticists, who replied in a very sprightly burlesque of Jonson, *Satiromastix, or The Untrussing of the Humorous Poet*. A rivalry between theatrical companies was the economic cause. *Cynthia's Revels*, an allegory on the manners of the Court, proves defective in comic gusto and indeed is a failure in all but certain occasional stylistic graces. The comedies written in his old age are of curious interest, but contribute nothing further to this discussion.

As a phase of Jonson's remarkable blending of comedy and satire, fun and moral earnestness, the conception of a number of his chief characters repays reëmphasis. With true comic spirit he makes fun of persons who act with smug self-righteousness in attempting to destroy evil. He makes us more sympathetic with the knavish Face than with Surly, who is chiefly seen in a righteous effort to un- cover the rogues in *The Alchemist*. Like Overdo, Jonson despises Bartholomew Fair and cherishes the maxims of Horace. Instead of making the reformer a hero, however, he draws him as an ass. Conversely, Jonson may enlist a certain admiration for his comic victims. Morose is a bit harsh to his nephew but, after all, apart from his one great failing, a dread of noise, he is a gentleman, a scholar, an individualist, and no despicable person. Jonson even ad- mires his courage; indeed, to judge from his minor poems, he hated the noise, filth, and vulgarity of the city hardly less than Morose. The seemingly robust poet was probably himself a little neurotic. The moralist is sunk in the comic playwright in the conclusion of at least three of his mas- terpieces: *Epicoene*, *The Alchemist*, and *Bartholomew Fair*. One even suspects that the satirical mood may have been a professional affectation with him, as it was certainly with many of his Augustan successors. The morality in his tragedies is serious enough, but his comedies must not be viewed in too dolorous a sense.

No Elizabethan dramatist rivals Jonson in his synthesis of satire and comedy partly because none remotely equals him in orchestral strength. Compared with his massive comedies, those of his more romantic contemporaries seem slight and often trivial. They lack his power to compress so much into the given space of a play, his conviction and bitterness in satire, his grasp of reality, his comic invention,

his constructive power, and the titanic force of his merci-
less mirth. Yet on this very account it becomes of interest
to note work of men who in accord with the spirit of the
age follow at some distance his flights of highly critical
humor. Two of the most brilliant comedies of the period
may be remembered in this regard, *Eastward Ho!* and
A Game at Chess. In the former play Jonson had a hand.
How much of it he wrote is a question impossible to
answer, but while he was doubtless instrumental in con-
ceiving the play, he presumably composed only a minor
part of it. His able assistants were Chapman and Marston,
both masters in the realistic comedy of humors. As a result
of this collaboration, *Eastward Ho!* is a sprightlier work
than any from Jonson's pen alone and a much better and
more vital play than any comedy solely by either Marston
or Chapman. Much more serious and realistic in its criticism of life than Beaumont's theatrical burlesque, *The
Knight of the Burning Pestle,* it may be designated as a
comedy of manners and as a partly satirical piece; and it
proves entertaining to many readers who find the undi-
luted Jonson unpalatable and heavy.

Its major plot is the age-old story of the industrious and
the idle apprentice as later immortalized in prints by Ho-
garth. The feminine side of London life is by no means
neglected, since there are contrasting portraits of the dutiful housewife and the social climber who aspires to be a
fine romantic lady. All the upstarts are in the end put
down, the idler and the prodigal rebuked, and the citizens'
virtues of piety and honest industry rewarded, though with
much irony and amusement.

The tale is a telling satire on the taste and morals of the
London middle class. The upstarts Quicksilver, Gertrude,
and Sir Petronel Flash talk an absurdly affected euphuism.
The honest tradesmen hold to a simple code of morality

suitable to their humble station in the middle class but
somewhat ridiculous in the eyes of a bohemian poet and
intellectual friend of the aristocracy. The last scenes are as
soul-searching as this type of comedy well can be. Quicksilver and Sir Petronel experience the pangs of conscience
while languishing in prison. The sentimental dreams of
Gertrude are dissipated by her bitter experience.

Eastward Ho! is thus no mean criticism of plebeian
ideals. On the other hand it is one of the most rollicking
and amusing of English comedies. Cold scorn at no time
puts out the fires of mirth. The virtuous characters are
absurd in their virtue, the wicked no less ridiculous in their
vices. The popular romances and even the conventions of
the popular theatre are parodied by the delightful rightness of fortuitous events. It is as though a purely humorous
god had created the world in a fit of holiday fooling. The
stars in their courses fight for a poetic justice that is com-
ically satisfying. Thus when the drunken crew are washed
ashore at various points on the Thames, what more appropriate than that the cuckoldy usurper Security, nightcap on
head, should swim ashore at Cuckold's Haven; that Win-
ifred should be rescued and her virtue saved at the village
dedicated to the chief of all virgin martyrs, Saint Catherine; that the shifty Quicksilver should find himself by the
gallows at Wapping; and that Petronel and Seagull,
worthless rascals both, should be cast up on the Isle of
Dogs? The supreme comic irony is that it is Saint Luke's
Day when Slitgut, the butcher's apprentice, faithful to
ancient tradition, affixes the symbolic antlers of cuckoldry
to the tree that has stood at the haven since the reign of
the royal cuckold-maker, King John. Yes, it would be hard
to find a play at once so instructive and diverting as this
excellent travesty of London life.

A Game at Chess, by Thomas Middleton, belongs virtu-

ally in a class by itself yet preserves a union of tartness and
fantastic humor reminiscent of Jonson. It is more serious
than the average Elizabethan comedy in that, contrary to
the rule, it deals primarily with public affairs. The author
congratulates the patriotic party that the projected marriage between the English Prince and the Spanish Princess
has failed to eventuate. Under the perspicuous but ingenious allegory of a game of chess the diplomatic negotiations
are related from the Protestant point of view. Although
Prince Charles had visited Spain, his proposed marriage
with the Infanta was checkmated. In the performance a
bag was placed on each side of the stage where the captured chessmen were thrown. Ignatius Loyola is introduced
in an amusing prologue. Much humor is had at the expense
of Gondomar, the witty Spanish ambassador, and still more
at that of the talented prelate, De Dominis, who argued
learnedly in behalf of Catholicism or Protestantism as one
or the other party offered him the better rewards. Each
was an eccentric and highly individualistic character lend-
ing himself readily to the pen of the amused satirist. Several scenes make excellent sport of the beguiling words
whispered by Jesuits into the ears of English women. The
comedy is in the better humor since it reflects the smile of
the triumphant, not the sneer of the defeated. Rising to
what was obviously a rare and important occasion on the
English stage, Middleton for once wrote a comedy with
exceptional care, for though the work cannot have been
long in process, it shows considerable polish. On the one
side we note the daring of the author and the seriousness
of his theme, on the other the gaiety of his style and audacity of his imagination, which employs an allegory not
unworthy of the most active fancy of Aristophanes or Jonson—or, one might add, of Lewis Carroll. Such a play

assures us that the bitter and yet jovial mood of Jonson, though rare, as any spiritual refinement must be, was neither peculiar to himself nor extinguished when he laid down his pen. It is, in fact, a mood older than Lucian and younger than Bernard Shaw.

CHAPTER TWELVE

FANTASTIC COMEDY

What need we fiddles, bawdy songs and sack,
When our own miseries can make us merry?
—FLETCHER

THE SPIRIT of the sixteenth and seventeenth centuries
which created the dramatic romances of the Shakespearean
period, with their implausible plots and readily accepted
theatrical conventions, lent itself to the rich development
of a fantastic comedy wherein mirth and farce surpass
satire and realism. Especially among the average and typical writers of the age this comic gaiety prevails. With
the important exception of Jonson, almost all the dramatists lean heavily upon a union of sentimental romance and
farce, the spirit of merriment ascendant and pervasive.
The medieval heritage of Elizabethan comedy is direct
and important. A few further exceptions, however, are
sufficiently notable, so that before considering the major
stem in the comic tradition it is convenient to recall the
less flourishing plants surrounding it.

Both before the great age of the theatre began and after
its main impetus had subsided, there flourished a conversational type of play by no means typical of Elizabethan
comedy as a whole. No major poet wrote for the popular
stage before Marlowe in 1587 or after the death of Fletcher
and the end of James I's reign in 1625. There is a curious
kinship, all differences notwithstanding, between the polite
euphuistic banter in the comedies of John Lyly and the
polished dialogue in James Shirley's *Hyde Park* and *Lady
of Pleasure*. Though both playwrights have a story to tell,
their chief concern here is with talk rather than with action.

All Lyly's plays reflect the elaborate and strangely charming pedantry of court life under Queen Elizabeth. Almost all were played by groups of children before their sovereign during the Christmas revels. The small group of genuinely social comedies by Shirley and his associates of the time of Charles I mirror the life of a wider circle of society, but are none the less comedies of polite manners. The difference is that between the Elizabethan courtiers and the Cavalier gentlemen. Indeed, a sophisticated and favored society is required to produce a fundamentally conversational theatre. While the populace always demands a wealth of action, the more educated classes will sometimes content themselves with the play of ideas. A conversational comedy was possible in England just after Renaissance culture had crossed the Channel in full force and before the great vogue of the popular theatre. It was possible once more when the public at large was withdrawing its support, leaving the stage to the Royalist faction. The great years of the Elizabethan theatre, national in its appeal, forbade such a development. Of Shakespeare's comedies only his early *Love's Labour's Lost* inclines toward Lyly's school of witmongering. The typical Elizabethan comedy was destined to owe more to humorous situations than to witty talk and more to romantic poetry than to colloquial dialogue. The reputation of the dramatists, especially in the nineteenth century, reveals the situation significantly. While critics have acknowledged some fascination in Lyly's art and some charm in Shirley's, they have expressed on the whole remarkably little enthusiasm for these playwrights. Unhappily, the minor Elizabethan drama has appealed chiefly to persons of a romantic temperament, who have followed Swinburne in extolling the great Elizabethans at the expense of Lyly and Shirley. Lovers of witty social comedy, it would seem, have turned from these neglected playwrights to the dramatists of the Restoration.

One of the most popular types of comedy during the Elizabethan period itself has met with even less applause from the historians. A truly popular comedy in the age of Marlowe was likely to contain some ill-ordered episodes founded on the most debased of the popular romances, interlarded with a vast amount of horseplay for the clowns. In fact, during the first years of the public theatre no actors seem to have been so enthusiastically received as the clowns themselves, who improvised much of their parts and excelled in pantomime. Their art remains today highly difficult to recover, and the plays in which they triumphed, such as the much-beloved *Mucedorus,* are conceded to have little or no literary value. The verse of the romantic scenes is childish, and the humor of the comic scenes, as even Shakespeare observed, quite inexplicable.

In the hands of playwrights of more than average skill, as Peele and Greene, whose dramatic activity was greatest about 1590, the romantic tradition produced some delightful works which can only dubiously be classed as comedies. Comedies they are, to be sure, in the sense that they have the conventional happy ending; but the farce scenes are subordinated to sentimental and romantic passages. The modern reader is likely to find even the serious scenes of these plays somewhat risible because of their extreme naïveté. In the last act of Greene's *Friar Bacon and Friar Bungay* the humble heroine has been "tried" by her courtly lover, who has written her an epistle declaring that he has cast her off forever. Accordingly she stands, in the dress of a nun, on the threshold of the cloister. From the irrevocable step her lover comes to rescue her. One of the courtiers puts the case to her with remarkable frankness:

Choose you, fair damsel, yet the choice is yours,—
Either a solemn nunnery or the court,
God or Lord Lacy: which contents you best,
To be a nun or else Lord Lacy's wife?

The ingenuousness of such passages is almost certain to produce a smile in the modern reader, while the original audience was probably more soberly inclined. There is much comic fantasy in Greene's *Friar Bacon*, but the play is not really a fantastic comedy. Though Bacon is indeed a "frolic friar," he is also a brother to Faust. There are many undeniably serious and even tragic scenes in Greene's unobtrusive masterpiece. Not even in his ultraromantic version of Ariosto in the play entitled *Orlando Furioso* does he view love so humorously as Shakespeare in *As You Like It*, *A Midsummer-Night's Dream*, and other of his light and masterful comedies. Peele's *Old Wives Tale*, its burlesque elements notwithstanding, was probably intended by its author first of all as sentimental romance. These early plays lead rather to the gay dramatic romances of the Fletcherian school than to the truly comic work of Fletcher and his associates.

As the sentimental drama passes from the earlier Elizabethans to the playwrights of the immediately succeeding group, however, the species takes a perceptible turn closer to true comedy without actually effacing itself and becoming the lighter type of play. While the major plot remains primarily serious and the general effect emotionally grave, two notable changes occur. A minor plot dominated by a character humorous in both the Elizabethan and the modern sense of the word grows important. And the major plot, though still essentially romantic, becomes in a measure intellectualized. A witty intelligence sits in control of the action. But since tragedy marks the ascendancy of emotion over reason and comedy that of reason over emotion, the step toward genuine comedy is unmistakable. Specimens of this development are two fine plays hovering between the typical dramatic romance and true comedy, namely Chapman's *Monsieur D'Olive* and Marston's *Dutch Courtezan*. In the former play the leading character in the humorous secondary plot, as often in Beaumont and Fletcher, gives the work its title. In its major action two highly serious and romantic love affairs are finally steered to happy endings by deft, intelligent scheming. The hero of *The Dutch Courtezan* cures his friend of a dangerous infatuation for the courtesan by having the friend accused of murder on seemingly unanswerable evidence. The situation is obviously grave, but the audience, unlike most of the characters, always knows the secret and anticipates a happy ending. This is only one episode in the comedy, but an important and indicative one. The play, too, has its lively comic underplot. Such plays are graver by far than *Twelfth Night*, which has its even more notable comic underplot centering on the eccentric Malvolio and a romance for its central theme that, despite its tenderness, remains essentially amusing. Were these and some other comedies by Chapman and Marston more typical, they would be given greater attention in the present volume than is granted other plays perhaps inferior but more representative. They are more vital works than any by the Cavalier school. We must also recall, if only to pass by, those excellent light satires (not true comedies) Chapman's *Widow's Tears* and Marston's *What You Will*.

Many of the light entertainments of the early Elizabethan stage, on the other hand, are properly farces rather than comedies. They descend from medieval farce, as admirably practiced by John Heywood during the first half of the sixteenth century, as well as from early adaptations of Plautus, who, Polonius reminds us, seemed the very type of the lightest possible theatrical diversion. The relation of Plautus and Terence to Elizabethan comedy is almost exactly that of Seneca to Elizabethan tragedy. Without the Latin background the mature English work could hardly have come into being, yet the native plays only become eminent, or classics in their own right, as they desert the narrow imitation of the classical models. Great indebtedness to the Latin comic poets is to be found in all the English playwrights from Lyly to Shirley, and the scholarly and intellectual Jonson is not materially more in debt to them than the ever-popular and lightheaded Thomas Heywood. But just as the early imitations of Seneca are relatively frigid, so the early adaptations of Plautus leave the modern reader or audience comparatively cool. The early versions of Latin comic themes, such as Udall's *Ralph Roister Doister* (c.1566) and Shakespeare's *Comedy of Errors* (c.1593), are competent farces rather than inspired comedies. Elizabethan drama has better offerings than these.

Of the rich and truly complex comedy of Shakespeare and Jonson little further need be said here. Each of the two major dramatists goes his own way, yet each is profoundly the child of his age by virtue of his audacious eclecticism. The first combines within his comedies all elements compatible with plays pleasant and humorous, the second all elements compatible with plays hilarious and yet satirical. The two express the brave and spacious times in which they lived. Their comedies have at once more reality and more poetry, more fantasy and more penetration, than any written by their contemporaries. They show vastly more fresh invention and less reliance upon the mere tricks of the theatre than works by their fellow dramatists. Although their comic situations are often implausible, they never appear hackneyed; and although their realism is often pointed, it never becomes prosaic.

The minor comic dramatists from Greene to Shirley at all times run a number of favorite theatrical conventions to death. Whether the scene is Cheapside or Phrygia, the technique remains much the same. Their fantasy, in short, is not always that pure gold that glistens in *A Midsummer-Night's Dream*. For example, borrowing the notion of disguise from the ancients, the Elizabethans at times carry the trick to most unfortunate extremes. False beards and false faces must have fairly littered their property rooms. Even historical themes are subjected to this popular rage, so that such a work as the anonymous *Look about You,* which purports to be an English chronicle-history play, abounds in ridiculously rapid changes of face. Proteus becomes an evil genius of the stage. Many charming plays, to be sure, as *Twelfth Night,* freely employ the device. A disguise that conceals sex has considerable possibilities for comedy. But since the typical Elizabethan sin is excess, the playwrights show small discretion in knowing when to stop. The Elizabethan mind naturally proved even more lawless in comedy than in tragedy. Thus if we dismiss the lighthearted romances and consider only the more legitimate fantastic comedies, we find the number of really distinguished plays, at least for the early part of the period, relatively small. Shakespeare's predecessors wrote poetic dramas that are not quite comedies, while his successors wrote comedies that are not quite poetic. Jonson was too massive a genius to be followed closely even by his own admiring "tribe." Ford and Massinger had no great comic genius, while Webster, Middleton, and Dekker were as a rule notoriously careless in comic writing. Heywood lacks substance; and therefore the only really eminent comic dramatists besides Shakespeare and Jonson are Beaumont and Fletcher. Yet at least forty or fifty admirable comedies were produced. A few of them, as *Eastward Ho!*, have already been considered in these pages. It remains for us to examine some phases of the spirit of fantastic comedy as they appear in some of the better, though typical, plays by Dekker, Heywood, Middleton, Shirley, and Beaumont and Fletcher. Mirth and comic gusto inspire them all, from the innocent humors of the true Elizabethans to the controlled gaiety of the accomplished Cavaliers.

In Peele and Greene romance tends to outdistance comedy, as it also does in Dekker's extraordinary dramatic fantasy, *Old Fortunatus*. One of the first successful comedies in which humor surpasses romance is Dekker's eternally delightful fantasy, *The Shoemaker's Holiday*. The play was produced in 1599, so that, like most of its author's best dramatic work, it belongs literally to the Elizabethan period, Dekker's genius as time advanced flowing chiefly into his pamphleteering. While aiming to give the London public what it wanted, Dekker here succeeded in expressing his own peculiar spirit in a really captivating manner. Beaumont treating the same story would certainly have written a burlesque. Dekker undoubtedly perceived the implausibility and the sentimental optimism of his tale, but enjoyed both and so left a sympathetic picture of the daydreams of the London shopkeepers and their apprentices. Scholars such as the authors of *Eastward Ho!* might, if they would, be supercilious toward the average citizen. But Dekker accepted all in the interests of his own charming art. For once he wrote a well-constructed play, kept to his mood and subject, and achieved a complete success. *The Shoemaker's Holiday* lacks, of course, the depths of his more serious *Honest Whore*, but more than offsets this with its naïve and unsurpassable mirth.

Dekker imagines a world in which sorrow itself is a jest,

where Simon Eyre, the merry shoemaker, presides as a comic deity over the scene. No one's ambition is seriously thwarted, crimes against society are viewed lightly or easily forgiven. Hearts at least are proof against time and temptation. Labor is an unmixed joy, and economic problems are either nonexistent or a jest. Merrily sing the apprentices as they work for an hour or more before breakfast, and merrily do they carol at the close of a long day. Everyone gains; no one loses. People eat and drink deeply and often, laughing at the idle play of shadows, eager to champion the right, seldom beguiled into wrong. Years bring increased fortunes to all. The industrious apprentice becomes a master of his trade; the enterprising master becomes Mayor of London. The play ends with a great ringing of the pancake bells that summon all the worthy prentices of London to feast in the Guildhall beside the King himself. The hard-working shoemakers forget their daily toil in joy at their annual holiday.

Possessed with the love of speech and song they rant and carol from dawn to night. Simon Eyre loves the exuberant rhetoric of the Elizabethan melodrama, decorating his harangues with tags from the playhouse. He is a comic Tamburlaine of Cheapside or a Falstaff in a state of innocence reveling in Paradise before the Fall. The gay music of the prentices must have been one of the chief attractions in the original performances of the work of this lyrical playwright. Dekker's love of song is indeed equally apparent from his early *Old Fortunatus* to his late *Sun's Darling*. The whole flavor of *The Shoemaker's Holiday* is compressed in such lyrical prattle as this:

> Cold's the wind, and wet's the rain,
>   Saint Hugh be our good speed:
> Ill is the weather that bringeth no gain,
>   Nor helps good hearts at need.

Trowl the bowl, the jolly nut-brown bowl,
   And here, kind mate, to thee:
Let's sing a dirge for Saint Hugh's soul,
   And drown it merrily.

One is reminded of the philosophical merriment of Feste in *Twelfth Night*.

Notwithstanding two or three really exquisite scenes of sentiment, written largely in rhyme, *The Shoemaker's Holiday* is a true comedy. Dekker more than indicates this in his dedication, "To all good fellows, professors of the Gentle Craft, of what degree soever." He ends his summary of the "argument" of the play as follows: "the merriments that passed in Eyre's house, his coming to be Mayor of London, Lacy's getting his love, and other accidents, with two merry Threemen's songs. Take all in good worth that is well intended, for nothing is proposed but mirth; mirth lengtheneth long life, which, with all other blessings, I heartily wish you. Farewell!" Where mirth is the prime end, even in a romantic play, true comedy is inevitable.

The singular glamour of this mirth and the unique music of this laughter are scarcely captured in another English play. There is too much of shrewdness of criticism and reality of life in Shakespeare's Falstaff scenes, or even in his *Midsummer-Night's Dream*, to produce quite the carefree abandon of this naïve author, and in the tremendously successful comedies by Middleton and Beaumont and Fletcher, there is, of course, much less of idealism and subtlety.

One of the most typical and animated of the lesser comedies of the age is Heywood's *Wise-Woman of Hogsdon*. The situations are almost all humorously conceived. Everything depends upon plot; and until the action gets fairly under way, the imaginative force of the design scarcely becomes apparent. With the last few scenes, however, a really brilliant theatrical development occurs, far more sprightly and alive than any work of merely commonplace imagination.

As often in Heywood, who amused plebeian audiences from about 1590 till forty years thereafter, *The Wise-Woman of Hogsdon* combines many illusions to real places and many touches of true realism with an inexhaustible wealth of fantastic plotting. Opening in the key of modest realism, in almost photographic manner it depicts a group of young men at a gambling table. Yet despite its realism the little scene has a fine economy of line and lithesomeness of rhythm. The plot rapidly enters upon a maze of bewildering disguises. At the Wise-Woman's house the morose Boyster is married to "the first Luce," though she takes him to be Chartley, while Chartley marries "the second Luce," mistaking her for the first. At this ceremony the second Luce is doubly disguised, first as a boy and then as another woman of the same name. The pairs are dispersed immediately after the ceremony; Boyster believes that he has been duped, and Chartley postpones living with the Luce he thought he married. An utterly fantastic low-comedy plot centers in the deception of an elderly and dignified gentleman, father of the fair Gratiana. This Plautine story, resembling also *The Taming of the Shrew*, depicts rival pedants seeking the hand of an heiress, one of the men being the hero in disguise. The doggerel rhymes and Latin puns carry us back to the somewhat academic comedy in Greene's *Friar Bacon and Friar Bungay*. The highly ingenious setting of the last act, however, affords a fine example of this frolic type of comedy at its best. Young Chartley has ruined his fortunes and broken many hearts. He has capriciously deserted the second Luce practically at the church door and, as we have seen, married her in secret, believing her to be the first Luce. Deflected in his ambitions by the more opulent heiress, Gratiana, he has contracted himself to marry this lady the next morning. To secure her hand he has told any number of lies, as that his father has offered them a large fortune. The night before the wedding he is decoyed to the Wise-Woman's house under the pretense that Luce number one, to whom he believes himself married, awaits him there to resign her station as his wife in exchange for the pleasure of becoming his mistress. Half a dozen doors enter into the Wise-Woman's hall. Behind each door stands a man or woman whom Chartley has deceived. As he repeats each lie, the wronged person issues from hiding to call him to account. Each time he leaves one discredited story by hurrying on to another. Breathless and overcome by numbers, he stands at the last a repentant man. His sins lie gently on his breast; all is easily forgiven; three weddings are hastily arranged; the second Luce drops her disguise; and the company departs for general rejoicings. The scene is one of the wittiest pieces of plotting in Elizabethan drama. Even the persons taking part in these preposterous events are somehow made real by the playwright's deft art. Rapid and unassuming as Heywood's style is, it proves much more adapted to comedy than to pure tragedy and by no means inadequate for a gay and primitive type of humor. The pleasantly bawdy language gives a touch of richness to the Aristophanic fancy. Our pedestrian comedy of the twentieth century may well seem worsted when compared with such an instance of the humor of London cockneys three centuries ago. A similar humor promised by our more animated moving pictures is too commonly drowned by floods of sentimentality.

If we regard Jonson as a writer of dramatic satire rather than of pure comedy, Middleton is perhaps the most important comic playwright of early Jacobean times save

Shakespeare. His very conception of fantastic comedy, midway between romantic poetry and the conservative comedy of manners, gives a centrality to his position. Fancy in Middleton is none the less itself because it inhabits Cheapside instead of Arden. Like Jonson he lays the scenes of his chief comedies in London; but unlike Jonson and in the spirit of the school of plebeian playwrights he puts no apparent limit upon his farfetched and implausible situations. His comedies have settings as homely as Jonson's with plots as fantastical as Shakespeare's. His better genius demanded both the realistic scene and the unreal situation. Thus his few attempts at comedy making no use of the London scene, as those undistinguished plays, *The Old Law* and *The Phoenix*, prove as lacking in vigor as his few experiments in play-writing without ingenious plots, such as two comedies always acknowledged to be weak, *Your Five Gallants* and *The Family of Love*. His successful formula for a light play is accordingly to reconcile a profusion of local coloring and allusions with a wealth of fantastic intrigue.

We have already seen Middleton as author of two tragedies which dispense with the glamorous style of most Renaissance drama and achieve poetic distinction through emotional sincerity and curt, trenchant speech. His best comedies follow suit. Four are unquestionably masterpieces: *A Trick to Catch the Old One*, *A Chaste Maid in Cheapside*, *Michaelmas Term*, and *No Wit, No Help like a Woman's*. There are other memorable though less brilliant performances: *A Mad World My Masters*, *Anything for a Quiet Life* (in which Webster was perhaps a collaborator), and *The Roaring Girl* (in which Dekker had a large share). His attempts at pure romance lack his foremost distinction, a biting style, while his excursions into pure realism become episodic, formless in plot, and uninspired in language. One of his best-known works, *A Fair Quarrel*, though it has lively comic scenes by William Rowley added to its first version, is so serious in its major plot as to be a dramatic romance or tragicomedy rather than a pure comedy. Like Middleton's tragedies it reveals much of his character as an artist, but it cannot be held to be one of his comedies or even to illuminate the subject of his comic style.

Despite the general similarity of his pure comedies, no formula can, of course, be found to fit them all perfectly. A group with exceptionally strong family likenesses, they still possess some individual qualities not to be totally disregarded. *A Trick to Catch the Old One* is the most consistently worked out; it has no secondary plots; its machinery moves as smoothly as a well-built watch; it even suggests the classical perfection of Molière. The English element in the play is the bold intrusion not of a secondary plot but of a secondary episode with the character of the unscrupulous lawyer, Dampit. He has no relation whatsoever to the major action, except as he also represents the lust for gain; he is indeed a grotesque and almost horrible caricature suggestive of Balzac or of Dickens. The sheer force of the brief Dampit scenes renders them among the most memorable passages in Middleton's works, proving their author to have been essentially a poet. *A Chaste Maid in Cheapside* is distinguished above all else, even in Elizabethan drama, for its successful and entertaining bawdiness. Swinburne's observation that the play has little chastity is one of the few understatements by that critic. Both in word and deed the play deals consistently with sex: a gloriously racy farce belonging to the fleshly school of poetry. Breathless in gaiety and immorality, it is perhaps more closely crowded with sheer fun, albeit coarse, than any rival in English comedy. Fun blossoms upon the tomb. All women, maids, wives, and widows, throng in tears to the funeral of the Chaste Maid. Those who have no pocket handkerchiefs brazenly lift their skirts to dry their eyes. Of all these plays focused upon money none pursues the theme more consistently or effectively than *Michaelmas Term*, for three acts chiefly realistic and in its conclusion a gayer and more comic *Volpone*. *A Mad World My Masters* is more episodic and less accomplished writing, a happy impromptu in the hilarious mood. In *The Roaring Girl* Middleton's acidity is softened by collaboration with the sweet-tempered Dekker. *Anything for a Quiet Life* is a more substantial but also a soberer production, with a falling off in comic verve. From this station we can, if we desire, proceed to the lowlier levels of Middleton's uninspired work, such as *Your Five Gallants*.

The realism of the plays needs small critical comment. All abound in racy pictures of London's social life, with special emphasis upon money. Comedy consists in getting money by wit and not by work. Conversely, man's sorriest lot is to work and get nothing. Usurious goldsmiths, stingy parents, and avaricious uncles fill half the scenes; witty sons, sprightly widows, and clever nephews occupy the rest. Passion is presented sincerely and effectively but without the slightest recourse to euphuism or to any other form of Renaissance rhetoric or poetic eloquence. Lamb called Heywood a prose Shakespeare, but the words apply still better to Middleton, who writes an imaginative and metaphorical verse that is still close to prose in its inspiration. Caricatures of impassioned lechers and misers remind us of Sir Epicure Mammon or Shylock; they add warmth and weight to Middleton's scenes. But they never rise in such flights of poetry as seriously to challenge the mundane spirit of the dramatist's work.

The fantasy in the plotting is likewise unmistakable.

Disguise is used in all the plays. It is wholly unlikely that anyone in real life could, like Witgood, hero of *A Trick to Catch the Old One,* pass off a prostitute for a wealthy widow upon two such cautious old usurers as Lucre and Hoard. The last act of *A Chaste Maid in Cheapside* employs the familiar plot of two lovers united by an escape in coffins from their parents, a funeral turning abruptly into a wedding. In *Michaelmas Term* the usurer Quomodo has a pair of devils for his servants who pass through an interminable number of disguises. In the last scenes of the play the familiar device is used of a man who reports himself dead to discover how the world will receive the news. *A Mad World My Masters* consists chiefly in a series of tricks, more ingenious for the poet to imagine than likely to succeed in reality, which a witty young man plays upon his hardhearted grandfather. Despite homely settings and an abundance of prose dialogue or of nakedly sinewy verse, fantastic is not too strong a word to describe such plotting.

One of Middleton's masterpieces, the somewhat neglected *No Wit, No Help like a Woman's,* may be taken for more detailed analysis of a style that in cold wit equals Sheridan and in farfetched plotting surpasses Gilbert and Sullivan. Here money and love divide the honors as motivating forces. Five of Lady Goldenfleece's six suitors seek her fortune rather than herself. Four of these pursue her as a wealthy widow. A lucky fifth seeks to avenge injuries which Lady Goldenfleece's late husband has done to the family fortunes. This plot reaches its climax when two boxes full of money and jewels, containing all the lady's wealth, become the visible objects of dispute. The other and more romantic plot still has its roots in a mercenary soil. Two babies have been transferred in infancy. Sir Oliver Twilight has put his infant daughter Grace to nurse with Mistress Sunset, a woman who, as her name suggests, suffers at the time from poverty. To secure the advantages of wealth for her own child, Mistress Sunset substitutes her own daughter for Grace, Grace accordingly being brought up as daughter to Sunset. This concern for wealth is not the only tie with London life. The acts abound in homely scenes and local allusions. A dinner and a wedding are presented with considerable attention to the customs of the times. Much fun is made of the superstitious faith in almanacs, a subject of constant ridicule among the more intellectual of the playwrights. Middleton proves himself a realist in more senses than one.

On the other hand the dramatist relies to the utmost upon the popular love of fantastic conventions of stage and story. The romantic plot depicts two pairs of lovers. Philip Twilight is in love with Jane, whom in the fourth act he supposes in horror to be his sister Grace and whom in the last act he happily finds to be Sunset's daughter. Sandfield, his friend, loves Grace, whom everyone supposes to be Jane and whom Philip's father wishes Philip to marry. Philip introduces Jane to his father as his long-lost sister, although he is secretly married to her and she is pregnant by him throughout the play. Philip's lost mother is also recovered, ransomed from the Dutch pirates by a witty scholar named Beveril. So much for one reel of fantasy.

The other is like it. Beveril is brother to Mistress Low-Water, a married woman whose husband has been ruined by the dead usurer, Goldenfleece. Mistress Low-Water's plots, however, recover the family fortune even without serious injury to Lady Goldenfleece. Disguising herself as a man, she easily proves to Lady Goldenfleece the worthlessness of her present suitors, such as Weatherwise and Sir Gilbert Lambstone, and by an amusing display of mannishness actually succeeds in marrying the widow. Without disclosing her sex she refuses to lie with the bride and moreover makes it possible for the indignant woman to lie with Beveril on the marriage night. Beveril already loves the widow and she admires him. Mistress Low-Water frees the widow from their marriage ties by accepting half her fortune and gladly sees her married to Beveril instead. Thus by pleasant trickery the entire Goldenfleece fortune comes, as it belongs, into the possession of the injured persons, half to Mistress Low-Water and half to her brother. The widow is happily married. Stage plotting and disguises can hardly be carried off more effectively or ingeniously than in this representative comedy. Its actions are well developd, its plots well knit, and, remarkable to say, the dialogue and in a sense the characterizations are sustained amid the whirl of action. Mistress Low-Water is especially amusing, the widow spirited, Beveril dashing, the mother notable at once for dignity and pathos, and even such minor parts as the almanac addict Weatherwise, the lecherous Sir Gilbert Lambstone, and the two Dutchmen have comic value. The imagery in the brisk dialogue often becomes genuinely imaginative and witty, while certain passages in the romance plot are even emotionally moving. The chief excursions into verbal and theatrical fancy are the two set scenes: first, the banquet where twelve sit at table beside twelve signs of the zodiac and, second, the masque at Lady Goldenfleece's wedding, where the four suitors who impersonate the four elements are, on misrepresenting Beveril's intentions, put to flight by the impromptu entrance of the four winds. Throughout the play the combination of wit and tenderness, realism and romance, must necessarily remind one of Shakespeare's comic art, as seen at its best in *Twelfth Night*, for example. Middleton and Shakespeare as comic poets both unblushingly gave the Elizabethan public what it desired. A fastidious taste three hundred years later may still relish their highly seasoned feast.

At times the carefree spirit of the Cavalier playwrights leads them across the border from sentimental romancing to romantic or fantastic comedy. Indeed, most of the lighter plays of the Cavalier period belong to this category. Fletcher really had more followers than Jonson, despite the prestige of the latter. All these dramatic fantasies have much in common. Between *The Widow*, a play in which Middleton himself had a major share, and Shirley's *Opportunity*, for example, there lies no marked difference. Since the graver suavity and more intellectual humor of *The Opportunity* render it the superior work, this may be cited as an instance of the last phase of true comedy before the closing of the theatres in 1642.

Shirley's play is a comedy of farfetched situations. The story comes directly from a Spanish source, but indirectly from Latin, Greek, Arabian, and Far Eastern legend. A traveler in a strange city is mistaken for a citizen who has been several years absent. The Duchess falls in love with him. He ambitiously aspires to her hand, but at the same time inconveniently falls in love with his supposed sister. A rival Duke is also suing for the hand of the Duchess. In a typical scene, virtually a parody of *Romeo and Juliet*, the Duke, himself in disguise, mistakes the Duchess on a balcony at night for the sister, while the traveler mistakes the sister for the Duchess. The comic idea behind the comedy, exhibited in both a major and a minor plot, is that only a maximum of audacity wins a fortune in this obtuse world. Because the traveler fails to snatch eagerly enough at the golden and unforeseen opportunities strewn in his path, he misses his promised reward. Naturally the play has a number of frankly humorous characters, as a clownish servant who impersonates a German prince and a vain and irritable father. The exotic setting, numerous love scenes, Petrarchan conceits, and facile poetry might lead one hastily to interpret the work as a sober dramatic romance. But Shirley is both less robust and less serious than the elusive Robert Greene. Beneath all his lines run the sparkling wit and quiet laughter of a sophisticated spirit. It is a pity that such graceful trifles as *The Opportunity* should so seldom ornament our libraries or our stage. Their very lightness is not easily duplicated; and in some respects they seem more precious than the type of strenuous Jacobean tragedy so well remembered in the works of Middleton, Webster, and Tourneur.

Lastly, one turns to the gay and highly accomplished comedies of Beaumont and Fletcher, robust comedies that come nearer to the broad farce of *The Taming of the Shrew* than to the sentimental romance of *The Winter's Tale*. Many of these great bonfires of mirth blazed for two centuries on the English stage. Fletcher's *Rule a Wife and Have a Wife*, for example, was long and justly applauded as one of the most actable and amusing of light plays. His *Wild-Goose Chase* received the compliment of much imitation. Here a witty lover named Mirabel first appears on the English stage, with a long and brilliant future before him. Three generations later Congreve was to write with this play in mind. As a burlesque of the dramatic absurdities of the hour perpetrated by Thomas Heywood and others, *The Knight of the Burning Pestle* had a briefer career on the old stage, but has been even more lovingly read and successfully revived in recent times. All these plays have ingenious and imaginative situations carried off with the utmost comic gusto.

Like *The Opportunity, Rule a Wife and Have a Wife*

owes its plot to a Spanish romantic source while a part of
the story goes far back into world literature. As in many
of its author's comedies, the mercenary motive is uppermost. A lady marries a man whom she takes to be a fool
with the expectation that he will serve meekly as her
"umbrella" against her future affairs. But he cheats her,
not she him. It develops that he has merely pretended
meekness in order to entrap her and her fortune and that
he is in fact a most masculine and commanding husband.
The lady soon becomes contented to live with so witty
and authoritative a man. The shrew is tamed, the female
wanderer reclaimed. The secondary plot neatly reverses
the situation, making an even score in the war of the sexes.
Here a woman outwits a man. The lady's servant beguiles
a braggart soldier into marriage by leading him to suppose that she and not her mistress owns a sumptuous
house. At first angry and chagrined, the man is ultimately
reconciled to the situation when he realizes that his wife
is, after all, truly witty and not incapable of successful
cheating to aid the family fortunes. Such is the singularly
felicitous story. Nowhere are two plots more happily interwoven or the good humor and good graces of Cavalier
thought more agreeably expressed. It is indubitably a comic
masterpiece, on the whole superior to *The Taming of the
Shrew* though of course beneath the merits of Shakespeare's more poetic comedies. Much resembling it and
almost equally brilliant are the two sparkling comedies,
Wit without Money and *The Scornful Lady*.

The *Wild-Goose Chase* is even more of a comic extravaganza. It depicts the humorous turns of fantastic courtship or, in other words, the Puckishness of Eros. Men and
women fated to come in the end into each other's arms
take up arms against each other in a series of ingenious
plots and counterplots. Again the war of the sexes is seen,

to the observer at least, to be a hilarious affair. In the
course of a few hours a shrew turns modest and then a
shrew once more. All the characters are at one time or
another victorious, although the women are represented
as on the whole more gifted in this weird wooing game
than the men. Much frank speaking on sex contrasts with
the devious ingenuity of the plot. This is true, hilarious
comedy, Aristophanic in its hyperbole. A climax is reached
when four women attack one of the men with knives.
Poor Belleur, the bashful man, vacillates between extremes of timidity and audacity. The heroine, Oriana,
now pretends to be at the point of a wealthy marriage
and now at the brink of death. In the end she wins Mirabel, the hero, by pretending to be an Italian heiress, though
whether or not he sees through her disguise the dramatist
deliberately leaves unclear. The turns in this race for
hearts occur with calculated abruptness. Repeatedly one or
the other lover seems to have entrapped his fated partner,
only to find the partner leaping aside with scornful laughter. Not all modern palates relish such extravagant and
robust fooling. It belongs to a different world indeed from
either the innocent poetry of Robert Greene or the dry
wit of William Congreve. But in itself it remains perfect;
the play is too rounded a work of art to escape the admiration of some readers in any age.

The Knight of the Burning Pestle, at once a more critical and a still more exuberant work, represents the torrential laughter of the Jacobean intellect at middle-class
Elizabethan romance. Lines such as those of Mucedorus
and the early popular romantic plays are faithfully given
by Beaumont and placed in a highly ludicrous setting.
With Cervantean humor the dramatist delights at the inconsistency between the romantic mental diet of the sentimental London citizens and their prosaic physical environ-

ment. Here is a sentimental love-story such as Heywood delighted to put on the stage: the adventures of Jasper, Luce, and Humphrey. Their love affairs are shown in a wholly ridiculous light. Here are humorous citizens, Merrythought and his scolding wife, substantially like the Simon Eyre and his spouse in Dekker's *Shoemaker's Holiday*. Here is Ralph, a burlesque of the popular hero of fiction, worthy of Ben Jonson at his best. And here are character sketches of a grocer and his wife even worthy of the creator of Christopher Sly and Mistress Quickly. Beaumont's play is the first of the four most uproarious burlesques in English, its successors being Buckingham's *Rehearsal*, Fielding's *Tom Thumb*, and Sheridan's *Critic*. The quintessence of Beaumont's work is contained in the harangue of Ralph dressed as the May-Lord. We encounter the gusto of a great comic spirit, always close to Shakespeare in poetry, humor, and humanity and further above his worst art than beneath his best. A review of the fantastic comedies may well close with a glimpse at this superlative example of hilarious humor:

London, to thee I do present the merry month of May;
Let each true subject be content to hear me what I say:
For from the top of conduit-head, as plainly may appear,
I will both tell my name to you, and wherefore I came here.
My name is Ralph, by due descent though not ignoble I,
Yet far inferior to the stock of gracious grocery;
And by the common counsel of my fellows in the Strand,
With gilded staff and crossed scarf, the May-lord here I stand.
Rejoice, oh, English hearts, rejoice! rejoice, oh, lovers dear!
Rejoice, oh, city, town and country! rejoice, eke every shire!
For now the fragrant flowers do spring and sprout in seemly sort,
The little birds do sit and sing, the lambs do make fine sport;
And now the birchen-tree doth bud, that makes the schoolboy cry;
The morris rings, while hobby horse doth foot it feateously;

The lords and ladies now abroad, for their disport and play,
Do kiss sometimes upon the grass, and sometimes in the hay;
Now butter with a leaf of sage is good to purge the blood;
Fly Venus and phlebotomy, for they are neither good;
Now little fish on tender stone begin to cast their bellies,
And sluggish snails, that erst were mewed, do creep out of their
    shellies;
The rumbling rivers now do warm, for little boys to paddle;
The sturdy steed now goes to grass, and up they hang his saddle;
The heavy hart, the bellowing buck, the rascal, and the pricket,
Are now among the yeoman's peas, and leave the fearful thicket:
And be like them, oh you, I say, of this same noble town,
And lift aloft your velvet heads, and slipping off your gown,
With bells on legs, and napkins clean unto your shoulders tied,
With scarfs and garters as you please, and "Hey for our town!"
    cried,
March out, and show your willing minds, by twenty and by
    twenty,
To Hogsdon or to Newington, where ale and cakes are plenty;
And let it ne'er be said for shame, that we the youths of London
Lay thrumming of our caps at home, and left our custom undone.
Up, then, I say, both young and old, both man and maid a-may-
    ing,
With drums, and guns that bounce aloud, and merry tabor
    playing!
Which to prolong, God save our king, and send his country peace,
And root out treason from the land! and so, my friends, I cease.

CHAPTER THIRTEEN

RISE AND FALL OF COMIC PROSE

Brief as the lightning in the collied night,
That, in a spleen, unfolds both heaven and earth . . .
—SHAKESPEARE

THE INCREASINGLY EXACT study of the externals of Shakespeare's style has familiarized scholars with his so-called period of prose, about 1598 to 1604, when he wrote as much prose as verse and much more prose than earlier or later in his career. It is also clear that among the plays usually assigned to these years the prose scenes are largely comic or satiric, not only in *The Merry Wives of Windsor, All's Well, Much Ado, Measure for Measure, Twelfth Night,* and *As You Like It,* but in the Falstaff episodes of *Henry the Fourth* and in *Hamlet.* In this vein the dramatist brought his prose to its perfection, thus bequeathing to the predominantly verse scenes of his ripest plays a new mastery of dramatic speech. This descriptive outline needs no further comment, though detailed study of certain aspects of Shakespeare's prose may always prove rewarding.

While it is another commonplace that Shakespeare is the mirror of his age, no one seems to have observed how faithfully he reflected, or rather slightly anticipated, his times by this temporary excursion into prose for purposes of comedy and satire. Neither the fact nor its causes have been closely examined. In English drama before 1598 verse often lyrical in spirit predominated even for comedy, while the leading playwrights after the rise of Fletcher, who began writing about 1605 or 1606, increasingly favor verse which, though often prosaic, is certainly not prose.

Although tragedy occasionally entertained prose as a guest, its home lay in comedy. Elizabethan tragedies predominantly in prose can be numbered on the fingers of one hand. Even in tragedy of the most domestic and bourgeois type, the playwrights chose verse as their prevailing medium. But there is more prose than verse in comedies from 1600 to 1610, and many of the most successful of these plays are almost wholly prose. As in Shakespeare, the prose of the tragedies is chiefly in scenes of comic relief. The following review of prose in the evolution of the drama before 1642 is accordingly directed to comedy.

The thesis must of course be understood as a statement of marked tendencies and not of inflexible rules. In the period before 1598 the euphuistic prose comedies of John Lyly afford a notable exception. But the same principles which determined Lyly's use of prose govern the later dramatists. George Gascoigne and George Peele at uncertain dates began early experiments in prose. There are always writers or works a little ahead or behind the general march of the times. So, too, while the major authors of the Fletcherian school, as Beaumont, Fletcher, Massinger, Shirley, and Ford, prefer verse to prose, several minor Cavalier playwrights show a relatively greater fondness for the humbler medium. The exceptions should not conceal the prevailing tides and crosscurrents of the times.

Obviously the course of comedy from the end of the fifteenth century to the close of the seventeenth is on the whole from verse to prose. Henry Medwell and John Heywood are acquainted only with verse and with rhymed verse at that. Congreve and Wycherley choose prose. On theoretical grounds one might assume the evolution to have been consistent throughout, rhyme steadily yielding to blank verse and this to prose. Such is not the case. For the simple hypothesis takes no account of the unpredictable burst of energy at the turn of the new century, the period of *Henry the Fourth, Hamlet*, and *The Alchemist*. Shakespeare, Jonson, and Chapman mastered comedy before tragedy. Some of the leading comedies belong to the last two or three years of the sixteenth century. With these plays the maturity of prose as a dramatic vehicle begins. In the first five or six years of the new century were written the chief comedies by Marston, Middleton, and Webster, all conspicuous for the use of prose. Even the earliest plays by Beaumont, who as a member of the Tribe of Ben is more of an Elizabethan in comedy than Fletcher, show liking for prose. But under the influence of Fletcher and with the retirement of all the half dozen just-mentioned masters of comedy, a new school is born. The Cavalier tradition supplants the Elizabethan. Jonson's followers are for the time being few and undistinguished, Fletcher's numerous and successful. If Cavalier comedy is not poetic after the manner of *A Midsummer-Night's Dream*, at least it is generally romantic and couched in verse. The change in style accompanies a change in temper. Comedy loses its robust spirit, becoming less a criticism of life, more an idle game of too facile theatrical conventions. Humor deteriorates as prose declines. Fletcher is, of course, one of the most irresponsibly minded of men; often highly humorous, he is never profoundly humorous. Massinger, a superb master of romance, proves singularly weak in humor. Ford wholly lacks comic gusto. And Shirley cares more to charm his audience with his cleverly manufactured fantasies than to arouse hilarious or derisive laughter. Pure comedy sinks to its ebb tide in the humble prose of Dick Brome and a few aristocratic authors who lack even Brome's honest standards of professionalism.

How sharply the tide of inspired prose comedy rises and falls within a comparatively short time seems to have escaped the notice of dramatic historians. Prose in the new realistic comedy was mastered almost simultaneously by Shakespeare and Chapman, a year or two later by Jonson, and in rapid succession by Marston, Webster, and Middleton. The last became for the first decade of the new century the most enthusiastic practitioner of the craft. Although the canon and chronology of his works still remain uncertain, it is safe to say that practically all his true comedies were written before 1610 and the best of them, as well as the greater number, before 1606-7.

It is significant that all the leaders in this movement lived on after 1610, when the wave of prose comedy subsided; they then turned to other tasks or lost their original grasp of the medium. Leading the movement by a few years, Shakespeare definitely passed from comedy to tragedy about 1604. His latest so-called comedies are, of course, dramatic romances and largely verse. Chapman and Webster turned to tragedy. Marston also seems to have preferred tragedy to comedy before his retirement from all play-writing to take holy orders in 1609. Middleton's brilliant early comedies were followed after a few inactive years by his even more brilliant but less numerous tragedies. It is probable that at the time of his tragic writing he had a hand in *The Widow,* a romantic drama containing work by Fletcher of the type which supplanted realistic comedy and was couched predominantly in verse. After writing *Bartholomew Fair* Jonson lost his mastery of comedy, became fatigued, and leaned more frequently upon verse. The peculiar energy which lay rather in the need and nature of the times than in the leadership of any one man, even if that man was Shakespeare, subsided with the prolongation of James's reign. The movement was too

bitter and brilliant to last long. There were personal qualities which playwrights, nurtured in the last years of Elizabeth, were powerless to pass on to the new generation. On
the one hand their technical mastery resembled a material
possession, left intact to Fletcher and again bequeathed
by him to Shirley, who possessed this treasure unimpaired.
But on the other hand the soul is not transferable, and
this the Elizabethans could not give to their successors.
When the chief Restoration dramatists fifty years later
remade English comedy, they created a style more nearly
resembling Shirley's verse broken down entirely into prose
than the more imaginative prose in the great plays of the
first decade of their own century.

Prose is the only, or almost the only, medium in *The
Merry Wives of Windsor*, in Chapman's *May Day* and in
Chapman, Jonson, and Marston's *Eastward Ho!*, in Jon-
son's *Epicoene* and *Bartholomew Fair*, in Dekker and
Webster's *Northward Ho!* and *Westward Ho!*, in Mid-
dleton's *Trick to Catch the Old One, Your Five Gallants,
Family of Love*, and *Michaelmas Term*. It predominates
in *Much Ado, As You Like It, Twelfth Night*, and *All's
Well*, in Jonson's *Every Man in His Humour, Every
Man Out of His Humour, Cynthia's Revels*, and *Poetaster*,
in Marston's *Malcontent, Parasitaster*, and *Dutch Courtezan*, in Dekker and Marston's *Satiromastix*, in Chapman's
Humorous Day's Mirth, Monsieur D'Olive, and *Widow's
Tears*, and in Middleton's *Mad World My Masters* and
Anything for a Quiet Life. Middleton's *No Wit, No Help
like a Woman's* is about a third prose, and most of the
scenes which he wrote for *The Roaring Girl* are in this
form. His ribald though almost lyrical fantasy, *A Chaste
Maid in Cheapside*, alone among his lighter plays has a
predominance of verse. Some of the less assured masters
of comedy also felt the force of the movement. Dekker's

Shoemaker's Holiday and *Honest Whore* are half prose and Day's *Law Tricks, or Who Would Have Thought It,* wholly so. Heywood on the other hand, an inveterate romanticist of the bourgeois species, clings largely to verse in comedies that almost always prefer the ideal to the real. Of his many light plays only *The Wise-Woman of Hogsdon* and *The Late Lancashire Witches,* the latter written partly by Brome, contain much prose.

Let us glance at the contrasting pictures of comedy before and after the movement already defined. Shakespeare, as we have seen, set the key, since his early and late styles distinctly favor the verse form. In the mid-Tudor period even farce clung to verse, as shown conspicuously by *Gammer Gurton's Needle* and *Ralph Roister Doister.* While Lyly was introducing his own euphuism into play-writing, his contemporaries held largely to verse. Peele's *Arraignment of Paris* is wholly in that medium and the comedies of Greene are largely so. Prose came by about 1590, however, to be used generally for farcical scenes of more or less low life. All Shakespeare's clowns use some prose and most of them nothing else. His early inclination to use more prose than was at the time conventional appears, for example, in important speeches by Petruchio, where Shakespeare deserts the verse medium of his source.

The spread of prose remained at first distinctly gradual. Euphuistic or affected prose preceded realistic or poetic prose in the chief scenes of the comic stage. The former appears in the scene in which Portia dissects her suitors. The traditional prose in farce reaches its apotheosis in the Falstaff episodes. As a general medium for realistic comedy, prose appears first dominantly in Chapman's *Humorous Day's Mirth.* His romantic *Blind Beggar of Alexandria,* a still earlier work, contains considerable prose,

but his realistic comedy of manners is very largely prose.
Jonson uses prose more and more freely in his first humor
comedies, attaining his perfect style in the polished dialogue of upper-class life found in *Epicoene* and in the
rude speech of the vulgar reflected in *Bartholomew Fair*.
It is typical of him that he turns his back on the license
of his age. Only a small fraction of the comedies of the
first decade of the seventeenth century are wholly prose;
only a similar fraction are entirely verse. The representative comedy is a blend in which prose on the whole predominates. Although Jonson's mature comedies are
never romantic, they are more or less serious. The more
serious, as *The Alchemist* and *Volpone,* are in verse, the
more farcical, as *Epicoene* and *Bartholomew Fair,* in
prose. Only his plays produced earlier than *Volpone* blend
the two. Jonson himself is merely typical in accepting both
styles in comedy, although like others he uses more prose.
Each of the masters of prose comedy composed, to be
sure, one or more light plays chiefly in verse. Shakespeare,
for example, wrote *The Two Gentlemen of Verona,*
Chapman *All Fools,* Marston *What You Will,* Middleton
A Chaste Maid in Cheapside, and Jonson his *Volpone*
and *Alchemist.* Verse ceases to be an important factor in
comedy only with the Restoration. But for over a decade
it did resign its ascendancy.

The early predominance of verse comedies and the rise
of comedy in prose seem more generally recognized by
students than the backward turn of Cavalier comedy to
verse again. Consequently a few more details are worth
mentioning here. It is well known that the Fletcherian
school prefers tragicomedy to tragedy and comical romances to pure comedies. A romantic play has been defined as one in which the major plot is seriously conceived,
whatever may be the lightness of the minor plot. The

subordination of pure comedy greatly reduces the amount
of prose. The Beaumont and Fletcher canon includes some
fifty-five plays. Two comedies predominantly in prose are
early works and chiefly by Beaumont, *The Woman Hater*
and *The Scornful Lady*. Two others chiefly by Fletcher,
though probably under the literary influence of Beaumont
and Middleton, are largely prose, *Wit without Money*
and *The Coxcomb*. The remaining plays are all over-
whelmingly in verse. Such rollicking comedies as *Rule a
Wife and Have a Wife* and *The Woman's Prize, or The
Tamer Tamed,* for example, are exclusively and remarkably so. There can be no question which medium these
men prefer.

In all the fifteen plays commonly ascribed solely to
Massinger the only prose scene is a brief episode in *The
Emperor of the East,* where an empiric talks medical jar-
gon that even Massinger could not stomach in verse. Similarly Ford's unimpressive comedies are almost wholly in
verse. Over prose this distinguished poet had no mastery.

Shirley writes tragedy, romance, and true comedy in
much the same proportion as Fletcher. Again, like the
tragedies, all the romances are largely or wholly in verse.
The sole author of over thirty extant plays, most of them
fairly light in tone, he wrote only two with more prose
than verse, these being among his earliest works. His tendency, with his age, is to write ever more and more in
verse. The early *Love Tricks* is about three-fifths prose;
The Witty Fair One, belonging to the same period, approximately two-thirds prose. *The Bird in a Cage* divides
the two media equally. *The Arcadia,* of uncertain date and
authorship and a dubious claim to be called comedy, recalls Sidney's great novel by several prose scenes. Only a
few trifling passages occur in this medium in *The Changes,
or Love in a Maze, The Grateful Servant, The Example,*

The Opportunity, The Gamester, The Ball (where one character who speaks broken English uses prose), *The Constant Maid,* and *The Imposture.* Even the best of Shirley's realistic comedies of London life, with their mildly censorious flavor, have verse alone, as his comic masterpieces, *Hyde Park* and *The Lady of Pleasure.* Shirley, in short, does nothing to arrest the descent of the comic medium to a graceful, artificial, unpoetic verse.

If these are the facts, how shall we account for the rather sudden rise and fall of powerful comic prose? The causes, as already indicated, are broadly what we should suppose them to be. The playwrights chose their medium with unfailing tact. Where romance, fantasy, and idealism dominate, verse is the leading medium; where intellectualism, realism, and satire dominate, the dramatists prefer prose. Verse depicts the passions, prose the manners, of men. Verse presents the soul of the universal man, prose distinguishes idiosyncrasies of character, humorous contrasts, and clashes of personality as revealed to a scientific scrutiny. One is serious, the other humorous. One symbolizes the tragic brotherhood, the other the comic incongruities of humankind. Comic dissonance is commonly resolved into verse harmony in a final scene.

In the immediate background of the poetic Elizabethan drama stands the lyrical medieval drama with a content ideally constituted for stanzaic verse. Marlowe's Tamburlaine is a new Herod bent on cruel war, his Faustus an Everyman seduced by Humanism. Strong traces of the poetic generalizing dominant in the mystery and morality plays persist in such works as Dekker's *Old Fortunatus,* Greene and Lodge's *Looking Glass for London,* and Peele's *David and Bethsabe.* The age of miracles had not passed for the audience that enjoyed Greene's *Friar Bacon and Friar Bungay.* The authors of *George a Greene* and

The Death of Robert, Earl of Huntingdon wrote with heroic fifteenth-century ballads ringing in their ears. The chief figures in John Heywood's farces are so conventionalized by centuries of tradition as to be substantially minor comic deities, the Vulcans and the Momuses of medieval lore. Similarly that favorite figure of a realistic or satirical stage, the prodigal son, still popular in the sixteenth century, was nevertheless universally accepted as the picturesque symbol of the repentant sinner. The romantic love-scenes of the Tudor drama hark back to the medieval lyric, as many speeches in *Romeo and Juliet* betray. The decorum of princely life always demanded formal expression. All these subjects the playwrights naturally presented in verse and often in rhyme. In short, the typical subject-matter of the comical-romantic drama before the last two or three years of the sixteenth century invited as a rule no serious break with the verse tradition. The only grave challenge to the predominance of verse was made by the facetious moralist, John Lyly, and his euphuistic prose was itself more highly mannered and artificial than any verse of the period. His case deserves special scrutiny.

In an epoch of verse drama Lyly's prose justified itself, for unlike most of his rivals Lyly was a witty and graceful entertainer with courtliness and without poetical afflatus. As a result his work has been favored by critics who frankly condone literary affectation and has been condemned by those who, like Swinburne, assume a passion for poetical enthusiasm. The great age of the English theatre begins and ends on curiously similar notes. Lyly's comedies celebrate the formalities of the Tudor Court, Shirley's romances voice the graceful taste of Cavalier society. Each remains a fundamentally social expression rather than an exercise of truly creative imagination. Lyly manufactures phrases, Shirley intrigues in equally cold

blood. Lyly's style was perfectly adapted to a social situation. His plays befitted both the child-actors and the
court festivals in which the children performed. Instruct-
ing both young and old in pleasant myth and useful moral,
they are couched in a prose actually the ideal of the courtly
affectations of the hour. Such eloquence was used in speech
and in writing, as recorded orations and such correspond-
ence as the Spenser-Harvey letters show. Lyly's mytho-
logical comedies are thus the finer breath or spirit of
polite manners, not, of course, literal reproductions of
human actions but nevertheless emanations of aristocratic
life. In rare moments of slightly higher purity and idealism they rise to brief lyric expression; for the most part
their legitimate and natural home rests in prose. Wherever
euphuism appears, as it does occasionally in later drama,
it carries with it this social implication. As in *The Merchant of Venice*, it introduces passages of decorative and
self-conscious prose into plays elsewhere distinguished by
romantic fervor.

But although the great movement of the English drama
was born, and died, in swathings of the Court, it flung
these gay garments aside as superfluous to its strenuous
manhood. The mature drama, as we know, expressed the
nation, including the Court but not the Court merely.
Its intellectual and aesthetic life was directed by men of
high genius, not manufactured by facile craftsmen serving
the will of Court or queen or king. George Chapman and
not John Lyly chalked out its course.

It is unfortunate that perhaps the most fascinating of
all Elizabethan comedies from a historical point of view
should be one of the most tiresome plays of the period to
read. Chapman, who later acquired a fine command of
comedy, as author of *An Humorous Day's Mirth* suffered
from his besetting fault of allowing his reach to exceed

his grasp. This play contains the first full-length portrait of the favorite type-character of the age, the melancholy man, here named Dowsecer. It is a comedy of manners based on the dishumoring of men and women, each ridden by his or her idiosyncrasy. Inchoate as the play is, it apparently preceded Jonson's humor comedies and probably helped to inspire them. It consists in a cool, reasonable, analytical examination of a group of representative people. Chapman's uncommon purpose led him to discover more readily than his contemporaries the fitness of prose as a comic medium and for a particular subject-matter. The great translator of Homer was spacious enough in imagination to be also one of the founders of the prose comedy of wit and manners.

The actual quality of Chapman's prose in *An Humorous Day's Mirth* is hardly notable. The important thing here is not that he used prose well but that he used it extensively and with sound aesthetic intention. His happier prose in *Monsieur D'Olive* and *The Widow's Tears* shows him in this vein at last at his best. His friend Jonson was meanwhile framing the massive but none the less vital periods of his prose plays. Jonson achieves both the sophisticated eloquence of the humanist orator and the untrammeled and spontaneous eloquence of the man in the street. He employs prose as man's finest tool for sharpening ideas, as his surest means for expression of character or personality. "Language most shews a man; speak, that I may see thee," he declared. With such ideals prose became his dominant vehicle.

Prose may of course legitimately be poetic, and in the hands of the more romantic of the Elizabethans it becomes hardly less ornate and eloquent than their verse. The Elizabethans use poetic prose instead of poetic verse in scenes for some reason calling for the more familiar me-

dium. A desire to wed to language more intellectual analysis, witty expression, humorous gusto, topical allusion,
detailed portraiture of manners, or robust colloquialism
than verse readily admits leads dramatists to prefer prose.
Many of the finest passages in Shakespearean roles from
Rosalind to Falstaff thus exhibit prose inspired by the
poetic imagination, passages of the richest poetic texture
and warmest coloring. Even in the age of euphuism the
banalities of spurious and conventional eloquence more
readily vitiated verse than prose. So for at least a few
years playwrights found in prose the fresher and more
flexible comic medium. It may be sharp and staccato, as
in speeches by Beatrice and comedies by Thomas Middle-
town, or baroque and intricate, as in courtly passages in
The Winter's Tale and harangues by John Fletcher;
seraphically lyrical, as in *The Tempest* and in the finest
scenes by Thomas Dekker, or pleasantly colloquial, as in
All's Well and in humbler scenes by Thomas Heywood;
dashing and impetuous, as in speeches by Mercutio and by
some young gallant drawn by Francis Beaumont, or keenly
philosophical, as in *Troilus and Cressida* and in John
Marston. Elizabethan prose has a myriad varied uses, all,
however, distinct from those of verse. Only two types of
subject matter it refuses as foreign to its own nature,
namely, tragic passion and conventional and sentimental
romance.

Why the love of satire and realism characterized English drama in general and comedy in particular during the
first decade of the seventeenth century is a large question.
The scientific influences reaching England not only from
Italy but from all parts of the Continent already under
the spell of the new learning aided this condition. Translations from Italian comedy, as Gascoigne's *Supposes* and
Chapman's *May Day*, were themselves likely to be in

prose. The rapid rise of the scientific spirit in England, both in natural and psychological science, helped in creating the intellectual climate for a powerful prose comedy. It was inevitable that as the eminently secular spirit acquired a popular theatre and turned its eyes upon the externals of the social scene, it should bring the language of the stage into close alignment with that of life. Jonson summed up the whole problem in his defiant manifesto of the new comedy, demanding "language such as men do use." For a few robust and crowded years men enjoyed the keen and often cruel light which Jacobean theatrical prose shed upon their own lives. Presently they shrank before this brilliance, shielding themselves behind the comfortable cloak of romance, while the muffled and muted verse of Fletcher, Massinger, and Shirley supplanted the metallic prose of Shakespeare, Jonson, and Marston. The prose movement was a brief splendor. It in no way led to the prose of Restoration comedy and had no ancestors in the earlier Tudor period. Like Shakespeare himself, it came and went unpredictably.

CHAPTER FOURTEEN

CONCLUSIONS

...What seest thou else
In the dark backward and abysm of time?
If thou remember'st aught ere thou camest here,
How thou camest here thou mayst.

—SHAKESPEARE

IN ONE of his remarkable notebooks Byron observes that any major poet mediates between past and future, assimilating more of the past and anticipating more of the future than his fellow men. The world is a perpetual wound or fissure between two broken parts. The poet delights us by healing some of this wound, by soldering some of this break. It has been our object in the foregoing chapters to indicate repeatedly how much of the medieval remains in the Elizabethan playwrights and how often the Cavalier dramatists anticipate the comic or tragic moods of the Restoration. The conclusion of our studies turns primarily to this topic, with special reference to the medieval inheritance in the earlier dramatists and particularly in their master spirit, Shakespeare.

There are two ways of plotting the change from the older to the newer style in the English drama of the Renaissance. One is to arrive at an approximate date to fix the watershed between the two movements. Such a date, as already stated, would be virtually that of Shakespeare's retirement from the stage, or about 1611. Thereafter the drama becomes increasingly more aristocratic and less national, the tragedies more sentimental, the comedies more realistic and polite. Tragicomedy forges ahead of tragedy. The theatre is yearly becoming more stereotyped.

The second way of plotting the change from the earlier to the later style is to consider the men chiefly involved in the respective movements. To be sure, this course is no more fully satisfactory than the search for a significant chronology. Authors of the younger school had done important writing before 1611; authors of the older school had not all finished their work by that date. The two groups necessarily overlap each other. And even a single writer may be keenly sensitive to the attractions of both styles. He may be converted from the earlier to the later; or without the least feeling of incongruity he may create to some extent a fusion of the two styles, however inconsistent this course may be. Nevertheless the weight of his influence bears as a rule clearly in one direction. Leading playwrights of the earlier and more robust school are Kyd, Marlowe, Marston, Tourneur, Middleton, Webster, Dekker, Heywood, and Shakespeare. The corresponding playwrights of the later and more courtly school are Beaumont, Fletcher, Massinger, Shirley, and Ford. In his immense vitality and in certain of his marked characteristics Jonson is an Elizabethan. For with all his reason, he is an enthusiast, a strongly imaginative and a highly creative and original genius. Although he despises the people, he is as much a popular author as an aristocratic one. Even the most conservative school must have its vigorous beginners. Jonson's influence was ultimately in the direction of the newer style, and from his burly comedies was finally to be drawn much of the inspiration and the doctrine which produced Congreve's polished masterpieces.

A few more of the possible objections to this account must be faced. A playwright may forge ahead of his times in one play and lag behind them in another. Thus Fletcher anticipates the heroic play in certain of his tragedies, but harks back to Shakespeare in a few of his lighter works.

While some of his comedies, as *The Noble Gentleman* (with Beaumont), are clearly comedies of manners, suggestive of Shirley's *Lady of Pleasure* and of the Restoration stage, others are gigantic farces on the wars of the sexes, such as his continuation of *The Taming of the Shrew*, entitled *The Woman's Prize, or The Tamer Tamed*, his *Wild-Goose Chase* and *Rule a Wife and Have a Wife*. At least in one phase of his thinking, then, he continues the themes of such plays as *As You Like It* and *A Midsummer-Night's Dream*. His subject is the absurdity of mercurial passion, not the absurdity of unconventional manners. Even these exceptions, however, fail to obscure the major lines that mark the Cavalier from the Elizabethan drama.

These are, roughly sketched, the two schools. Although Webster continued to write tragedies after 1611, his style had been created and, according to the argument of this book, his masterpiece written at an earlier date. Middleton and Rowley seem to have produced their most stirring tragedies slightly later; but their minds had also been formed, and their chief comedies written, during the first decade of the century. Jonson's tragic writing as well as most of his comic writing was complete by this time. Chapman had finished all his important dramatic work. Meanwhile Beaumont and Fletcher had just begun theirs. Most of Beaumont's work and by far the greater part of Fletcher's and Massinger's still remained to be done. Shirley was not to emerge till a dozen years later. As Shakespeare's last dramatic romances show, he had felt the coming of the new fashions. But he never really resigned himself to them. And his retirement may have been due to his awareness that a tradition alien to his own was about to take possession of the English stage.

Thus far we have failed to reach any considerable depth

in seeking the character or explanation of the sweeping change which overtook the theatre about 1611 and brought a wholly new group of leaders to the fore. Nor does any analysis of Shakespeare and of Machiavellian skepticism, as that by Wyndham Lewis, in *The Lion and the Fox*, prove entirely satisfactory when its terms are applied to the drama as a whole. As the years advanced Machiavelli and his skepticism were not more prominent, but, on the contrary, were forgotten. Shakespeare is certainly more "modern" than Fletcher in the sense that he remains the more alive today. The tragedies of the post-Shakespearean period were more feudal in setting, more idealistic, more optimistic and romantic than ever. The rational, critical, and scientific temper failed to reach the English stage in any powerful way during the period of Charles I. Tragedy and tragicomedy became as a rule speciously archaistic, as in Davenant's heroic plays. The Cavalier drama may be modern, but it certainly is not Machiavellian. How, then, shall we interpret the change?

The best explanation is to be found in the loss of that curious poise or equilibrium between medieval and modern influences which rendered the Elizabethan age so restless and the drama until 1611 so vital a form of expression. The whole drama became paler and less exciting as it approached the closing of the theatres in 1642. In any serious sense it was both less medieval and less modern. It was less alive. But what vitality and promise it did possess was modern and forward-looking. Tragedy was growing a less significant form as it approached that ultimate frigidity to be reached in the middle of the eighteenth century. The comedy of manners, on the contrary, was the promising stem. While Jonson throughout the seventeenth century was forced to divide the laurels with Fletcher, by the eighteenth century the former was recog-

nized as the more important figure. It must be confessed
that modernity spoke with a relatively frail voice in the
drama from Fletcher to Shirley. Meanwhile in English
drama the medieval influences had declined steadily and
vastly since the rise of the public theatres in 1576, while
the modern influence had arisen—even though in 1630
these were not present in great power. The outstanding feature of the entire movement is the tenacious hold of the
medieval heritage for many years and its rapid decline
after 1611. To use an architectural metaphor, Gothic influences were still present in marked degree in work of
Kyd, Marlowe, Peele, Greene, Marston, Dekker, Middleton, Webster, Heywood, and Shakespeare and especially in
the many popular and now virtually forgotten playwrights
who labored during this period. They are not present with
anything like the same prominence in the Cavalier type of
play, over which the genius of Inigo Jones presides with
benign patronage. When Shakespeare was born, London
was architecturally a medieval city. When Fletcher died
it was rapidly becoming a baroque one. Shakespeare's
Globe Theatre was medieval; Inigo Jones's design for the
Cockpit Theatre at Whitehall was Romanesque. The
drama in its evolution tells a similar tale.

No one has ever supposed or is ever likely to suppose
that the Elizabethan drama is a medieval phenomenon.
Written for the most part in a verse form unknown to
the Middle Ages, it is inspired by many feelings and
ideas thoroughly new to its own times. These features are
well understood. That the Elizabethan is a Renaissance
drama has become almost a platitude, that it is also
medieval has remained almost a secret. During Elizabeth's
reign England abruptly became cosmopolitan, newly conscious of France, Italy, and Spain under the spell of the
Renaissance; it was stirred to its depths by the Reforma-

tion and reformed in its economic and social structure. It was clearly not the England of Malory and Caxton. Shakespeare and his comrades had no predecessors in the fifteenth century or earlier who stood really close to them in the spirit. The new playhouses and theatrical companies represented a type of theatrical life wholly unknown to the times of Henry VIII. The Elizabethan theatre is a modern institution. But it differs from the Renaissance theatre on the Continent precisely in that it is also the more strongly affected by medieval survivals. Like all else truly Elizabethan, it is eclectic. The Renaissance came later to England than to France; the Middle Ages also lingered longer in memory.

Edmund Spenser, the chief nondramatic poet of the times, exhibits the situation most clearly. His great poem is a curious compound of the old and the new. So heterogeneous a work would be difficult to discover abroad. Cervantes, Ariosto, and Ronsard seem simple beside the Englishman. Spenser affects an obsolete English, remembers the chivalric romances with an extraordinary grasp of detail, cherishes innumerable types of medieval imagery, and idealizes the feudal and religious codes of the Middle Ages. On the other hand, of course, he rejoices in the new classical learning, is fully aware of all the chief contemporary literature abroad, has read and digested Machiavelli and Bodin as well as Calvin and Melanchthon, knows Bruno and the radical astronomers, is a lover of Renaissance painting, costume, architecture, and gardening, and bends to every new wind of doctrine or idea. Even John Donne, who in poetry led a revolt from Spenser, enjoyed a profound Jesuit training and trailed clouds of medieval darkness throughout all his learned and perplexing works. He retains memories of the medieval night as Spenser of the medieval day. Certainly no one thinks of Donne primarily as a neoclassical poet. As the two chief nondramatic poets of the period show, the Elizabethan mind resembles the architecture of Oxford fifty years ago: a conjunction of the Gothic and the baroque.

English scholarship and criticism have been slow to recognize the medieval survivals in Shakespeare and his fellow dramatists. Although medieval plays were much edited in the last century, the Elizabethan mind was not studied in relation to the medieval. Of late, to be sure, some important contributions to the field have been made. One of the most stimulating of Shakespearean scholars, W. W. Lawrence, in his book *Shakespeare's Problem Comedies,* traces the medieval background of a limited number of the dramatist's plays and shows the probable attitude of the audience as determined by tradition. R. W. Chambers, in his brilliant paper read before the British Academy in 1937, discussed the medieval spirit in which *Measure for Measure* was conceived, showing the guiding thought of the play to have been based on the theological doctrine of mercy. Willard Farnham has recently published a study of the medieval heritage of Elizabethan tragedy. These scholars may be regarded as in advance of their times in emphasizing the medieval background. While research has, of course, traced innumerable features of Shakespeare's plays, as words and allusions, to their origins in the Middle Ages, interpretations of the evidence are still relatively rare. It may be significant that E. K. Chambers, the great historiographer of both the medieval and the Elizabethan stage, closes his researches with the death of Shakespeare, doubtless well aware that a radically new chapter in the history of the drama commences at approximately that date.

The reasons for the comparative neglect of this important field are scarcely obscure. The reverence of the usual English criticism for Shakespeare's creative genius, for the Italian Renaissance, and for the Protestant Reformation has helped to conceal the germs of much of the dramatist's thought and expression. It has long been customary to address Chaucer as the father of English poetry and to write of this poetry as though it were written in another language. English thought and literature of the fifteenth century have been relatively little studied by literary historians. A Protestant view of Shakespeare has unquestionably prevailed. No one has attempted to organize what is actually known of his medieval heritage as a whole.

It will accordingly be useful to sketch briefly some of the notable survivals of medieval thinking among the Elizabethan dramatists, with special reference to Shakespeare, whose most powerful imagination comprehended more of the medieval past than was given to any of his contemporaries to entertain. The briefest inspection reveals that Greene, Dekker, Heywood, Chettle, Munday, Haughton, and the more popular playwrights retained medieval influences in a large proportion. The Renaissance is first felt as an aristocratic movement.

To begin with we may consider the matter of cosmology. Elizabethan playwrights still believed in a Ptolemaic universe with astrological influences, and their audience, at least for the most part, believed in alchemy. The physical universe in which they lived was, then, almost identical with Chaucer's. Their world had barely been disturbed by rumors of modern science. Marlowe as a dramatist caught a brilliant glimpse of men climbing to knowledge infinite—a glimpse and little more. The still overwhelming medieval conditions in this respect cannot be regarded as unimportant. The plays abound in moving references to a static universe in which man and the stars engage in the same spiritual contentions visioned by Chaucer in *The Knight's Tale*.

In the background of the Elizabethan drama is also a theology still largely medieval, the presence of conservative ecclesiastical institutions and a vivid memory of others only recently vanished from England and still active abroad. Marlowe's greatest play, *Doctor Faustus*, depicts the conflict between the medieval and the Renaissance man, giving the palm to the former. Peele and Greene elaborately dramatize Biblical stories. Shakespeare delights in allusions to theology and is unusually sympathetic with his many nuns and friars. He writes as a man who, whatever his personal beliefs or their relevance to his plays, has at least experienced a fair amount of religious education. Hamlet has certainly studied theology at Wittenberg even if he has, oddly enough, learned later to doubt its validity by a reading of Montaigne.

This book has dealt at considerable length with the homiletic character of Elizabethan tragedy and its exploitation of the sense of sin. An eminently Christian and medieval feeling for wickedness gives the principal emotional vitality to the tragedies or, in other words, to the most serious works of Kyd, Marston, Tourneur, Middleton, Webster, and Jonson. Contrary to the rule, Shakespeare is here less medieval than most of his fellow dramatists, although in such an early play as *Richard the Third* the Christian character of the ethics, with its dualism of good and evil and emphasis upon conscience, is predominant. It recurs magnificently in *Macbeth*. The neopagan Fletcher was the son of a bishop. It is more illuminating that Marston, ceasing to be a playwright, became an Anglican priest. We must not forget the impressive religious prose of such men as Nash, Greene, Lyly, Hey-

wood, and Dekker. No one would, of course, contend
that the Elizabethan drama is religious in the sense that
the churchly drama of the Middle Ages is religious. But,
viewing the work of the Elizabethans too casually and
with too-modern eyes, we easily overlook the important
degree to which their work is Christian. As Professor
Farnham has shown, their doctrine and practice of tragedy
is basically that of Boccaccio and Lydgate, the medieval
idea at times altered but never forgotten.

The fears and horrors of a supernatural world carrying
the mind back to the medieval and the primitive are far
from absent from the Elizabethan stage. Kyd devised, to
be sure, an academic, neoclassical, and Senecan ghost, but
Hamlet's ghost comes directly from the medieval purgatory. Marlowe, Dekker, and Jonson bring devils on the
stage. Heywood and Middleton add witches. We have
examined with some detail the admirable witch scenes in
The Witch of Edmonton, by Dekker, Ford, and Rowley.
Macbeth would be a pale tragedy without its hell-inspired
hags.

Magic in almost all forms goes back to the Middle
Ages. A magician who controls wind and wave, like Prospero, no matter how belated in time, is a child of the
medieval centuries. There are many important magicians
in the great Elizabethan plays, so that we may speak not
metaphorically of their mighty magic. Prominent among
them are Faustus, Bacon, and Fortunatus. There are
astrologers, oracles, and fortunetellers. Prophecies are
numerous and always fulfilled. Superstitions are repeated
so often that more plays than one deserve the title of
Peele's charming fantasy, *The Old Wives Tale*. White
magic is almost as common as black, and the dramatists
frequently find themselves in the world of Puck and the
fairies. The universe is, then, not the modern world

fashioned by science but a much older and more primitive one. The more plebeian the Elizabethan playwright, the fonder he is of superstition.

That the ethics of the dramatists is in large part medieval has just been indicated in reference to their frequent exploitation of the experience of sin. The second chapter of this book discusses in some detail thirteen plays deeply affected by this viewpoint. The third chapter considers three, all written after 1611, only superficially touched by it. This proportion is a fair index to the general temper of the period. The seven deadly sins, the view of a world of good and evil men, of the absolute good or evil of any action, of strict personal responsibility, and of a virtually feudal loyalty demanded to existing orders of society dominate the ethical thought of the drama.

Shakespeare is almost oblivious to the moral problems of an industrial and commercial world. Although other playwrights glance at the rising trade and industry of London, their attitude is generally most unsympathetic. Ben Jonson is certainly against the political cause of the citizens. Only Dekker and Heywood actively espouse the interests of the new classes, and they hardly entertain a new social philosophy. Dekker's *Shoemaker's Holiday*, for example, celebrates the guild and apprentice systems as these had existed for centuries. The pageants of the Lord Mayors, to which several playwrights lent their aid, were themselves of medieval origin. In short, the new mercantile spirit finds no adequate expression in the Elizabethan theatre.

Many of the dramatists, on the contrary, delight in looking backward across the annals of English history. When a patriotic Elizabethan looked backward he could gaze only into the Middle Ages. Thus Shakespeare writes his long series of plays on the Wars of the Roses. We have seen that every English reign since the Conquest and many earlier and semilegendary periods were treated by the dramatists. But it is of greater importance that in dramatizing the chronicles they by no means departed from the spirit of medieval history itself. Holinshed's chronicle is much more a medieval than a modern treatment of the past. The ideas in plays dealing with Jack Straw, the Earl of Warwick, Thomas Cromwell, and Sir Thomas More would hardly have seemed strange to the historical personages whom they celebrate. If Marlowe's *Edward the Second* distorts history, it distorts it chiefly to make the past not brighter but darker and more primitive than it was.

The culture of both the medieval folk and the feudal aristocracy is thus mirrored on the Elizabethan stage. We have glanced at folklore in connection with magic. The work of Peele, Greene, Heywood, Dekker, and Shakespeare is full of homely superstitions. Even Jonson in his scientific way remembers them. The Middle Ages are perpetuated by their popular beliefs, and the popular songs, ballads, and tales of wonder find their way into such diverting drama as the anonymous *George a Greene*. The graver scenes of the Elizabethan dramatists meanwhile preserve the spirit and circumstance of chivalry— the feudal rituals, loyalties, rivalries, and beliefs. Both the old classes, then, high and low, are equally noted by the playwrights. It is wholly in keeping with these currents of thought that Shakespeare recalls the popular belief that on Christmas Eve the cock sings all night long; it is wholly in keeping that all the ideals of the very perfect gentle lover are met in Troilus, and of the generous and valiant knight in Hector. Othello believes in a magic handkerchief, Caliban in the supernatural hag, his mother.

Amorous idealism was one of the favorite infirmities or glories of the Middle Ages. Shakespeare and his fellow dramatists delight in the theme. Sometimes they accept it enthusiastically, ascending to the dizziest heights of poetry upon its wings. Sometimes they stoop to subject it to a new and sharper skepticism. The divine afflatus in the portraits of Romeo and Juliet, Orlando and Rosalind, Ferdinand and Miranda is impossible to imagine without a romance tradition still close and warm. Even the stronger conception of love and devotion represented in Paulina and Hermione has its debt to medieval feeling. Troilus is quite as medieval a character in Shakespeare as in Chaucer. Moreover, the medieval notion of the war of the sexes is richly developed by the comic dramatists, as appears in such a typical piece as *The Taming of the Shrew*.

Modern scholarship has often pointed to the infatuation of the Renaissance not only with love but with friendship, not only with the amoretti but with more mature and masculine devotion. Friendship, it will be recalled, is the theme of one of the six books of *The Faerie Queene*. The immediate source of such stories as appear in Edwards' *Damon and Pythias*, in *The Merchant of Venice* or *The Two Gentlemen of Verona* may lie in Renaissance literature, but it is pertinent to consider that the theme is nowhere more popular than in medieval fiction. The friendship of Gawain and Launcelot, for example, heightens the tragedy of *Le Morte d'Arthur*. It is a favorite subject with all the Elizabethan dramatists, as notably with Lyly, Peele, Greene, Marston, and Chapman. And it colors more scenes in Shakespeare than a too-casual and modernistic reader will suppose.

Ideals of love and friendship lead us directly to medieval romance as a source for ideas, plots, and situations. Storytelling of all sorts is almost as important to the

Elizabethans as to Chaucer. A majority of the plays produced before 1600 contain dramatizations of romance material. It is amusing to recall that when Dekker wished to satirize Ben Jonson he put him in a play with a scene in the reign of William Rufus and a plot redolent of medieval manners and literature. Shakespeare's *As You Like It* has its roots in a verse tale of the Middle Ages. *Cymbeline* carries us back to a large number of medieval stories. The stolen children, the magic potions, the wager for chastity, the cruel stepmother, and the enmity of Britain and Rome are commonplaces of romantic legend. Shakespeare's *Troilus and Cressida* is based on a tale once told by Chaucer, his *Pericles* on a story by the fourteenth-century poet, John Gower, who as a stage personage fittingly speaks the prologue. He had a hand in *The Two Noble Kinsmen*, another dramatization of Chaucerian material, altered from its original more in manner than in substance. After 1600, to be sure, the chief playwrights gradually drew away from romantic sources but never divorced themselves wholly. Even Massinger writes of the Courts of Love, and Shirley of St. Patrick's Purgatory.

Allegory and personification retained for the Elizabethan playwrights some of the fascination which they held for medieval poets and dramatists. Jonson's *Cynthia's Revels* is almost as much an allegory as a medieval morality play. His *Volpone* carries on the allegorical beast fable. His *Staple of News* has important allegorical figures, although this type of Aristophanic writing was, significantly enough, more in favor with him as a young man than as an old one. All the earlier dramatists are fond of allegorical scenes. Peele has them in most of his plays. Greene and Lodge's *Looking Glass for London and England* is in a sense an allegory, applying as it does the story of Jonah to the life of Britain. Marlowe's *Doctor Faustus* contains allegorical elements such as scenes presenting the seven deadly sins and good and evil angels. Dekker's *Old Fortunatus*, with its long episodes depicting Fortune and Virtue, becomes half an allegory. Heywood's most charming play, *Love's Mistress*, is an allegorical treatment of the legend of Cupid and Psyche. Where the masque intrudes upon the drama, as in *Love's Labour's Lost*, *As You Like It*, and *The Tempest*, allegorical personification in some degree indebted to medieval tradition appears. The language of the poets is still rich in colorful personifications with similar indebtedness to one of the outstanding features of medieval imagery and verse.

The evolution of poetic style from medieval to Elizabethan, a subject too seldom treated by students, shows much more continuity than at first sight appears. The medieval style and the Elizabethan, that of Malory and that of Shakespeare, seem at a glance highly dissimilar. They are so; but there are likenesses easily overlooked. A style very like euphuism had developed in England by the early sixteenth century, as the sermons of Bishop Fisher, co-martyr with Sir Thomas More, evince. The aureate or gilded eloquence reached Shakespeare through earlier and equally artificial poets, as John Skelton, another contemporary of More. Skelton's unrestrained and eloquent panegyric or vituperation closely resembles that of Nash or any other representative Elizabethan.

The Elizabethan drama is full of fine ranting and bombast. So is the medieval drama. It was, indeed, precisely the ambition of Marlowe and his followers to out-Herod Herod, the voluble villain of the mystery cycles. And just as, by contrast, in their tender scenes these cycles can be remarkably simple, so can Greene or Dekker or Shakespeare. Such contrasts eighteenth-century English virtually eliminated. Elizabethan English was in truth a new and

wonderfully flexible speech, but it was not without important roots in the immediate past.

Its tone of rhetorical didacticism, for instance, it owes
largely to the earlier tradition. Elizabethan poetic drama
abounds in passages such as Portia's praise of mercy, a
type of declamation much on the wane in the Cavalier
period. As is well known, Portia's speech derives from
Gower. The playwrights, of course, learned much of their
rhetoric from sixteenth-century handbooks and collections
of aphorisms, such as the famous *Adagia* of Erasmus. But
like euphuism itself, Elizabethan eloquence as a whole
had a long tradition behind it. A typical case is Shakespeare's image for adversity as a jewel in the head of a
toad. The figure appears frequently. It occurs, for example, in Nash's first pamphlet, *The Anatomy of Absurdity*, and is derived from medieval bestiaries, the collections of fantastic allegorical fables on animals. The
lonely dragon in his fen to which Coriolanus likens himself is a typical metaphorical ornament plucked from the
medieval world of fancy and fable.

At first sight the versification of the blank-verse Elizabethan drama may appear totally unlike that of its medieval antecedents. But a more thoughtful inspection shows
some very significant inheritances. To state the case
broadly, the English drama was genuinely a poetic drama
from its inception in the fourteenth century till approximately the death of Shakespeare. It was largely written in
verse; and such prose as appeared was a poetic prose.
Thereafter it has been increasingly in prose, and what verse
has appeared has been largely prosaic. It is true that the
proportion between verse and prose is in the Cavalier
drama only a little more favorable to prose than in the
Elizabethan. But it is also true that the Cavalier dramatists are relatively mediocre poets compared with the

Elizabethan. The sheer poetic gifts of the earlier group are incomparably greater than those of the later. It is even fair to say that any one of the major Elizabethan playwrights is more of a true poet than any member of the school of Fletcher. The Cavalier idiom for drama, then, is relatively prosaic. Its rhetorical style is presently to evolve into the decorous fustian of the well-formulated heroic play. In tragedy the verse becomes oratorical, as we have noted in Fletcher's *Bonduca* and in Massinger's *Duke of Milan*. In comedy the verse becomes colloquial, as may be seen in Fletcher's and Massinger's *Elder Brother*. This comedy was twice printed during the Cavalier period, once as blank verse and once as prose. It makes little difference. Shirley's verse is similarly designed to be read as prose. This is certainly not intended in the case of Marlowe's verse, nor is it likely that even Shakespeare's last plays or the tragedies of Middleton or Webster, familiar as their verse often becomes, should be so understood. There is an unmistakable evolution. Medieval drama is almost wholly lyrical in form and often exquisitely lyrical in spirit. Much of the Elizabethan drama of the years of Shakespeare's apprenticeship is also highly lyrical both in spirit and in form. The love scenes in *The Spanish Tragedy* and in *Antonio and Mellida* are in a lyrical verse and commonly rhymed. Marlowe is celebrated for his highly lyrical passages. Obviously *Romeo and Juliet* and *A Midsummer-Night's Dream* have the artificial movement and disciplined enthusiasm of the finest lyrical verse. They have well been compared to an operatic style. Even if Shakespeare's verse becomes decreasingly lyrical as it grows increasingly dramatic, it never entirely loses a potentiality for lyrical expression, as *Antony and Cleopatra* best shows. And such elements appear in all the Elizabethan playwrights, notably in Peele,

Greene, Chapman, Dekker, Heywood, and Tourneur.
Jonson can be lyrical even in the movement of his massive
prose. So, too, can Middleton. Nor should too much attention be given here to the songs freely interspersed
throughout all the major playwrights. (Massinger alone
seems to have been without the song-writer's gift.) The
Cavalier playwrights employ song as often as the Elizabethans, although throughout the entire period the plays
acted by the children's companies are the most profuse in
singing. Fletcher was a wonderful writer of songs, as
shown in his lyrical drama, *The Faithful Shepherdess*.
He supplies a link in the lyric art between Shakespeare
and Milton. But his songs lack the afflatus of the lyrics of
a true Elizabethan, as Thomas Dekker. And the important consideration here is the presence of a strict lyrical
and musical form in the non-lyrical passages of the Elizabethan plays quite obviously lacking in similar parts of
the Cavalier works.

Behind these facts lie many highly significant aspects
of the Renaissance theatre. As time advances acting clearly
becomes less formalized and more naturalized. There is
less ritual, pantomime, and balance, more of the informal,
the colloquial, and the realistic. It is all a continuous stream
of evolution, though its swiftest current flows at about the
time of Shakespeare's retirement. Even the largest units
of dramatic form show the effect of this movement, which
had reached its critical stage by 1611.

Medieval theory and practice had evolved two principal
dramatic types, namely tragedy and farce. These types
came to the Elizabethans buttressed, to be sure, by the
classical examples of Seneca and Plautus, but not determined by these or other classical sources. Shakespeare began his career by writing historical tragedies on the fall of
princes and comedies of a distinctly farcical gusto. He never

lost his love for clowning, as Autolycus, the Old Shepherd, and his son in *The Winter's Tale* sufficiently indicate. The humor of Middleton's early comedies is still largely that of the sixteenth-century jestbook. But the succeeding movement in the theatre tended to reduce tragedy to tragicomedy and to elevate and transform farce into high comedy of polite manners. Tragedy and comedy themselves took on new form and spirit. The playwrights in direct descent from Fletcher to Shirley contribute much to this evolution, while the typical Elizabethans, as Chapman, Webster, and Marston, contribute little to it. The current began to flow strongly away from the long-established theatrical traditions only upon the ascendancy of the Fletcherian school.

Although emphasis in the preceding pages has fallen upon the force of the medieval inheritance in plays before 1611 rather than on the decline of such influence in the typical plays thereafter, the tendencies are so evident that no elaborate effort is required to trace the evolution through the later years. For each positive conclusion regarding the medieval influence in the earlier period one may assume a negative one for the later. A new cosmology, a new and less exciting view of religion and morals, superstition, and magic arise. Sin, witchcraft, and the devils mean less. That history is less treated becomes less important here than the extinction of interest in the faithful dramatizing of chronicles written in the medieval spirit. The dramatists are making a new folklore of their own. Distinctively medieval ideas, enthusiasms, and institutions grow far less conspicuous. Ideas of friendship and love grow rapidly less medieval and more modern. Plots from medieval literature or tradition are fewer. Imagery from medieval sources becomes relatively scarce. Catholic theology or the medieval bestiary, for example, no longer has the figura-

tive value in the dramatic language which it held for the
contemporaries of Shakespeare. The prevailing type of
allegory or personification ceases to be brightly colored by
medieval usage and acquires an Augustan whiteness. The
dramatic verse, as we have seen, loses its ancient lyrical
spirit, and the lyrics themselves lose their ethereal quality,
so that we are swiftly passing from the lyrical atmosphere of *The Shoemaker's Holiday* to that of *The Beggar's Opera*. Comedy becomes more natural, and tragedy
more artificial. Finally, the conscious and avowed attitude
towards things medieval changes. The eclectic Elizabethans of the period of Stow's pious description of London
or of Holinshed's patriotic chronicle of England were still
inordinately proud of their medieval heritage. No con-
certed prejudices against medieval art or the medieval
period had arisen in an audience daily thronging a theatre
built in a medieval style. But as the Stuarts continued upon
the throne and as Inigo Jones, Van Dyck, and their associates revolutionized English taste, the dogma of the Dark
Ages came into being. Even by the time of Shirley, under
a growing classicism the Middle Ages were becoming at
once despised and ignored. What is more important still,
the ties were actually weakening. English culture as expressed in the theatre of necessity felt this shift of wind
and change of climate most sharply at the commencement
of the seventeenth century. These conditions afford the
easiest critical means to distinguish and to explain one of
the most vital changes in English dramatic history.

The story, as already indicated, may be corroborated in
the history of nondramatic poetry. Gascoigne, Spenser,
Donne, and Drayton obviously stand far closer to the
Middle Ages than Suckling, Herrick, Marvell, and Milton. A typical Restoration poet and parodist of Dryden,
such as Matthew Prior, may have a sentimental and an

antiquarian affection for the Middle Ages. But culturally he stands in another world. It is the world for which preparation has been made upon the stage as early as the period of Philip Massinger and James Shirley.

Yet the drama has far closer ties with the Middle Ages than the nondramatic literature. To perceive this we may revert to the views presented in the Introduction of this book and to a consideration of the manner in which the plays were written and produced as distinguished from a direct study of the dramatic literature itself. The frequent anonymity and significant habits of collaboration are typically medieval. And the English theatre from 1576 to 1611 was principally the heir of the medieval theatre because, like that theatre, it was wholly national, addressed to all classes of the community. The Elizabethan stage is the last great communal expression in art following the waning of the Middle Ages and in this respect above all others has its kinship with medieval culture. Studies in both Shakespeare and his contemporaries are best illustrated today by much-needed evidence regarding their hitherto superficially interpreted medieval inheritance. Such study should not make them more remote from ourselves. On the contrary, it should make them more alive by presenting them as they really are.

The last words of our analysis concern the two major playwrights, Jonson and Shakespeare, with special reference to their cultural backgrounds and to the arguments of preceding chapters. Jonson's relation to medieval culture is sufficiently important and unusual to warrant particular attention. He began his career as a typical romantic Elizabethan writing chronicle-history plays on medieval England doubtless not greatly unlike Shakespeare's. Only the titles of such works survive. But although he early ceased to collaborate with popular romanticists such as

Chettle and Haughton and became the great prophet of
rationalism and neoclassicism in England, to the end of
his life he also retained strong traces of these early influences. With a medieval passion for allegory, an insatiable
intellectual curiosity, and a basic tolerance which made all
accessible phases of medieval culture of interest to him,
he kept in touch with England's past. When his library
burned, he lamented the loss of many annotated folios of
the schoolmen. He imitated Skelton, showed a thorough
acquaintance with Chaucer, Gower, and Lydgate in the
citations in his *English Grammar,* and was at least a student of folklore and medieval legend. When he writes a
pastoral drama, he celebrates Robin Hood instead of
Daphnis; and if Robin becomes for him in part a
Cavalier gentleman in exile, he remains also a medieval
outlaw. The legends of Christmas he loves as truly as
Shakespeare. Jonson has a Gothic weakness for eccen-
tricity. As Dekker well argued, if justice were done he
himself should be in his *Every Man in His Humour.*
He can be as stern a moralist as any Christian preacher or
he can be as broad and goliardic a humorist as Chaucer.
The father of English neoclassicism, he is, then, ample
enough in soul to remain still in living contact with much
that is typically medieval. Like Shakespeare and his generation as a whole, he, too, is partially medieval and partially modern, though the modern is present in him in a
greater proportion. Although a rationalist, he is hardly
urbane and consequently prepares the way for the light
comedy of wit without actually inventing it. He may be
called the Moses of the Augustan migration, looking into
the promised land without entering fully into it.

In the general field of Elizabethan drama Shakespeare
is both more and less of an exception than Jonson. In point
of style the two are equally individual, one achieving the

highest perfection of eloquence, the other of poetry. Shakespeare is the less unusual in generously accepting the conventions of his own age, while Jonson leads the way to new. Only because of his superlative genius does Shakespeare stand dramatically apart from his contemporaries. Far better than Jonson he represents the equable balance of medieval and Renaissance influences that defines the eclectic Elizabethan temper, for in him the medieval heritage is obviously stronger than in Jonson. It is more a heritage of the heart than of the head, more spontaneous and less academic. Shakespeare's early life in a provincial town, in contrast with Jonson's education in London, matured the medieval influences in the former more fully. For Stratford was certainly less susceptible than London to the initial impact of new ideas.

Shakespeare's position is a broad one not only in the character but in the merits of his work. Throughout this book it has been apparent that his own art sometimes sinks below the best works of his contemporaries, although more often it equals or far surpasses them. This holds true in all fields of his endeavor. Thus our argument has been that there are other Elizabethans who wrote more powerful tragedies than *Titus Andronicus*, more attractive historical plays than *Henry the Sixth*, and more charming comedies than *The Two Gentlemen of Verona*. More has been said of some of the less popular of Shakespeare's plays—works standing in interest between his weakest and his strongest productions—than of his masterpieces. This is because when putting forth more than his least but less than his greatest powers he comes the closest to his chief comrades. We have considered *Love's Labour's Lost* in relation to plays dealing with Renaissance ideas, *Richard the Second* as typical of the Elizabethan chronicle-history play, *The*

Winter's Tale in the light of the sentimental tragicomedies, *Cymbeline* in comparison with the heroic extravaganzas of Fletcher, *All's Well That Ends Well* in connection with the Cavalier romances, *The Merry Wives of Windsor* as representative of the comedies of manners, *Measure for Measure* in view of the satirical comedies, and *A Midsummer-Night's Dream* as an instance of the comedy of pure fancy. Especially between Shakespeare's less popular but still mature work and the masterpieces of his contemporaries the closest likenesses are to be found. In these pages relatively little has been said regarding *Hamlet* and *Othello*, and still less concerning *Macbeth*, *King Lear*, and *Antony and Cleopatra*. As the first few chapters are designed to show, he surpassed his age in nothing more clearly than in his deeper insight into the nature of tragedy. He outdistances his immediate rivals here not only in merit but in kind. But any general study of the art or literature of a brilliant age leaves heights unexplored. Some peaks rise above the zone of comfortable habitation, exposed to all eyes but scaled if at all only by the most adventurous hand and foot. In so far as Shakespeare rests in his age, he represents it in nothing more conspicuously than in his balance of medieval and modern thought. In so far as he soars above it, he achieves poetic eminences peculiar to himself, which are without the province of a general dramatic or literary historian to discuss. This book has aimed consistently to picture Shakespeare in relation to his times but not to consider the ultimate heights of his art. In a sense one can write of him effectively only in relation to his comrades. His ultimate magic warns us in his own words: "The rest is silence."

To the modern reader Shakespeare must be both the beginning and the end of any study of Elizabethan drama.

That he is a legitimate part of his age appears unmistakably in the original popularity of his plays. It is of greater interest, however, to reflect on his own attitude towards his associates. From first to last he was at one with them. He singled out Marlowe personally for praise. He assimilated many ideas from Lyly, Greene, Marlowe, Kyd, Marston, and Jonson. His collaboration with other playwrights and especially with Fletcher further shows how spontaneously he associated himself with the movement in which he played the major role. It is impossible to suppose that he viewed coolly the best work by the above-mentioned men as well as that by dramatists such as Middleton and Chapman. That he was generally far more imaginative than they in the same or similar types of writing cannot have lessened his pleasure in their achievements. The nineteenth-century romanticists were mistaken in asserting that Shakespeare spins his art solely from the depths of his own personality, while the more prosaic of later historical scholars are equally mistaken in inferring that he merely modifies the work of his contemporaries. Through a supreme imaginative sensitivity he spontaneously became a living part of his times. Thus the three recognized phases of his art—his euphuistic preciosity, his imaginative profundity, and his suave sentimentality—these we have seen to be the quintessence of three successive decades in the history of English dramatic poetry: so sensitively was he attuned to the rapidly changing temper of the age of which he himself formed the most conspicuous part. The poet who admirably represents his times should be seen through the age, and the age itself should be viewed through him. One way to appreciate the Elizabethan and Jacobean drama is to imagine what delight Shakespeare derived from it and what his own attitudes towards it may have been. We understand it best as we attempt to view it through his own piercing and glowing eyes. As we conceive his joy at this rich pageant of human life, we realize the fullest measure of enthusiasm which this dramatic literature is capable of evoking.

BIOGRAPHICAL AND
BIBLIOGRAPHICAL NOTES

BIOGRAPHICAL AND
BIBLIOGRAPHICAL NOTES

THE FOLLOWING brief lists of printed plays and other books are in no case given as formal bibliographies, but are presented in the hope that they may prove useful and suggestive to the reader of English plays not already a specialist in the subject. The annual bibliography published since 1921 for the Modern Humanities Research Association is an important current review of this field as of so many others. The bibliography in the *Bulletin* of the Shakespeare Association of America, also appearing annually, is especially valuable. Likewise the bibliography published annually in *Studies in Philology* is important. The standard summaries of scholarly work under three of the major fields are all the work of E. K. Chambers: *The Medieval Stage, The Elizabethan Stage,* and *William Shakespeare.* For the background of the present book the second is of the greatest value, since it contains critical bibliographies and biographical sketches of all dramatists between 1559 and 1616. The first of the following lists aims to give a convenient enumeration, by authors, of all the extant plays of the chief dramatists from 1576 to 1642, with short biographical summaries and a brief list of critical works wherever possible. After the title of each play is given the approximate date of its first stage production followed by the date of its first publication, the latter marked "pub." A desirable modern edition of each author is also noted. Eighty-five of the best non-Shakespearean plays are in the popular "Mermaid Series" under the general editorship of Havelock Ellis.

The following list includes about three-quarters of the plays produced from 1576 to 1616, printed before 1660 and extant today. It also includes about half the plays first produced between 1617 and 1642. There is a list of anonymous plays appearing between 1576 and 1611, and there are four additional lists giving titles of books chiefly of recent date and directly or indirectly illuminating to the study of Elizabethan and Jacobean drama. No mention is made of periodical literature.

A List of Plays by the Chief Dramatists, 1576–1642
with Dates, Biographical Notices, Modern Editions
and Critical Works

ALEXANDER, SIR WILLIAM, EARL OF STIRLING (c.1568-1640)

Alexander wrote closet dramas in the Senecan tradition. After studying in Glasgow and Leyden, he traveled widely in Europe and was tutor to Prince Henry, gentleman extraordinary of the Privy Chamber, and governor of the English territories in North America. He wrote excellent lyrics. There is no record of his plays on the stage. They were published under the general title of *The Monarchick Tragedies* and form a sequence. All are dignified and highly polished compositions.

> Darius, pub. 1603.
> Croesus, pub. 1604.
> The Alexandrean Tragedy, pub. 1607.
> Julius Caesar, pub. 1607.
> Kastner, L. E., and H. B. Charlton, eds., The Poetical Works of Sir William Alexander, Earl of Stirling, 1921.

BEAUMONT, FRANCIS (c.1584-1616), and JOHN FLETCHER (1579-1625)

Since the works of these two playwrights have never been separated in editions of their plays, it will be convenient to treat the two together here.

Beaumont, the son of a Leicestershire justice of the Common Pleas, was a student at Oxford and in the Inner Temple. He became a close friend of Ben Jonson, who is said to have sought his advice in play-writing. Beaumont collaborated in many plays with Fletcher, especially from about 1606 to 1612. He wrote nondramatic poems as well. A more responsible artist than Fletcher, he is believed to have taken the leading hand in the plays which they produced together. He seems to have written little independently. He was buried in Westminster Abbey.

Fletcher was the son of a minister who became bishop of London. Like Beaumont, he belonged to a family which produced other poets than himself. Stories about him indicate that he was the jovial, carefree person we would infer him to have been from his plays. His portrait in the National Gallery shows a handsome and somewhat effeminate man, with clothes as loosely fitting as his own dramatic works. Although he was the most popular play-wright after the retirement of Shakespeare, little is really known of his life.

It is certain that the plays published under the joint names of the two men contain many works by Fletcher alone, both before and after Beaumont's death, and that other authors, especially Massinger, were contributors. No one supposes that the riddles of authorship or chronology raised by the plays can be more than partially solved. The following list is based chiefly on the conclusions of E. H. C. Oliphant, although no account is taken of that scholar's tentative suggestions as to the hands of some of the less distinguished playwrights. The plays were published in two folios: the first, with thirty-four plays, edited by Shirley, in 1647, the second in 1679 with eighteen more.

By Fletcher without Beaumont

Bonduca, 1606 (later revised), pub. 1647.

The Women Pleased, 1606(?), pub. 1647.

The Woman's Prize, 1607, pub. 1647.

The Faithful Shepherdess, 1609, pub. 1609.

The Night Walker, c.1609, pub. 1640.

The Wild-Goose Chase, c.1609(?), pub. 1652.

Monsieur Thomas, c.1611, pub. 1639.

The Honest Man's Fortune, 1613, pub. 1647.

Valentinian, 1613, pub. 1647.

Four Plays in One, c.1614, pub. 1647.

Wit without Money, 1614, pub. 1639.

The Chances, 1615, pub. 1647.

The Mad Lover, 1616, pub. 1647.

The Loyal Subject, 1618, pub. 1647.

The Humorous Lieutenant, 1619, pub. 1647.

The Laws of Candy, 1619, pub. 1647.

The Island Princess, 1621, pub. 1647.

The Pilgrim, 1621, pub. 1647.

BEAUMONT and FLETCHER: FLETCHER ALONE (*Continued*)
The Maid in the Mill, 1623, pub. 1647.
Rule a Wife and Have a Wife, 1624, pub. 1640.
A Wife for a Month, 1624, pub. 1647.

BY BEAUMONT AND FLETCHER ALONE

The Faithful Friends (authorship problematical), 1606, pub.
1679.
The Nice Valour, 1606, pub. 1647.
The Noble Gentleman, 1606(?), pub. 1647.
Wit at Several Weapons, 1606, pub. 1647.
The Woman Hater, 1606, pub. 1607.
Cupid's Revenge, c.1608, pub. 1615.
Philaster, 1609, pub. 1620.
The Knight of the Burning Pestle (mainly Beaumont),
1610, pub. 1613.
The Captain, 1611, pub. 1647.
A King and No King, 1611, pub. 1619.
The Maid's Tragedy, 1611, pub. 1619.
The Scornful Lady, c.1614, pub. 1616.
Love's Pilgrimage, 1615, pub. 1647.

BY BEAUMONT, FLETCHER, AND MASSINGER

Thierry and Theodoret (Beaumont questionable), 1608,
pub. 1621.
The Beggars' Bush, 1609, pub. 1647.
The Coxcomb, 1609, pub. 1647.

BY FLETCHER AND MASSINGER

The Fair Maid of the Inn, 1606(?), pub. 1647.
Love's Cure, 1606, pub. 1647.
The Elder Brother, 1614, pub. 1637.
The Bloody Brother (probably with Chapman), 1615(?),
pub. 1639.
The Knight of Malta, 1616, pub. 1647.
The Queen of Corinth, 1616, pub. 1647.
A Very Woman, 1616, pub. 1655.

Barnavelt, 1619, pub. 1883 from MS.

The Custom of the Country, 1620, pub. 1647.

The Double Marriage, 1620, pub. 1647.

The False One, 1620, pub. 1647.

The Little French Lawyer, 1620, pub. 1647.

The Prophetess, 1622, pub. 1647.

The Sea Voyage, 1622, pub. 1647.

The Spanish Curate, 1622, pub. 1647.

The Lover's Progress, 1623, pub. 1647.

By Fletcher and Shakespeare

The Two Noble Kinsmen, 1613, pub. 1634.

Bullen, A. H., ed., Works of Beaumont and Fletcher, Variorum Edition (only 4 vols. issued), 1904-12.

Gayley, C. M., Beaumont the Dramatist, 1914.

Glover, A., and A. R. Waller, eds., Beaumont and Fletcher, 1905-12.

Oliphant, E. H. C., The Plays of Beaumont and Fletcher, an Attempt to Determine Their Respective Shares and the Shares of Others, 1927.

Tannenbaum, S. A., Beaumont and Fletcher, a Concise Bibliography, 1938.

Wilson, J. H., The Influence of Beaumont and Fletcher on Restoration Drama, 1928.

Brome, Richard (?-1652)

The playwright was for many years a servant or amanuensis to Ben Jonson. His activity as a dramatist commenced about 1630. He imitated not only his master but Dekker and Fletcher, writing both comedies of manners and romantic plays. He enjoyed protesting his own humble place as man and author, and indeed his social rank is often reflected in his work. *The Northern Lass* and *A Jovial Crew* are commonly held his best plays.

The Court Beggar, 1632, pub. 1653.

The Northern Lass, pub. 1632.

Novella, 1632, pub. 1653.

The Sparagus Garden, 1635, pub. 1640.

BROME (*Continued*)
> The Antipodes, 1638, pub. 1640.
> A Jovial Crew, 1641, pub. 1641.
> The City Wit, pub. 1653.
> The Damoiselle, pub. 1653.
> The Mad Couple Well Matched, pub. 1653.
> The Queen's Exchange, pub. 1657.
> Covent Garden Weeded, pub. 1659.
> The English Moor, pub. 1659.
> The Lovesick Court, pub. 1659.
> The New Academy, pub. 1659.
> The Queen and the Concubine, pub. 1659.

Brome, Richard, The Dramatic Works, Pearson's reprint, 1873.

CARY, LADY ELIZABETH (1586-1639)
Lady Cary, afterwards Lady Falkland, was a patroness of letters and one of the more gifted of noble authors. Only one of her plays is extant. It is a typical example of scholarly closet drama, written on neoclassical lines especially close to the French.
> Mariam, c.1604, pub. 1613.

Dunston, A. C., ed., Mariam, Malone Society Reprints, 1914.

CHAPMAN, GEORGE (c.1559-1634)
Chapman first comes to light as a writer of philosophical poetry (*The Shadow of Night,* 1594). He anticipated Jonson in the realistic comedy of humors and wrote as well romantic comedies and tragedies of a political and philosophical nature, remarkable for their luxuriant style. He completed Marlowe's *Hero and Leander* (1598). His chief work he considered to be his great translation of Homer, finished in 1625, but he also translated a large number of Greek and Latin poets. His hand has been traced in Fletcher and Massinger's *Bloody Brother* and in the anonymous *Sir Giles Goosecap.*
> The Blind Beggar of Alexandria, 1596, pub. 1598.
> An Humorous Day's Mirth, 1597, pub. 1599.
> Charlemagne, c.1600, pub. 1920 from MS.

The Gentleman Usher, c.1602, pub. 1606.

May Day, 1602(?), pub. 1611.

All Fools, c.1604, pub. 1605.

Bussy D'Ambois, 1604, pub. 1607.

Monsieur D'Olive, 1604, pub. 1606.

Eastward Ho! (with Jonson and Marston), 1605, pub. 1605.

Charles, Duke of Byron, 1608, pub. 1608.

The Widow's Tears, c.1608, pub. 1612.

The Revenge of Bussy D'Ambois, c.1610, pub. 1613.

Chabot Admiral of France (with Shirley), c.1613, pub. 1639.

Caesar and Pompey, not acted when written, pub. 1631.

Ellis, Havelock, George Chapman, 1934.

Parrott, T. M., ed., The Plays of George Chapman, 1910-14.

Solve, N. D., Stuart Politics in Chapman's Tragedy of Chabot, 1928.

Tannenbaum, S. A., George Chapman, a Concise Bibliography, 1938.

CHETTLE, HENRY (c.1560-c.1604)

Chettle entered authorship by way of his partnership in a printing business. He associated with Greene and Nash in pamphleteering, his most interesting nondramatic work being *Kind-Heart's Dream*. His contemporaries write of him as modest, good-natured, humorous, and fat. Dekker refers to him affectionately in his *Knight's Conjuring* (1607), speaking of him as dead. He wrote many plays now lost, always apparently in a romantic and popular style. Among his collaborators were Munday, Haughton, and Dekker.

Hoffman, 1603, pub. 1631.

Farmer, J. S., ed., Hoffman, 1913.

Jenkins, Harold, The Life and Work of Henry Chettle, 1934.

DANIEL, SAMUEL (c.1563-1619)

Daniel is one of the chief poets of the period. After studying at Oxford he traveled abroad on diplomatic service and later be-

DANIEL (*Continued*)

came a tutor to the daughter of the Earl of Cumberland. One of his best poems is an epistle to her mother. His sonnet series, *Delia* (1592), contains parallels to Shakespeare's. He also wrote poems representing the same popular taste for English history which appeared on the stage. His *Civil Wars* (1595) may be compared with *Richard the Second*. His nondramatic masterpiece is a verse essay on learning, *Musophilus* (1599). Called by William Browne "the well-languaged Daniel" and eminent for his restrained eloquence as an English stylist, in his plays he deserts the popular English tradition in favor of more decorous foreign models. His masque, *Tethys' Festival*, is memorable.

Cleopatra, c.1593, pub. 1594.

Philotas, 1604, pub. 1605.

The Queene's Arcadia, 1605, pub. 1606.

Hymen's Triumph, 1614, pub. 1615.

Grosart, A. B., ed., The Complete Works in Verse and Prose of Samuel Daniel, 1885-96.

DAVENANT, SIR WILLIAM (1606-68)

In his early work Davenant showed more clearly than any other playwright the tendencies leading to Restoration taste. In his literary theories he renounced the poetic abandon of the Elizabethans and found equal place for colloquialism and for heroic ranting. His *Siege of Rhodes* (1656) launched the English opera on its course. His epic, *Gondilbert* (1651), written during imprisonment, is one of the oddest of literary experiments. He wrote tragic extravaganzas, polite and affected comedies, and excellent songs. After the Restoration he became one of the leading theatrical managers.

The Just Italian, 1624, pub. 1630.

Albovine, King of the Lombards, pub. 1629.

The Cruel Brother, pub. 1630.

The Wits, 1633, pub. 1636.

The Platonic Lovers, pub. 1636.

The Unfortunate Lovers, pub. 1643.

Love and Honour, pub. 1649.

Harbage, Alfred, Sir William Davenant, Poet Venturer, 1935.
Maidment, J., and W. H. Logan, eds., The Dramatic Works
of Sir William Davenant, 1872-74.
Nethercot, A. H., Sir William Davenant, 1938.

DAY, JOHN (c.1574-c.1640)
Day is one of the gayest of English dramatists. Expelled at the
age of eighteen from Cambridge for stealing a book, he became
one of the group of romantic playwrights including Chettle,
Dekker, and Haughton. Later he wrote independently for the
Children of the Queen's Revels. Adjusting his style to the changing taste, he was equally witty in the Elizabethan and in the
Cavalier manner. His typical style is a less ethereal echo of *A
Midsummer-Night's Dream*. His most original work is an allegory, *The Parliament of Bees*. He has been plausibly associated
with *The Maid's Metamorphosis* and the *Parnassus* plays. His
salacious repartee was destined to shock Swinburne.

The Blind Beggar of Bethnal Green, 1600, pub. 1659.
Law Tricks, 1604, pub. 1608.
The Isle of Gulls, 1606, pub. 1606.
Humour Out of Breath, 1607, pub. 1608.
The Travels of Three English Brothers, 1607, pub. 1607.
The Parliament of Bees, c.1612, pub. 1641.
Bullen, A. H., ed., The Works of John Day, 1881.

DEKKER, THOMAS (c.1572-1632).
Born in London, more than any other playwright he associated
himself with the life and spirit of the city. He wrote much nondramatic work in prose and some in verse, usually employing a
highly poetic style. His pamphlets, many of them having a pious
flavor, deal especially with the lower classes and the plague. *The
Gull's Hornbook* is a prose satire glancing at theatrical audiences.
Most of his plays were written in collaboration. Despite his genius,
he was always something of a hack writer; he shifted his style
to accord with more successful, but not always more gifted,
playwrights.

Old Fortunatus, 1599, pub. 1600.
The Shoemaker's Holiday, 1599, pub. 1600.

DEKKER (*Continued*)
   Patient Grissell (with Chettle and Haughton), 1600, pub.
      1603.
   Satiromastix (with Marston), 1601, pub. 1602.
   Sir Thomas Wyatt (with Webster), 1602, pub. 1607.
   The Honest Whore (with Middleton), Part I, 1604, pub.
      1604; Part II, 1605, pub. 1630.
   Westward Ho! (with Webster), 1604, pub. 1607.
   Northward Ho! (with Webster), 1605, pub. 1607.
   The Whore of Babylon, c.1606, pub. 1607.
   The Roaring Girl (with Middleton), c.1610, pub. 1611.
   If It Be Not Good, the Devil Is in It, c.1611, pub. 1612.
   Match Me in London, c.1613, pub. 1631.
   The Virgin Martyr (with Massinger), c.1620, pub. 1622.
   The Witch of Edmonton (with Ford and Rowley), c.1623,
      pub. 1658.
   The Wonder of a Kingdom (with Day), 1623, pub. 1636.
   The Sun's Darling (with Ford), 1624, pub. 1656.
   The Noble Soldier (with Day and Samuel Rowley), c.1631,
      pub. 1634.
Hunt, M. L., Thomas Dekker, 1911.
Shepherd, R. H., ed., The Dramatic Works of Thomas Dek-
   ker, 1873.

FIELD, NATHAN (1587-1633)
   Field, the son of a celebrated preacher, was educated at Mulcaster's famous Merchant Taylors School. He acted as one of the
Children of the Queen's Revels in Jonson's *Cynthia's Revels* in
1600. On maturity he became one of the most successful actors
of his day. He was a friend and admirer of Jonson. His own
plays show him to have had a fund of sentiment, a liking for witty
dialogue, and a snatch of Jonson's intellectualism. They deal in
a traditional vein with the character of women. His later work as
a collaborator, though possibly extensive, is hard to trace. It includes *The Fatal Dowry*, written with Massinger (1632).
   A Woman Is a Weathercock, 1609, pub. 1612.
   Amends for Ladies, 1611, pub. 1618.

Brinkley, R. F., Nathan Field, the Actor Playwright, 1928.
Verity, A. W., ed., Nero and Other Plays, Mermaid Series, 1888.

FLETCHER, JOHN, see under Beaumont, Francis

FORD, JOHN (1586-c.1640)
Derived from a prominent family in Devon, Ford was engaged in law studies in 1602. An affected and introverted character, throughout his life he was fascinated by ideas of a decadent chivalry, as appears in his early work, *Honor Triumphant*, or *The Peers' Challenge* (1606). He came much under the influence of Burton's *Anatomy of Melancholy*. His powerful imagination getting the better of his unfortunate temperament, he attained considerable scope in tragedy, but he had small ability in comedy. He collaborated with Dekker, Middleton, and others and may possibly have written an anonymous play, *The Queene* (pub. 1653).

The Lover's Melancholy, 1628, pub. 1629.
'Tis Pity She's a Whore, c.1628, pub. 1633.
The Broken Heart, c.1629, pub. 1633.
Love's Sacrifice, 1630, pub. 1633.
The Chronicle History of Perkin Warbeck, c.1633, pub. 1634.
The Fancies Chaste and Noble, c.1635, pub. 1638.
The Lady's Trial, 1638, pub. 1639.
Sargeaunt, M. J., John Ford, 1935.
Vocht, Henri de, ed., John Ford's Dramatic Works, 1927.

GREENE, ROBERT (1558-92)
Born in Norwich, 1558, Greene took an M. A. at Cambridge before 1583 and a degree at Oxford five years later. Autobiographical references in many of his prose works, whatever falsifications they may contain, are doubtless adequate to prove that he married, deserted his wife and child, and lived a makeshift life in London. He adapted many romances from French, Italian, and classical sources. His most eloquent story is *Menaphon*, interspersed with lyric poetry. In the last two years of his brief career he wrote his notorious conycatching pamphlets on Elizabethan

GREENE (*Continued*)

cheats and his own confessions, as *Never Too Late*, *Greene's Mourning Garment*, *Greene's Farewell to Folly*, and *Greene's Groats-Worth of Wit Bought with a Million of Repentance*. In the last of these he renounced poetry and denounced the poets, including Shakespeare. His plays are among the most charming of pre-Shakespearean romances.

>   Alphonsus, King of Aragon, c.1587, pub. 1599.
>   Friar Bacon and Friar Bungay, c.1589, pub. 1594.
>   A Looking Glass for London and England (with Lodge), c.1590, pub. 1594.
>   James the Fourth, c.1591, pub. 1598.
>   Orlando Furioso, c.1591, pub. 1594.
>   Collins, J. C., ed., The Plays and Poems of Robert Greene, 1905.
>   Dickinson, T. H., ed., The plays of Robert Greene, Mermaid Series, 1909.
>   Jordan, J. C., Robert Greene, 1915.

GREVILLE, FULKE, LORD BROOKE (1554-1628)

A schoolmate of Sir Philip Sidney, Greville was early attached to him. The two exchanged views on life and literature, and Greville wrote a memoir of Sidney c.1610. Although a successful courtier under Elizabeth, James, and Charles, he regarded this friendship at the chief glory of his life. He studied at Jesus College, Cambridge. His highly reflective and idealistic mind appears in his sonnets and verse essays, as well as in his neoclassical plays, which are likewise substantially essays on politics and morals. He owed much to Spenser as well as to Sidney.

>   Alaham, c.1600, pub. 1633.
>   Mustapha, c.1605, pub. 1609.
>   Grosart, A. B., ed., The Works in Verse and Prose Complete of the Lord Brooke, 1870.

HAUGHTON, WILLIAM (c.1575-1605)

Little is known of this playwright's life, but, like others with whom he collaborated, he was at times impecunious, since he went to prison for debt in 1600. He was associated with Day, Chettle, Dekker, and Rowley. Only one play entirely his own survives.

Englishmen for My Money, 1598, pub. 1616.

Greg, W. W., ed., Englishmen for My Money, Malone Society Reprints, 1912.

HEYWOOD, THOMAS (c.1574-1641)

The most bourgeois of all the successful playwrights of the time, Heywood enjoyed a long career, more remarkable for industry than for consistency or genius. He wrote massive and naïve compilations on diverse themes, as mythology, good women, and the angels. He translated writings by Erasmus, Ovid, Lucian, and Sallust. A volume entitled *Lives of All the Poets* is most unhappily lost. In 1633, after a career of over forty years as a dramatist, he stated that he had written the whole or greater part of two hundred and twenty plays. He wrote pageants for the city of London and an *Apology for Actors*. Among his notable qualities are tenderness, fancy, and occasionally a remarkable fidelity to daily life.

The Four Prentices of London, c.1592, pub. 1615.

King Edward the Fourth, 1599, pub. 1599.

How a Man May Choose a Good Wife from a Bad, 1602, pub. 1602.

The Royal King and the Loyal Subject, c.1602, pub. 1637.

A Woman Killed with Kindness, 1603, pub. 1607.

The Wise-Woman of Hogsdon, c.1604, pub. 1638.

If You Know Not Me, You Know Nobody, 1605; Part I, pub. 1605, Part II, pub. 1606.

The Rape of Lucrece, c.1606, pub. 1608.

Fortune by Land and Sea (with Rowley), c.1609, pub. 1655.

The Golden Age, 1610, pub. 1611.

The Silver Age, 1610, pub. 1613.

The Brazen Age, 1610, pub. 1613.

The Iron Age, 1610, pub. 1632.

The Captives, 1624, pub. 1921 from MS.

The English Traveller, c.1624, pub. 1633.

HEYWOOD (*Continued*)

The Fair Maid of the West, 1631, pub. 1631.

A Maidenhead Well Lost, 1632, pub. 1634.

A Challenge for Beauty, c.1634, pub. 1636.

The Late Lancashire Witches (with Brome), 1634, pub. 1634.

Love's Mistress, 1634, pub. 1636.

Clark, A. M., Thomas Heywood, Playwright and Miscellanist, 1931.

Heywood, Thomas, The Dramatic Works, Pearson's reprint, 1874.

JONSON, BENJAMIN (1572-1637)

Jonson was born in Westminster after the death of his father, who was a minister of Scottish extraction. His stepfather was a bricklayer. He became an actor and a playwright on or before 1597. In 1598 he killed Gabriel Spencer, a fellow actor, in a duel. Twice he encountered serious difficulties with the dramatic censorship. From the accession of James he achieved great success as a writer of masques for the Court. The leading spokesman for the neoclassical culture that was rapidly winning its way in England and a man of great learning and personal force, he won innumerable friends and admirers and made several enemies. He seems to have known virtually all the leaders in the public, intellectual, and artistic life of London. In 1619 he visited the poet Drummond in Scotland, whose notes on their conversations are of high interest. Besides his plays he wrote poems chiefly imitative of the Latin classics, a commonplace book, *Discoveries*, several translations, and an English grammar. A man of amazing power and breadth, he became the greatest realist among English dramatists. His reputation, which declined during the romantic period, is now probably on the ascent.

The Case Is Altered (possibly with an unknown collaborator), 1597, pub. 1609.

Every Man in His Humour, 1598, pub. 1601.

Every Man Out of His Humour, 1599, pub. 1600.

Cynthia's Revels, 1600, pub. 1601.

The Poetaster, 1601, pub. 1602.

Sejanus, 1603, pub. 1605.

Volpone, 1606, pub. 1607.

Epicoene, 1609, pub. 1612.

The Alchemist, 1610, pub. 1612.

Catiline, 1611, pub. 1611.

Bartholomew Fair, 1614, pub. 1631.

The Devil Is an Ass, 1616, pub. 1631.

The Staple of News, 1625, pub. 1631.

The New Inn, 1629, pub. 1631.

The Magnetic Lady, 1631-32, pub. 1640.

The Tale of a Tub, 1634 (first version c.1597), pub. 1640.

The Sad Shepherd (unfinished), pub. 1641.

Dunn, E. C., The Art of Ben Jonson, 1925.

Herford, C. H., and P. Simpson, eds., Ben Jonson (standard edition), 1925-38.

Knights, L. C., Drama and Society in the Age of Jonson, 1937.

Noyes, R. G., Ben Jonson on the English Stage 1660-1776, 1935.

Smith, G. Gregory, Ben Jonson, 1919.

Swinburne, A. C., A Study of Ben Jonson, 1889.

Symonds, J. A., Ben Jonson, 1886.

Tannenbaum, S. A., Ben Jonson, a Concise Bibliography, 1938.

KYD, THOMAS (1558-94)

The son of a London scrivener, whose profession he apparently entered, Kyd attended the Merchant Taylors School. He is generally thought to have written a lost play on Hamlet. Among his translations is an English version of Garnier's tragedy, *Cornélie*. He was arrested in 1593 on charges of a political nature. At the same time he denied any complicity in the atheistic views of which his friend Marlowe had been accused. Broken in health, he died intestate the following year. Devoted to the neo-Senecan school of play-writing, he nevertheless took a leading hand in shaping the course of popular English tragedy.

KYD (*Continued*)

The Spanish Tragedy, c.1589, pub. 1594.

Soliman and Perseda (questionably his), c.1590, pub. 1599.

Boas, F. S., ed., The Works of Thomas Kyd, 1901.

LODGE, THOMAS (c.1557-1625)

Lodge, the son of a lord mayor of London, lived an active and adventurous life, his dramatic work being a minor episode. He was educated at the Merchant Taylors School, Oxford, and Lincoln's Inn. As a writer he defended the cause of the actors against the moralists and wrote charming lyrics, Ovidian poetry, satires, and prose romances. Among his novels is *Rosalind, Euphues' Golden Legacy*, the story dramatized by Shakespeare in *As You Like It*. After making several long voyages, he studied medicine at Avignon, practicing at Oxford and in Flanders. On his professing Catholicism, he was forced to leave England, but permitted to return in 1610. He collaborated with Greene in *A Looking Glass for London and England* and probably had a hand in other romantic plays, but his only extant work compromises between classical and English traditions.

The Wounds of Civil War, c.1588, pub. 1594.

Paradise, N. B., Thomas Lodge, the History of an Elizabethan, 1931.

Tenney, E. A., Thomas Lodge, 1935.

Wilson, J. D., ed., The Wounds of Civil War, Malone Society Reprints, 1910.

LYLY, JOHN (c.1554-1606)

This facetious moralist was grandson of William Lyly, a famous headmaster of Saint Paul's Grammar School. He was probably born in Canterbury. After taking his M. A. at Oxford in 1575, he came to London, began writing, and entered the service of the Earl of Oxford, but was unfortunate in securing preferment. He was a member of Parliament, 1589-1601. His most successful prose work is the elegant and didactic novel, *Euphues, the Anatomy of Wit* (1579). All his plays were written for the

child-actors and for Court performance. As a rule Ovidian in their
plot, they are no less elaborate in their style than commonplace in
their morality. Lyly had an immense influence on literary form
and a considerable effect in the development of drama.

Campaspe, 1584, pub. 1584.
Galathea, 1584, pub. 1591.
Sapho and Phao, 1584, pub. 1584.
Endymion, 1588, pub. 1591.
Love's Metamorphosis, c.1589, pub. 1601.
Midas, 1589, pub. 1592.
Mother Bombie, c.1589, pub. 1594.
The Woman in the Moon, c.1593, pub. 1597.
Bond, R. W., ed., The Complete Works of John Lyly, 1902.
Feuillerat, A., John Lyly, 1910.
Jeffery, V. M., John Lyly and the Italian Renaissance, 1928.
Wilson, J. D., John Lyly, 1905.

MARLOWE, CHRISTOPHER (1564-93)
The son of a shoemaker in Canterbury, he studied at the King's
School in that city and, through one of Archbishop Parker's
scholarship's, at Cambridge, taking his M. A. in 1587. His *Tamburlaine*, which brought new poetical life to the English stage,
appeared almost immediately thereafter. The leading role was
well adapted to the great actor, William Alleyn. Marlowe's nondramatic poems consist chiefly of translations together with his
brilliant *Hero and Leander*. He associated with a group of free-
thinkers which included Raleigh. Marlowe was under serious
charges of this nature when he was killed at a tavern at Deptford.
Evidence suggests a conspiracy against him. No greater calamity
has befallen the English drama.

Tamburlaine, c.1587, pub. 1590.
Doctor Faustus, c.1588, pub. 1604.
The Jew of Malta, c.1589, pub. 1633.
Edward the Second, c.1592, pub. 1594.
Dido Queen of Carthage (with Nash), c.1593, pub. 1594.
The Massacre at Paris, 1593, pub. n.d.

MARLOWE (*Continued*)

Bakeless, John, Christopher Marlowe, 1937.

Boas, F. S., Marlowe and His Circle, a Biographical Survey, 1929.

Case, R. H., ed., The Works and Life of Christopher Marlowe, 1930-33.

Ellis-Fermor, U. M., Christopher Marlowe, 1927.

Henderson, Philip, And Morning in His Eyes, a Book about Marlowe, 1937.

Tannenbaum, S. A., The Assassination of Christopher Marlowe, 1928.

———— Christopher Marlowe, a Concise Bibliography, 1937.

MARSTON, JOHN (1576-1634)

The son of a Shropshire lawyer and an Italian mother, he strikingly exhibited the influence of Italian on English and Puritan thought. On graduating from Oxford he proceeded with law studies in the Middle Temple. The satirical flavor found in all his work appears strongly in his first two volumes, *The Metamorphosis of Pygmalion's Image and Certain Satires* (1598) and *The Scourge of Villainy* (1598). Several of his plays bear evidence of his relations with Jonson, to whom he was alternately friendly and hostile. Many were written for the children's companies. He left play-writing about 1608, entered holy orders, and in 1616 held the living of the magnificent church at Christchurch, Hampshire. His wife was daughter of a minister. Jonson maliciously observed: "Marston wrote his father-in-law's preachings, and his father-in-law his comedies."

Antonio and Mellida, 1599, pub. 1602.

What You Will, 1601, pub. 1607.

The Dutch Courtezan, 1603, pub. 1605.

The Malcontent (enlarged by Webster), 1604, pub. 1604.

Parasitaster, or The Fawn, c.1605, pub. 1606.

Sophonisba, 1606, pub. 1606.

The Insatiate Countess (with William Barksteed), c.1610, pub. 1613.

Bullen, A. H., ed., The Works of John Marston, 1887.

Wood, H. H., ed., The Plays of John Marston, 1934-38.

MASSINGER, PHILIP (1583-1640)

Massinger was born at Salisbury, the son of a highly valued retainer in the household of the Earl of Pembroke. He studied at Oxford, but without graduating went to London, where he seems to have supported himself somewhat precariously as a dramatist. A few of his works have led some biographers to suppose him to have been a Roman Catholic, although the evidence is not conclusive. Whatever his religion, his plays indisputably show a liberal prejudice politically. He collaborated with many playwrights, especially Fletcher, after whose death he became the leader in the Cavalier drama. His original plays are usually more marked by eloquence and idealism than by sprightliness or humor. He is especially admirable as a dramatic romancer and storyteller.

The Duke of Milan, c.1618, pub. 1623.

The Unnatural Combat, c.1619, pub. 1639.

The Maid of Honour, c.1621, pub. 1632.

The Bondman, 1623, pub. 1624.

The Parliament of Love, 1624, pub. 1805.

The Renegado, 1624, pub. 1630.

A New Way to Pay Old Debts, c.1625, pub. 1633.

The Roman Actor, 1626, pub. 1629.

The Great Duke of Florence, 1627, pub. 1636.

The Picture, 1629, pub. 1630.

The Fatal Dowry (with Field), c.1630, pub. 1632.

Believe as You List, 1631, pub. 1848.

The Emperor of the East, 1631, pub. 1632.

The City Madam, 1632, pub. 1658.

The Guardian, 1633, pub. 1655.

The Bashful Lover, 1636, pub. 1655.

Cruickshank, A. H., Philip Massinger, 1920.

Cunningham, Francis, ed., The Plays of Philip Massinger, 1870.

Tannenbaum, S. A., Philip Massinger, a Concise Bibliography, 1938.

MIDDLETON, THOMAS (1580-1627)

Middleton was born in London, went to Oxford, and later probably studied law in London. His first book was *The Wisdom of Solomon Paraphrased* (1597). He began play-writing about 1600, supplementing this activity by composing pageants for the city. He was appointed city chronologer in 1620. After writing many racy and realistic comedies, some in collaboration with Dekker, about 1616 he began collaborating in more serious plays with William Rowley. His bold political satire, *A Game at Chess*, brought him and its actors into trouble. His pithy and satirical style won him a conspicuous place among the playwrights.

The Old Law (later revised by Massinger), 1599(?), pub. 1656.

Blurt Master Constable (doubtfully Middleton's), 1601, pub. 1602.

The Phoenix, c.1603, pub. 1607.

The Family of Love, c.1606, pub. 1608.

A Mad World My Masters, c.1606, pub. 1608.

Michaelmas Term, c.1606, pub. 1607.

A Trick to Catch the Old One, c.1606, pub. 1608.

Your Five Gallants, c.1607, pub. 1608.

A Chaste Maid in Cheapside, c.1612, pub. 1630.

No Wit, No Help Like a Woman's, c.1613, pub. 1657.

A Fair Quarrel (with Rowley), 1616, pub. 1617.

The Widow (with Fletcher and others), c.1616, pub. 1652.

The Witch, c.1617, pub. 1778.

Hengist, King of Kent (known also as The Mayor of Quinborough), c.1618, pub. 1661.

Anything for a Quiet Life (possibly with Webster), c.1621, pub. 1662.

More Dissemblers besides Women, c.1621, pub. 1657.

The Changeling (with Rowley), c.1623, pub. 1653.

The Spanish Gipsy (with Ford and Rowley), 1623, pub. 1653.

Women Beware Women, c.1623, pub. 1657.

A Game at Chess, 1624, pub. 1625.

Bullen, A. H., ed., The Works of Thomas Middleton, 1885.

MUNDAY, ANTHONY (c.1553-1633)

The son of a London draper, Munday was apprenticed to a stationer, but turned early in life to slightly more original literary activity, supporting himself also as an actor and a pursuivant. He devised many city pageants. That he sought popularity with the city appears in all his works as well as in the designation of himself on his title pages: "Citizen and Draper of London." He engaged in Protestant propaganda, composed ballads, translated romances, collaborated with the plebeian school of playwrights, and wrote several patriotic chronicle-history plays, all of which activities made him the butt of Jonson and the more educated of the dramatists.

John a Kent and John a Cumber, 1594.

The Death of Robert, Earl of Huntingdon (with Chettle), 1598, pub. 1601.

The Downfall of Robert, Earl of Huntingdon, 1598, pub. 1601.

Sir John Oldcastle (with Drayton, Hathaway, and Wilson), 1599, pub. 1600.

Brooke, C. F. Tucker, ed., Sir John Oldcastle, in The Shakespeare Apocrypha, 1908.

———— John a Kent and John a Cumber, Students' Facsimile Edition (of MS), 1914.

Farmer, J. S., ed., The Death of Robert, Earl of Huntingdon, Students' Facsimile Edition, 1913.

———— The Downfall of Robert, Earl of Huntingdon, Students' Facsimile Edition, 1913

Turner, J. C., Anthony Munday, an Elizabethan Man of Letters, 1928.

NASH, THOMAS (1567-c.1600)

Nash was the son of a minister in Suffolk. He studied at Cambridge, (1582-88), and traveled briefly on the Continent. On coming to London he wrote some of the most imaginative books of the period in a series of prose satires, religious tracts, essays, and fantasies. He was one of the scholarly group of authors, collaborating with Marlowe and Jonson. His notorious literary quarrel

NASH (*Continued*)

with the pedantic Gabriel Harvey was silenced by the censor. His best-known work is the picaresque novel, *Jack Wilton, or The Unfortunate Traveller*. Although he composed several plays, including the lost *Isle of Dogs*, for which he was imprisoned in 1597, his only unaided extant work for the stage is a fanciful compromise between drama, morality play, and masque.

Summer's Last Will and Testament, 1592, pub. 1600.

McKerrow, R. B., ed., The Works of Thomas Nash, 1904-10.

PEELE, GEORGE (c.1557-1596)

George Peele was born in London, the son of James Peele, a writer of pageants in the medieval tradition. He went to grammar school in Christ's Hospital, of which his father was clerk, and thence to Oxford. In London he acquired the reputation of being a free liver, a wit, and a scholar. It is chiefly his wit which is celebrated in *The Merry Conceited Jests of George Peele* (1605). He wrote elegantly for the Court, at times without literary conscience for the popular theatre but frequently with true fancy and lyrical afflatus. Marlowe's sudden success was instrumental in determining much of his dramatic style.

The Arraignment of Paris, c.1584, pub. 1584.

The Battle of Alcazar, c.1589, pub. 1594.

Edward the First, c.1591, pub. 1593.

David and Bethsabe, c.1593, pub. 1599.

The Old Wives Tale, c.1593, pub. 1595.

Bullen, A. H., ed., The Works of George Peele, 1888.

PORTER, HENRY

Nothing whatever is known of Porter's personal life, although it is a conjecture that he was a musician. He wrote several plays for Henslowe's company between 1596 and 1599, no doubt intended to satisfy the more popular taste. His only extant work justifies the view of Meres in his *Palladis Tamia*, that he was one of "the best for comedy amongst us."

The Two Angrey Women of Abingdon, c.1598, pub. 1599.

Greg, W. W., ed., The Two Angrey Women of Abingdon, Malone Society Reprints, 1912.

RANDOLPH, THOMAS (1605-35)

Randolph went to Westminster School and Trinity College, Cambridge. At the age of twenty he became acquainted with Ben Jonson, who recognized him as a young man of much wit and learning. A warm friendship immediately sprang up. Randolph wrote charming and familiar verse and some highly convivial and witty comedy. His masterpiece, however, is his pastoral drama, *Amyntas*. No writer for the stage better exhibited the lighter phase of the Cavalier spirit. His authorship of *Hey for Honesty* (pub. 1651) is conjectural.

Aristippus, or The Jovial Philosopher, 1629, pub. 1630.
Amyntas, 1632, pub. 1638.
The Jealous Lovers, 1632, pub. 1632.
The Muses' Looking Glass, 1632, pub. 1638.
Hazlitt, W. C., ed., Poetical and Dramatic Works of Thomas Randolph, 1875.
Smith, G. C. M., Thomas Randolph, 1927.

SHAKESPEARE, WILLIAM (1564-1616)

Nothing within our knowledge of Shakespeare's personal life distinguishes him from the greater number of his fellow playwrights whom he so far surpasses in art. Like Marlowe and Munday he sprang from middle-class stock, like Dekker and Kyd he was denied a university education, like Nash and Greene he came to London from the country, like Marston and Tourneur he wrote poems as well as plays, like Chapman and Massinger he enjoyed some noble patronage, and like his fellow actors, Alleyn and Burbage, he acquired a considerable fortune. During his childhood and younger manhood he lived in the once quiet town of Stratford; most of his active life he spent as a prominent partner of the leading theatrical company in London; while his last four or five years he passed chiefly away from the literary world again in the town of his birth. Romantic criticism has sometimes obscured the light in which he appeared to his contemporaries. He seems to have been personally affable and well liked. His plays were the most popular of the times, and his genius was rather quietly recognized, although the neoclassical standards dominant

SHAKESPEARE (*Continued*)

in the upper-class world and best represented in criticism by Ben Jonson often deprived him of unqualified praise. So Webster in the prefatory epistle to his *White Devil* (1612) eulogizes most highly the work of playwrights learned in the classics and fond of imitating them, as Chapman, Jonson, and Beaumont and Fletcher, while he commends for "right happy and copious industry," almost with equal praise, Shakespeare, Dekker, and Heywood, representatives of an avowedly native school of the drama. These three names are given in exactly the order in which we should arrange them today. Shakespeare was the acknowledged leader in the popular, Jonson in the neoclassical, school of the theatre.

The following conjectural chronology of Shakespeare's plays is taken from the most exhaustive of recent biographies, that by E. K. Chambers. This scholar gives a slightly different chronology in his *Elizabethan Stage*, which preceded his *William Shakespeare* by seven years. Progress in this field has probably been made during the last decade, but complete accuracy is obviously impossible.

2 Henry the Sixth, 1590-91, pub. 1623.

3 Henry the Sixth, 1590-91, pub. 1623.

1 Henry the Sixth, 1591-92, pub. 1623.

The Comedy of Errors, 1592-93, pub. 1623.

Richard the Third, 1592-93, pub. 1597.

The Taming of the Shrew (based on The Taming of a Shrew), 1593-94, pub. 1623.

Titus Andronicus, 1593-94, pub. 1594.

Love's Labour's Lost, 1594-95, pub. 1598.

Romeo and Juliet, 1594-95, pub. 1597.

The Two Gentlemen of Verona, 1594-95, pub. 1623.

A Midsummer-Night's Dream, 1595-96, pub. 1600.

Richard the Second, 1595-96, pub. 1597.

King John, 1596-97, pub. 1623.

The Merchant of Venice, 1596-97, pub. 1600.

1 Henry the Fourth, 1597-98, pub. 1598.

2 Henry the Fourth, 1597-98, pub. 1600.

Henry the Fifth, 1598-99, pub. 1600.

Much Ado about Nothing, 1598-99, pub. 1600.

As You Like It, 1599-1600, pub. 1623.

Julius Caesar, 1599-1600, pub. 1623.

Twelfth Night, 1599-1600, pub. 1623.

Hamlet, 1600-1601, pub. 1603.

The Merry Wives of Windsor, 1600-1601, pub. 1602.

Troilus and Cressida, 1601-2, pub. 1609.

All's Well That Ends Well, 1602-3, pub. 1623.

Measure for Measure, 1604-5, pub. 1623.

Othello, 1604-5, pub. 1622.

King Lear, 1605-6, pub. 1608.

Macbeth, 1605-6, pub. 1623.

Antony and Cleopatra, 1606-7, pub. 1623.

Coriolanus, 1607-8, pub. 1623.

Timon of Athens, 1607-8, pub. 1623.

Pericles (with a collaborator, possibly Wilkins), 1608-9, pub. 1608.

Cymbeline, 1609-10, pub. 1623.

The Winter's Tale, 1610-11, pub. 1623.

The Tempest, 1611-12, pub. 1623.

Henry the Eighth (with Fletcher), 1612-13, pub. 1623.

The most useful edition for careful study is the *Arden Shakespeare* (1899-1924) under the general editorship of W. J. Craig and R. H. Case, giving a volume to a play. Facsimiles of the First Folio (1623) and the quartos should be consulted. The *Tudor Shakespeare* in small single volumes is convenient. A good collection of the plays in one volume is that edited by G. L. Kittredge (1936). No attempt will be made here to deal with the vast number of good editions or valuable commentaries. A collection of Shakespeare's sources is to be found in W. C. Hazlitt's *Shakespeare's Library* (1875). Samuel Johnson's Preface to his *Shakespeare* remains probably the finest critical essay. A brief list of some of the more recent books on Shakespeare follows:

Adams, J. Q., A Life of Shakespeare, 1923.

Anders, H. R., Shakespeare's Books, 1904.

Anderson, R. L., Elizabethan Psychology and Shakespeare's Plays, 1927.

Babcock, R. W., The Genesis of Shakespearean Idolatry, 1931.

SHAKESPEARE (*Continued*)

Bartlett, John, A New Complete Concordance to the Dramatic Works of Shakespeare, 1894.

Black, M. W., and M. A. Shaaber, Shakespeare's Seventeenth-Century Editors, 1937.

Boas, F. S., Shakespeare and the Universities, 1923.

Bradby, Anne, ed., Shakespearean Criticism 1915-1935, 1936.

Bradley, A. C., Shakespearean Tragedy, 1926.

British Academy, Aspects of Shakespeare, Being (9) British Academy Lectures, 1933. (Subsequent lectures may be consulted separately.)

Campbell, L. B., Shakespeare's Tragic Heroes, Slaves of Passion, 1930.

Campbell, O. J., Comical Satyre and Shakespeare's Troilus and Cressida, 1938.

Chambers, E. K., William Shakespeare, 1930.

Charlton, H. B., Shakespearean Comedy, 1938.

Croce, Benedetto, Ariosto, Shakespeare, and Corneille, 1920.

David, Richard, The Janus of the Poets, 1934.

Fripp, E. I., Shakespeare, Man and Artist, 1938.

Gollancz, Israel, ed., A Book of Homage to Shakespeare, 1916.

Granville-Barker, H., Prefaces to Shakespeare, 1927-37.

——— and G. B. Harrison, A Companion to Shakespeare Studies, 1934.

Green, Henry, Shakespeare and the Emblem Writers, 1870.

Kellner, Leon, Restoring Shakespeare, a Critical Analysis of the Misreadings in Shakespeare's Works, 1925.

Knight, G. W., The Imperial Theme, 1931.

——— Principles of Shakespearian Production, 1936.

——— The Wheel of Fire, 1930.

Lamborn, E. A. G., and G. B. Harrison, Shakespeare, the Man and His Stage, 1923.

Lawrence, W. W., Shakespeare's Problem Comedies, 1931.

Lee, Sidney, Shakespeare and the Modern Stage, 1906.

Lewis, Wyndham, The Lion and the Fox, 1927.

MacCallum, M. W., Shakespeare's Roman Plays and Their Background, 1910.

Mackail, J. W., The Approach to Shakespeare, 1930.

Menon, C. N., Shakespeare Criticism, 1938.

Murray, J. M., Shakespeare, 1936.

Naylor, E. W., Shakespeare and Music, 1931.

Nicoll, Allardyce, Studies in Shakespeare, 1928.

Odell, G. C. D., Shakespeare from Betterton to Irving, 1920.

Onions, C. T., A Shakespeare Glossary, 1911.

Pollard, A. W., Shakespeare's Folios and Quartos, 1909.

Quiller-Couch, A. T., Shakespeare's Workmanship, 1919.

Raleigh, Walter, Shakespeare, 1911.

Ralli, Augustus, A History of Shakespearean Criticism, 1932.

Raysor, T. M., ed., Coleridge's Shakespearean Criticism, 1930.

Rylands, G. H. W., Words and Poetry, 1928.

Schücking, L. L., Character Problems in Shakespeare's Plays, 1922.

Smith, D. Nichol, Shakespeare Criticism, a Selection, 1916.

—————— Shakespeare in the Eighteenth Century, 1928.

Spencer, Hazleton, Shakespeare Improved, 1927.

Spurgeon, C. F., Shakespeare's Imagery and What It Tells Us, 1934.

Stoll, E. E., Art and Artifice in Shakespeare, 1933.

—————— Shakespeare Studies, Historical and Comparative in Method, 1927.

Thorndike, A. H., The Influence of Beaumont and Fletcher on Shakespeare, 1901.

Wilson, J. D., The Essential Shakespeare, 1932.

SHIRLEY, JAMES (1596-1666)

Shirley was born in London and studied at the famous Merchant Taylors School, at Oxford, and at Cambridge. He became an Anglican minister in 1619, but retired upon his conversion to the Church of Rome, becoming master of the grammar school at St. Albans. About 1625 he gave up teaching for play-writing. He was fortunate at Court, earned the approval of Charles, and wrote an impressive masque, *The Triumph of Peace* (1634). For about four years (1637-40) he wrote for the theatre at Dublin. His many smoothly written plays are pleasant but unin-

SHIRLEY (*Continued*)

spired, showing the transition in taste from the age of Shakespeare to that of Dryden. Although recapitulating old characters and plots, they are conceived in a new spirit.

Love Tricks, 1625, pub. 1631.

The Brothers, 1626, pub. 1652.

The Maid's Revenge, 1626, pub. 1639.

The Wedding, 1626, pub. 1629.

The Witty Fair One, 1628, pub. 1633.

The Grateful Servant, 1629, pub. 1630.

Love's Cruelty, 1631, pub. 1640.

The Traitor, 1631, pub. 1635.

The Ball, 1632, pub. 1639.

The Changes, or Love in a Maze, 1632, pub. 1632.

Hyde Park, 1632, pub. 1637.

The Bird in a Cage, 1633, pub. 1633.

The Gamester, 1633, pub. 1637.

The Young Admiral, 1633, pub. 1637.

The Court Secret, not acted, pub. 1634.

The Example, 1634, pub. 1637.

The Opportunity, 1634, pub. 1640.

The Coronation, 1635, pub. 1640.

The Lady of Pleasure, 1635, pub. 1637.

The Duke's Mistress, 1636, pub. 1638.

The Constant Maid, c.1638, pub. 1640.

The Royal Master, 1638, pub. 1638.

The Arcadia (authorship questionable), c.1639, pub. 1640.

The Gentleman of Venice, 1639, pub. 1655.

The Humorous Courtier, c.1639, pub. 1640.

The Politician, 1639, pub. 1655.

St. Patrick for Ireland, c.1639, pub. 1640.

The Doubtful Heir, 1640, pub. 1652.

The Imposture, 1640, pub. 1652.

The Cardinal, 1641, pub. 1653.

The Sisters, 1642, pub. 1652.

Forsythe, R. S., The Relations of Shirley's Plays to the Elizabethan Drama, 1914.

Gifford, W., and A. Dyce, eds., Dramatic Works and Poems by James Shirley, 1833.

Nason, A. H., James Shirley, Dramatist, 1915.

SIDNEY, SIR PHILIP (1554-86)

Sidney's father was a leading statesman and lord deputy of Ireland. Sidney enjoyed the most intensive education which study at Oxford and travel abroad could afford, associating with Bruno, Languet, and many of the leading figures in Europe. Veronese painted his portrait. He was active in politics, boldly offering advice on state matters to Elizabeth. His death was caused by wounds received at the battle of Zutphen. As a thinker, writer, and all-accomplished gentleman he made a profound impression on his times. His *Defense of Poesie* expresses the prevailing views on literature and drama, his poems to Stella are among the finest of English lyrics, while his *Arcadia* is the chief of English pastoral romances. It supplied the story of Gloucester and his two sons in *King Lear*. Sidney's only dramatic work, like Milton's *Comus,* may be called either a masque or play.

The Lady of May, c.1579, pub. 1598.

Bill, A. H., Astrophel, 1937.

Myrick, K. O., Sir Philip Sidney as a Literary Craftsman, 1935.

Parks, E. W., and R. C. Beatty, eds., The Lady of May, in The English Drama, 1934.

Wilson, Mona, Sir Philip Sidney, 1932.

TOURNEUR, CYRIL (?-1626)

Little is known of his life or works. He appears to have been employed for several years in foreign service. His authorship of *The Revenger's Tragedy* has been questioned, but is perhaps no more dubious than the ascription of other Elizabethan plays less often challenged. Like Marston, whom he followed in other respects, he began his literary career with the production of a satire, *The Transformed Metamorphosis,* in 1600. The two plays commonly ascribed to him are examples of somber and satirical tragedy.

TOURNEUR (*Continued*)

The Revenger's Tragedy, c.1606, pub. 1607.

The Atheist's Tragedy, c.1609, pub. 1611.

Nicoll, Allardyce, The Works of Cyril Tourneur, 1930.

WEBSTER, JOHN

The dates of Webster's birth and death and all the data of his personal life are lost in conjecture. He is chiefly known as author of two tragedies carrying on the vein of philosophical melancholy prevalent from Kyd to Tourneur. He gives evidence of special regard for Chapman and for the type of classicism which Chapman represents. A serious writer of serious plays, he also wrote in the more popular romantic style and relaxed to some brisk but undistinguished comedy. His horizons were broadened by collaboration with Marston (q. v.) and Dekker (q. v.).

The White Devil, c.1610, pub. 1612.

The Duchess of Malfi, 1613, pub. 1623.

The Devil's Law Case, c.1620, pub. 1623.

Brooke, Rupert, John Webster and the Elizabethan Drama, 1916.

Lucas, F. L., ed., The Complete Works of John Webster, 1927.

WILKINS, GEORGE

Nothing is known of Wilkins' private life, although he wrote pamphlets and plays from about 1604 to 1608. Little of his dramatic writing seems to have been published, but he has been associated with the anonymous *Yorkshire Tragedy* and is usually held the author of the first two acts of Shakespeare's *Pericles*. The only extant play under his name is a typical instance of the dramatization of a contemporary crime.

The Miseries of Enforced Marriage, 1607, pub. 1607.

Farmer, J. S., ed., The Miseries of Enforced Marriage, Students' Facsimile Edition, 1913.

WILSON, ROBERT

There is little assurance as to Wilson's life or what works he wrote, but he appears to have produced plays from 1580 to 1590 on political topics in the medieval allegorical manner and popular romantic plays thereafter till about 1600.

> The Three Ladies of London, c.1581, pub. 1584.
> The Three Lords and Three Ladies of London, c.1589, pub. 1590.
> The Cobbler's Prophecy, c.1592, pub. 1594.
> Farmer, J. S., ed., The Three Ladies of London, Students' Facsimile Edition, 1911.
> ———— The Three Lords and Three Ladies of London, Students' Facsimile Edition, 1911.
> ———— The Cobbler's Prophecy, Students' Facsimile Edition, 1913.

YARINGTON, ROBERT
Yarington is mentioned only on the title page of his play, which betters Wilkins' *Miseries of Enforced Marriage* by dealing with two crimes, one contemporary, the other imaginary.

> Two Lamentable Tragedies, c.1597, pub. 1601.
> Farmer, J. S., ed., Two Lamentable Tragedies, Students' Facsimile Edition, 1913.

A Selective List of Anonymous Plays, 1576–1611

Alarum for London, An, pub. 1600 (W. W. Greg, ed., Malone Society Reprints, 1913).

Arden of Feversham, c.1590, pub. 1592 (in C. F. Tucker Brooke, ed., The Shakespeare Apocrypha, 1908).

Caesar's Revenge, c.1594, pub. 1607 (F. S. Boas, ed., Malone Society Reprints, 1911).

Cromwell, Thomas, Lord, c. 1600, pub. 1602 (in C. F. Tucker Brooke, ed., The Shakespeare Apocrypha, 1908).

Edward the Third, The Reign of King, c.1594, pub. 1596 (in C. F. Tucker Brooke, The Shakespeare Apocrypha, 1908).

Every Woman in Her Humour, c.1607, pub. 1609 (J. S. Farmer, ed., Students' Facsimile Edition, 1913).

Fair Em, c.1590, pub. 1631 (in C. F. Tucker Brooke, ed., The Shakespeare Apocrypha, 1908).

Fair Maid of the Exchange, The, c.1602, pub. 1607 (questionably included in editions of Thomas Heywood).

George a Greene, the Pinner of Wakefield, c.1592, pub. 1599 (F. W. Clarke, ed., Malone Society Reprints, 1911, and questionably included in editions of Robert Greene).

Goosecap, Sir Giles (plausibly ascribed to Chapman), 1602, pub. 1606 (J. S. Farmer, ed., 1912).

Grim the Collier of Croydon, 1600, pub. 1662 (J. S. Farmer, ed., Students' Facsimile Edition, 1913).

Henry the Fifth, The Famous Victories of, c.1586, pub. 1598 (J. S. Farmer, ed., Students' Facsimile Edition, 1913).

Histriomastix (a play revised in 1599 by Marston), 1589-99, pub. 1610 (J. S. Farmer, ed., Students' Facsimile Edition, 1912).

Jack Drum's Entertainment (partly by Marston), 1600, pub. 1601 (J. S. Farmer, ed., Students' Facsimile Edition, 1912).

Jack Straw, The Life and Death of, c.1592, pub. 1593 (J. S. Farmer, ed., Students' Facsimile Edition, 1911).

Jeronimo, The First Part of, c.1604, pub. 1605 (included in editions of Thomas Kyd).

John, The Troublesome Reign of King, c.1590, pub. 1591 (J. S. Farmer, ed., Students' Facsimile Edition, 1911).

Leire, c.1592, pub. 1605 (W. W. Greg, ed., Malone Society Reprints, 1907).

Locrine, c.1591, pub. 1595 (in C. F. Tucker Brooke, ed., The Shakespeare Apocrypha, 1908).

London Prodigal, The, c.1604, pub. 1605 (in C. F. Tucker Brooke, ed., The Shakespeare Apocrypha, 1908).

Look about You, c.1599, pub. 1600 (W. W. Greg, ed., Malone Society Reprints, 1913).

Love and Fortune, The Rare Triumphs of, c.1582, pub. 1589 (in Dodsley's Old Plays, 1874).

Maid's Metamorphosis, The (possibly by Day), 1600, pub. 1600 (J. S. Farmer, ed., Students' Facsimile Edition, 1912).

Merry Devil of Edmonton, The, c.1603, pub. 1608 (in C. F. Tucker Brooke, ed., The Shakespeare Apocrypha, 1908).

More, Sir Thomas, c.1596 (MS edited by C. F. Tucker Brooke in The Shakespeare Apocrypha, 1908).

Mucedorus, c.1596, pub. 1598 (in C. F. Tucker Brooke, ed., The Shakespeare Apocrypha, 1908).

Parnassus, The Pilgrimage to and Return from, c.1601 (MS edited by W. D. Macray, 1886).

Parnassus, The Return from, or The Scourge of Simony, c.1602, pub. 1606 (Oliphant Smeaton, ed., 1905).

Puritan, The (possibly by Middleton), 1606, pub. 1607 (in C. F. Tucker Brooke, ed., The Shakespeare Apocrypha, 1908).

1 Richard the Second, c.1593 (MS edited in Jahrbuch der deutschen Shakespeare-Gesellschaft, XXXV, 1899).

Richard the Third, The True Tragedy of, c.1593, pub. 1594 (in W. C. Hazlitt, ed., Shakespeare's Library, 1875).

Second Maiden's Tragedy, The, 1611 (MS edited by W. W. Greg, Malone Society Reprints, 1909).

Selimus, c.1592, pub. 1594 (W. Bang, ed., Malone Society Reprints, 1908).

Stukeley, Captain Thomas, 1596, pub. 1605 (J. S. Farmer, ed., Students' Facsimile Edition, 1911).

Taming of a Shrew, The, c.1589, pub. 1594 (F. S. Boas, ed., 1908).

Timon, c.1585 (MS edited by W. C. Hazlitt in Shakespeare's Library, 1875).

Trial of Chivalry, The, c.1600, pub. 1605 (J. S. Farmer, ed., Students' Facsimile Edition, 1912).

Warning for Fair Women, A, c.1598, pub. 1599 (J. S. Farmer, ed., Students' Facsimile Edition, 1913).

Wily Beguiled, c.1600, pub. 1606 (W. W. Greg, ed., Malone Society Reprints, 1912).

Wisdom of Doctor Dodypoll, The, c.1599, pub. 1600 (J. S. Farmer, ed., Students' Facsimile Edition, 1912).

Yorkshire Tragedy, A, c.1606, pub. 1608 (in C. F. Tucker Brooke, ed., The Shakespeare Apocrypha, 1908).

Books on the Drama

Archer, William, The Old Drama and the New, 1923.

Bateson, F. W., English Poetry and the English Language, 1934.

Boas, F. S., The University Drama in the Tudor Age, 1914.

Bradbrook, M. C., Themes and Conventions in Elizabethan Tragedy, 1935.

Cambridge History of English Literature, The, Vols. V-VI, 1910.

Chambers, E. K., The Elizabethan Stage, 1923.

—————— The Medieval Stage, 1903.

Clark, E. G., Elizabethan Fustian, 1937.

De la Bère, R., John Heywood, Entertainer, 1937.

Dunn, E. C., The Literature of Shakespeare's England, 1936.

Eliot, T. S., Elizabethan Essays, 1934.

Ellis-Fermor, U. M., The Jacobean Drama, 1935.

Farnham, Willard, The Medieval Heritage of Elizabethan Tragedy, 1936.

Greg, W. W., Pastoral Poetry and Pastoral Drama, 1906.

Harbage, Alfred, Cavalier Drama, 1936.

Motter, T. H. V., The School Drama in England, 1929.

Pearson, L. E., Elizabethan Love Conventions, 1933.

Reed, A. W., Early Tudor Drama, 1926.

Ristine, F. H., English Tragicomedy, Its Origin and History, 1910.

Schelling, F. E., The Elizabethan Drama 1558-1642, 1908.

—————— The English Chronicle Play, 1902.

—————— English Literature during the Lifetime of Shakespeare, 1928.

Smith, G. G., Elizabethan Critical Essays, 1937.

Spencer, Theodore, Death and Elizabethan Tragedy, 1936.

Sykes, H. D., Sidelights on Elizabethan Drama, 1924.

Symons, Arthur, Studies in the Elizabethan Drama, 1919.

Thorpe, Willard, The Triumph of Realism in Elizabethan Drama, 1928.

Ward, A. W., A History of English Dramatic Literature to the Death of Queen Anne, 1875-99.

Wells, H. W., Poetic Imagery, Illustrated from Elizabethan Literature, 1924.

White, H. O., Plagiarism and Imitation during the English Renaissance, 1935.

Books on the Historical Background

Black, J. B., The Reign of Elizabeth, 1936.

Burton, R., The Anatomy of Melancholy, F. Dell and P. J. Smith, eds., 1927.

Byrne, M. St. C., English Life in Town and Country, 1934.

Cheyney, E. P., A History of England from the Defeat of the Armada to the Death of Elizabeth, 1926.

Craig, Hardin, The Enchanted Glass, the Elizabethan Mind in Literature, 1936.

Creighton, Mandell, Queen Elizabeth, 1920.

Davis, W. S., Life in Elizabethan Days, 1930.

Fellowes, E. H., William Byrd, 1936.

Holinshed, R., Holinshed's Chronicle as Used in Shakespeare's Plays, A. and J. Nicoll, eds., 1927.

Judges, A. V., The Elizabethan Underworld, 1930.

Kelso, Ruth, The Doctrine of the English Gentleman in the Sixteenth Century, 1929.

Linthicum, M. C., Costume in the Drama of Shakespeare and His Contemporaries, 1936.

Mulcaster, Richard, Elementarie, E. T. Campagnac, ed., 1925.

Palmer, R. L., English Social History in the Making, the Tudor Revolution, 1934.

Raleigh, Walter, ed., Shakespeare's England, 1916.

Read, Conyers, The Tudors, Personalities and Practical Politics in Sixteenth Century England, 1936.

Salzman, L. F., England in Tudor Times, 1926.

Stow, John, A Survey of London, C. L. Kingsford, ed., 1908.

Wright, L. B., Middle-Class Culture in Elizabethan England, 1935.

Books on the Renaissance

Crane, T. F., Italian Social Customs of the Sixteenth Century and Their Influence on the Literature of Europe, 1920.

Crane, W. J., Wit and Rhetoric in the Renaissance, 1937.

Cunliffe, L. W., The Influence of Seneca on Elizabethan Tragedy, 1893.

Einstein, Lewis, The Italian Renaissance in England, 1927.

Fletcher, J. B., Literature of the Italian Renaissance, 1934.

Herford, C. H., The Literary Relations of England and Germany in the Sixteenth Century, 1886.

Lathrop, H. B., Translations from the Classics into English 1477-1620, 1933.

Lea, K. M., Italian Popular Comedy, a Study in the Commedia dell'Arte, 1560-1620, with Special Reference to the English Stage, 1934.

Lee, Sidney, The French Renaissance in England, 1910.

Matthiessen, F. O., Translation, an Elizabethan Art, 1931.

Painter, William, The Palace of Pleasure, H. Miles, ed., 1930.

Praz, Mario, Machiavelli and the Elizabethans, 1928.

Pulver, Jeffrey, Machiavelli, the Man, His Work, and His Times, 1937.

Rigal, E., Le Théâtre au XVII° siècle avant Corneille, in L. Petit de Julleville, ed., Histoire de la langue et de la littérature française, 1897.

——— Le Théâtre de la Renaissance, in L. Petit de Julleville, ed., Histoire de la langue et de la littérature française, 1897.

Scott, M. A., Elizabethan Translations from the Italian, 1916.

Underhill, J. G., Spanish Literature in the England of the Tudors, 1899.

Books on the Theatre

Adams, J. Q., Shakespeare's Playhouses, 1917.

Baldwin, T. W., The Organization and Personnel of the Shakespearean Company, 1927.

Campbell, L. B., Scenes and Machines on the Elizabethan Stage during the Renaissance, 1923.

Freeburg, V. O., Disguise Plots in Elizabethan Drama, 1915.

Green, A. W., The Inns of Court and the Early English Drama, 1931.

Greg, W. W., Dramatic Documents from the Elizabethan Playhouses, 1931.

Lawrence, W. J., The Physical Condition of the Elizabethan Public Playhouse, 1927.

Nicoll, Allardyce, Masques, Mimes, and Miracles, 1931.

Nungezer, E., A Dictionary of Actors and Other Persons Associated with the Public Representation of Plays in England before 1642, 1929.

Sharpe, R. B., The Real War of the Theatres, 1935.

Sprague, A. C., Shakespeare and the Audience, a Study in the Technique of Exposition, 1935.

Steele, M. S., Plays and Masques at Court during the Reigns of Elizabeth, James, and Charles, 1926.

Thorndike, A. H., Shakespeare's Theatre, 1916.

Young, William, ed., The History of Dulwich College, with a Life of the Founder, Edward Alleyn, and an Accurate Transcript of His Diary, 1889.

INDEX

Burns, Robert, 72
Burton, Robert, 128
Byron, George Gordon Byron, Lord, 250

Campbell, Oscar J., x
Cardinal, The (Shirley), 114
Carlyle, Thomas, 79, 87
Carroll, Lewis, 210
Cary, Lady Elizabeth, biography, 284
Case Is Altered, The (Jonson), 194
Castiglione, Baldassare, 94, 164
Catherine the Great, 196
Catiline (Jonson), 53-57
Catullus, 166
Cavalier Drama (Harbage), vii
Cavalier drama, use of term, vii, viii; scope, vii, 4, 11, 113; collaboration in, 3, 4, 10, 130, 270; close relation to Restoration, 4, 11, 178, 240, 250; compared with Elizabethan school, 11, 25, 28, 47 f., 64, 76, 109, 112 ff., 118, 119, 120, 161, 213, 219, 236, 240, 251 f., 253, 265 f., 268 f.; approach to Augustan era, 11, 253; decline of medieval inheritance, 11, 268 f.; conventional plot, 43; "unpleasant" or satirical tragedies, 45; *Othello* used as model, 61; audience, 67, 144, 146; sentimental tragedy, 112-29; key to enjoyment of, 113; playwrights, 114, 251; influenced by court life of Renaissance, 122; introspective aspect, 128; tragic extravaganza, 130-44; dramatic romances, 145-61, 163; the psyche, 163-75, 178; role of sex in, 163 f., 166, 174; treatment of polite manners, 176-88; fantastic comedy, 212-35; rise and fall of comic prose, 236-49
Cavalier psyche, 163-75, 178
Caxton, William, 255
Censorship, 84, 95, 96
Cervantes Saavedra, Miguel de, 255
Chambers, E. K., 256, 279
Chambers, R. W., 256
Changeling, The (Middleton and Rowley), 39-41

Changes, The (Shirley), 243
Chapman, George, 9, 39, 45, 83, 113, 119, 120, 127, 132, 183, 190, 197, 238, 239, 252, 262, 267, 274; dramatic works, 78 f., 83-94, 141, 240, 242, 246 f., 248, 284; biography, 284
Charles I, of England, vii, 4, 137, 182
Chaste Maid in Cheapside, A (Middleton), 187, 224, 225, 227, 240, 242
Chastity, cult of, 166, 174
Chaucer, Geoffrey, 9, 44, 159, 173, 257, 258, 262, 263, 271
Chettle, Henry, 20, 59, 257, 271; biography, 285
Children's companies, 267
Chivalrous ethics, 33, 79, 82, 166
Christian ethics, 33, 79, 82, 260
Chronicle History of Perkin Warbeck, The (Ford), 70, 98, 104-6, 107, 129
Chronicle-history play, 84, 98; *see also* History
Cicero, 55
City Madam, The (Massinger), 149
Classical background, 6, 7, 21, 23, 27, 32, 46, 58, 86, 87, 92, 189, 194, 217, 267
Clowns, role of, 214
Cockpit Theatre, 254
Collaboration among playwrights, 3, 4, 10, 130, 270
Comedy, classical background, 6, 7, 189, 194, 199, 217, 267; use of abstract names, in, 35; characteristics of pure, 146, 149, 190; of manners, 176-88, 253; of the Restoration, 178, 240; satirical, 189-211; complexity of elements, 190; fantastic, 212-35; medieval heritage, 212, 216; sentimental, 214 f.; rise and fall of prose in, 236-49; predominance of verse in, 242 f.; satire and realism characterize, 248
Comedy of Errors, The (Shakespeare), 146, 217
Complete Gentleman, The (Peacham), 178
Comus (Milton), 167, 172, 173-75